Islam and Modernity

D1202692

Critical Studies on Islam

Series Editors: Azza Karam (Director of the Women's Programme at the World Conference on Religion and Peace, New York) and Ziauddin Sardar (Editor of the critical international journal of contemporary art and culture, *Third Text*)

The Road to Al-Qaeda
The Story of Bin Laden's Right-hand Man
Montasser al-Zayyat

Islam in the Digital Age
E-Jihad, Online Fatwas and Cyber Islamic Environments
Gary R. Bunt

Iraqi Invasion of Kuwait
Religion, Identity and Otherness in the Analysis of War and Conflict
Hamdi A. Hassan

Transnational Political Islam
Globalization, Ideology and Power
Edited by Azza Karam

Hizbu'llah
Politics and Religion
Amal Saad-Ghorayeb

Islam and Modernity

Muslims in Europe and the United States

Iftikhar H. Malik

Pluto Press
LONDON • STERLING, VIRGINIA

First published 2004 by Pluto Press
345 Archway Road, London N6 5AA
and 22883 Quicksilver Drive, Sterling, VA 20166-2012, USA

www.plutobooks.com

British Library Cataloguing in Publication Data
A catalogue record for this book is available from
the British Library

ISBN 0 7453 1612 3 hardback
ISBN 0 7453 1611 5 paperback

Library of Congress Cataloging in Publication Data
Malik, Iftikhar Haider, 1949–
    Islam and modernity : Muslims in Europe and the United States
/ Iftikhar H. Malik.
        p. cm.
Includes bibliographical references and index.
    ISBN 0–7453–1612–3 — ISBN 0–7453–1611–5 (pbk.)
    1. Muslims—Europe. 2. Islam—Europe. 3. Europe—Ethnic
relations. 4. Muslims—United States. 5. Islam—United States.
6. United States—Ethnic relations. I. Title.
    D1056.2.M87M35 2003
    305.6'97104—dc21
                                              2003011896

10   9   8   7   6   5   4   3   2   1

Designed and produced for Pluto Press by
Chase Publishing Services, Fortescue, Sidmouth, EX10 9QG, England
Typeset from disk by Stanford DTP Services, Northampton, England
Printed and bound in the European Union by
Antony Rowe, Chippenham and Eastbourne, England

Contents

Critical Studies on Islam
Series Editors: Azza Karam and
Ziauddin Sardar

Islam is a complex, ambiguous term. Conventionally it has been used to describe the religion, history, culture, civilisation and worldview of Muslims. But it is also impregnated with stereotypes and postmodern notions of identity and boundaries. The diversity of Muslim peoples, cultures, and interpretations, with their baggage of colonial history and postcolonial present, has transformed Islam into a powerful global force.

This unique series presents a far-reaching, critical perspective on Islam. It analyses the diversity and complexity of Islam through the eyes of people who live by it. Provocative and thoughtful works by established as well as younger scholars will examine Islamic movements, the multilayered questions of Muslim identity, the transnational trends of political Islam, the spectre of ethnic conflict, the political economy of Muslim societies and the impact of Islam and Muslims on the West.

The series is built around two fundamental questions. How are Muslims living, thinking and breathing Islam? And how are they rethinking and reformulating it and shaping and reshaping the global agendas and discourses?

As Critical Studies on Islam seeks to bridge the gap between academia and decision-making environments, it will be of particular value to policy makers, politicians, journalists and activists, as well as academics.

Dr Azza Karam is a Program Director at the World Conference of Religions for Peace (WCRP) International Secretariat based in New York. She has worked as a consultant and trainer with the United Nations and various Middle Eastern and European NGOs, and has lectured and published extensively on conflict, Islam, the Middle East and the politics of development issues. Her books include *Women, Islamisms and State: Contemporary Feminisms in Egypt* (1998), *A Woman's Place: Religious Women as Public Actors* (ed.) (2002) and *Women in War and Peace Building* (forthcoming).

Ziauddin Sardar is a well-known writer. He is the editor of a critical international journal of contemporary art and culture, *Third Text*, and is considered a pioneering writer on Islam. He is the author of several books for Pluto Press, most recently *Islam, Postmodernism and Other Futures: A Ziauddin Sardar Reader*, edited by Sohail Inayatullah and Gail Boxwell.

Preface

At the sight of the title of this volume, one may legitimately ask the question: Why another book on Islam and the West? The plain answer is that this study does not look at Islam and the West as two perennial antagonists, but rather seeks to suggest a new paradigm of 'Islam in the West' and 'the West in Islam', without, of course, mono-lithising them, or neglecting their distinct ideological constellations and historical experiences. This book grew out of years of studying, teaching, travelling, debating and researching in the North Atlantic regions, with a simultaneous first-hand immersion in Muslim cultures and traditions. Most of the existing literature on Muslims, especially in the West, situates them as 'recent' immigrants and concentrates either on a single community or on just a handful of variables within one country. Studies focusing on wider, comparative realms either become narratives of contemporary issues, by ignoring historical evolution, or simply end up offering state-centred analyses. A few, however, include a substantial discussion on Muslim Spain and the earliest successful pluralism in Europe. With the exception of one or two books, none links the Muslim diaspora and modernity with the mainstream Muslim world itself. It is partly due to this factor that many readers fail to understand the implications of the 'Andalusia syndrome' – the fear of the complete disappearance of a Muslim community – increasingly apparent among certain Muslim sections, especially after 11 September and the Anglo-American invasion of Iraq. In the same vein, important topics such as Ireland, the European Union (EU) and slavery in the United States have remained unnoticed in many studies of Muslims in the West. While benefiting from the existing country-centred scholarship, the present volume attempts to take the debate forward within the dynamics of an intriguing interface between Islam and modernity.[1]

The manuscript of this book was still in its embryonic stage when the terrorists struck at New York and Washington on 11 September 2001. Since then we have witnessed the evolution of a new bicultural relationship within a changed geopolitical environment. While, on the one hand, the United States retaliated with severe vengeance and other Western governments began profiling and apprehending Muslim activists and organisations, Muslims in general found themselves in an intense predicament. The terrorists attacked the financial and military centres of the United States, but these acts of frustration and desperation also made millions of Muslims across the globe hostages to grave militarist and racist reactions. No other single act could have damaged pluralism so intensely, especially at the expense of Muslim communitarian and cultural heritage. The last decade or so, in general, has proved an excruciatingly testing time for Muslims, who have faced one trying predicament after another. After the painful Rushdie affair, ethnic cleansing and mass rapes in Bosnia, the first Gulf War and the agonising Ayodhya crisis in India, the horror-stricken faces of impoverished Afghans emerging from the debris of a decimated country haunted every concerned person. The bloodshed in Palestine, Chechnya, Kashmir and Gujarat, largely unleashed by state-led forces, and fears of the US-led anti-terror campaign being extended to other regions defined as the 'axis of evil' by President George W. Bush, brought stark anguish to Muslim consciousness.

The Anglo-American invasion of Iraq in 2003, largely contested and opposed by global opinion, heralded two new socio-political scenarios. Firstly, it was felt that in a unipolar world, Washington, duly aided by London, will undertake all types of militarist ventures irrespective of global attempts at dissuasion. The war against Iraq was opposed not only by global Muslim communities; the opposition came from all over the world, especially from within the North Atlantic regions. London, San Francisco, Rome, New York, Washington, Paris, Madrid and Berlin witnessed demonstrations unprecedented in their known history. Though the United Nations, Muslim groups and the anti-war global coalitions failed to deter President George W. Bush and Prime Minister Tony Blair from pursuing a fierce war on Iraq, the politicisation of the diverse communities in a world-wide peace movement was a feat of no less significance. It equally dispelled the view that ethno-religious minorities such as Muslims were antagonistic towards integration. On 15 February 2003, 2 million protesters marched across London, with Muslims, socialists, anarchists, churchgoers, women, students and senior citizens forming a massive rainbow of plural ethos, never seen before in the country's past. Such a scene was repeated several times across other towns and cities in Europe and North America.

Secondly, the invasion of Iraq may have signalled the failure of moral and legal objections to war amidst a growing critique of Islam by influential opinion makers such as Bernard Lewis, Daniel Pipes,

Oriana Fallaci, Silvio Berlusconi, Frank Graham and Pat Robertson; but criticism from the Pope, Nelson Mandela, Arundhati Roy and Jimmy Carter, as well as other notables, reassured Muslims that the West was not single-mindedly against Islam per se. While the world grieved over the unnecessary deaths and looting in Iraq without the Western troops finding any weapons of mass destruction – the main justification for this invasion – the greater accent on democracy, accountability, pluralism and a just global order became the focus of a wide-ranging critical opinion. It was felt that the entire country must not be made to suffer for the sake of a few unwanted individuals – often protected by vested interests in the first place. Simultaneously, it became clear that demolishing a regime may be easy, but as witnessed in Afghanistan, Iraq and Palestine, establishing peace and true democracy may prove a painstaking job requiring sustained and constructive engagement. The criticism of Anglo-American double standards in the developing world, even at the expense of moral and legal statutes, has never been so vocal before.

These volatile developments, of course, symbolised a grave margin-alisation of Muslim voices from the international forums. Not only was the United Nations sidelined by the Anglo-US insistence on war; the Organisation of the Islamic Conference (OIC) and the EU also found themselves in the doldrums. However, the sustained debate in liberal forums on the dangers of such a unilateralism, as vocally articulated in the print media, including the *Guardian*, *New Statesman*, *Liberation* and the *Mirror*, besides the flurry of critical books, electronic mail and specific television programmes, offered a counter-discourse from a global civil society seeking to be heard. While it is true that some Muslims, buckling under severe scrutiny, may have sought refuge in self-denial, others continued to reassert themselves through an aggressive and ruthless fundamentalism.

The unparalleled spotlight on Muslims is certainly unnerving, though many of them see in Islam something more than a ritualistic theology and would like to combine its humanism, frugality and tolerance with the scientific discoveries, rationalism and material progress of the West. Such reformist or modernist elements are equally perturbed over the hijacking of their heritage by a few hotheads, yet anti-Muslim sentiments and a pervasive Western indifference, coupled with a large-scale politico-economic disem-powerment within the Muslim world, prevent any major headway. However, many Muslims in the West have been reinterpreting their identity with reference to a synthesised discourse, while simultaneously fighting institutional racism and a theocratic nihilism – two similar hegemonies. Within a gloomy situation, this emerging fresher perspective may offer a silver lining.

This volume attempts to identify the strides and strifes, though it intentionally shies away from offering any futuristic judgement. It begins with an overview of Spanish Islam, then, treading its path through the European Union, ends with a discussion on the Islamic 'encounter' within the United States. Sociological arguments and historical evidence underpin the analysis within the context of a complex though not always hostile relationship between Muslim and 'Western' societies. Islam, in a historical sense, is neither a newcomer nor an eternal foe, and a pervasive Muslim unease remains one of the most seriously debilitating realities of our times. It is hoped that these chapters will add to our knowledge by offering a holistic overview of Islam in the West and the West in Islam.

Many individuals deserve my gratitude for making this research possible and they are too numerous to be named. However, Ziauddin Sardar, Anne Beech, Brian Griffin, Bill MacKeith, David Castle, Robert Webb, Anthony Winder and my own colleagues and students at Bath Spa University College deserve special thanks for their support and encouragement. I have shared my thoughts, hopes and cynicism with scores of Muslims and their friends across the four continents, all the way from *qahwakhanas* to *souks*, from mosques to *mohallas*, and from campuses to Sufi *zawiyyas*. My immediate family – Nighat, Farooq and Sidra – have offered unflinching encouragement at times when I should have been vacationing or relaxing with them.

Despite making numerous applications for financial support for the research necessary for this book, no funding was forthcoming, which speaks volumes about the state of institutional encourage-ment for such topics, especially when they are undertaken by 'hyphenated' and 'lone' academics. An ever-expanding teaching load without the luxury of any sabbatical turned the project into a race against the odds. However, such mundane challenges made the project even more exciting as I had to be puritanically frugal with the time and budgeting. It is hoped that scholars, students, policy makers and general readers will find the study worth the time, passion and effort.

Iftikhar H. Malik
Oxford
August 2003

Glossary

alim	a Muslim religious scholar
Andalusia syndrome	concern about the possible elimination or forced conversion of a Muslim community
anjumans	associations
biradari	kinship, extended family
churros	fritters
emir	a leader
fitna	feud or friction
fiqh	Islamic jurisprudence
Hispania	Spain
ijtihad	interpretive innovation
imam	one who leads prayers
insan-i-kamil	perfect person
khilafat	lit.: vice-regency – dynastic Muslim political rule
madrassa	a religious seminary
mahdi	the promised Messiah
mashaikh	Sufi leaders
Masjid-i-Kartaba	the Cordoba mosque
mihrab	a niche in a mosque, facing Makkah, from which the imam leads prayers
millet	trans-regional, trans-sectarian community
mofussil	indigenous, usually from non-urban background
mohalla	a locality within a township
muezzin	one who gives the call for prayer
mullah	a Muslim religious leader (usually a negative term)
mullahism	ritualism, theocracy
munshi	a scribe
mushairra	poetry recitals
muwashshah	a poetic genre in Muslim Spain
pir	a spiritual mentor
qahwakhana	tea stall
qasidah	a laudatory poem
razzia	a (tribal) raid
sharia	Islamic law

silsilahs	Sufi orders
souk	a bazaar
sufi	a mystic
taifa	faction
talib/taleb	a student of a religious seminary
taliban	pl. of *talib*
ulama	pl. of *alim*
umma/ummah	a united Muslim community, over and above differences.
zajal	a variant of *muwashshah*
zawiyya	a Sufi meeting place

1 Modernity and Political Islam: Contestants or Companions?

> There is a raging battle for the soul of religion between those who seek an accommodation with modernity and those who wish to stick strictly with the dogmatic certainties of the past ... This battle is not confined to Islam but rages in Catholicism and Judaism ... The hub of this battle is played out in the powerful sophisticated cities of the Western World, Paris, Rome, New York, London and indeed Dublin ... The struggle of Muslims for and against an accommodation with modernity is taking place, not just in Cairo, Tehran and Islamabad, but also among Muslims living in the West. The events of 11th September have brought the intensity of this struggle into sharp relief. (<www.Irishcatholic.ie/030321-mthtm>)

Within the triangular relationship between Western societies, the Muslim diaspora and the Muslim world, there is a rather complex though not always conflictive interface in which each influences the other. Major events since the end of the Cold War in 1989–90 have signalled some of the most significant developments in this respect with crucial ramifications for all three. Events have also intensified the quest for identity among Muslims with reference to tradition and modernity. This relationship is neither totally tension-free nor is it characterised by continual strife. While, historically speaking, modernity has generated a broad range of liberationist ideas and empowering institutions, it has also advanced some of the most violent practices including the slave trade, racism and ethnic cleansing – at least in their modern dimensions. Muslims have usually accepted modernity, though not always willingly, and, in several cases, the haphazard nature of modernising efforts has increased anxieties and tensions, generating violent and fundamentalist reaction. In some cases, modernising yet non-representative regimes have themselves coopted and promoted fundamentalist groups. So, while an unquestioned celebration of modernity may not be totally appropriate, the uncritical conformity with tradition shorn of human rights and reinterpretation is equally dangerous. The violent and fundamentalist reaction to the abrasive forces of modernity and globalisation is not confined to the world of Islam: in North America and across Europe, in Russia, India, Australasia and France, ultra-right forces are in the ascendant. In several Muslim countries, fundamentalists have been trying to assume centre stage by taking power, but it would be unfair to posit that the entire Islamic tradition is intolerant per se. However, judicious policies, universal political empowerment, economic stability, distributive justice, eradication of internal or regional conflicts and non-interference from outside are the prerequisites for effectively marginalising elements intent upon reducing a civilisational heritage such as Islam to a mere repressive dogma. The Westernised Muslim elite – the harbingers of modernity to the Islamic world – as well as their supporters elsewhere must urgently address the existing massive politico-economic alienation by offering accountable and transparent policies, otherwise violence and conflict will stay unabated.

However, it is important briefly to summarise some recent crucial developments and their imprints on Muslims before situating Islam – especially in the West – within the context of modernity.

The last few years have been a traumatic experience for Muslims across the world. Firstly, Salman Rushdie's publication of *The Satanic Verses* (1988) was met with anger and protests by many Muslims, who felt deeply hurt by his irreverence towards the Prophet, a consensus role model, or *insan-i-kamil* to them. Rushdie's satirical and arrogant attitude, combined with his own *Muslim* background, and with the continued marginalisation of the Muslim diaspora, especially in Britain, fuelled these protests. Many of the demonstrators, especially the younger generation, were, in fact, using the occasion to voice their own resentment against marginalisation in Western societies. Concurrently, certain exclusionary and alarmist sections used the anti-Rushdie demonstrations to reiterate their 'I-told-you-so' views on Islam. Liberals and other elements combined to portray Islam as an inherently anti-modern, anti-intellectual and anti-feminist ideology, which had refused to modernise itself. They were reluctant to look at a wider malaise within the context of a growing socioeconomic discontent spawning such protests.[1] The protesters torching the book in Bradford rekindled the stereotypes of Muslims *à la* Khomeini. Imam Khomeini's own fatwa against the British author in 1989 further aggravated the anger towards Islamic groups, which to many, had existed all along, below the surface, thanks to the legacy of the Crusades, colonialism, Orientalism and the continuing dominance of the West in international relations.

Secondly, Saddam Hussein's uncalled-for invasion of Kuwait further polarised the Muslim world as the Muslim nations and their umbrella organisation, the Organisation of the Islamic Conference (OIC), like the UN, proved unable to prevent another war in the region, coming so soon after the Iraq–Iran War. Muslim debilitation as a result of the region's politics became more apparent when the United States and its global alliance undertook to liberate an oil-rich Kuwait, and in the process ordinary Iraqis lost their lives in droves thanks to 'turkey shoots'. Amidst the agonising Middle Eastern imbroglio, Yugoslavia fell apart, leaving its Muslim communities vulnerable to the xenophobic forces of Greater Serbia and Greater Croatia. The painful Bosnian crisis, accompanied by widespread ethnic cleansing, gang rapes of thousands of Muslim women, the incarceration of countless Muslim men in concentration camps, and the sheer elimination of thousands in safe havens such as Srebrenica, once again exposed the peripheralisation of the Muslim factor in politics. Feelings of sheer helplessness and hurt pride reverberated all the more across the Muslim world as Russian nationalists mounted an annihilatory campaign in a defiant Chechnya. Muslims, to their discomfort, came to confront the painful vulnerability of small, disparate communities of co-religionists in the Balkans, the Caucasus, Palestine and Kashmir not long after the end of the Cold War. The Afghans, who earlier had been caught in the polarised world politics that occurred during the Cold War, put up a heroic fight against the Soviet invasion but now were divided into ethno-tribal configurations and, egged on by neighbours, engaged in killing sprees. As the world celebrated the fifth centenary of the Columbian expedition of 1492 and a burgeoning globalisation, Muslim communities bled profusely. For instance, Muslims accounted for three-quarters of the world's refugees.[2] The profusion of wars – mostly ethnic and rooted in politico-economic factors – was quickly interpreted by former Cold War protagonists as a 'clash of civilisations' in which Western civilisation was seen to be under a severe threat, mainly from Muslims. By the late twentieth century, Islam was the new bogeyman, Islamophobia was on the rise and Muslims were becoming the 'new Jews of the world'.[3]

Thirdly, in the new millennium, Muslim marginalisation within global politics became more apparent following the terrorist attacks on New York and Washington on 11 September 2001. The Saudi dissident Osama bin Laden and his Taleban hosts in Afghanistan dangerously reinforced pervasive negative images of Muslims. Not only did a poor country like Afghanistan become the focus of a sustained and devastating bombing campaign causing death and destruction on an enormous scale, but Muslim communities in other disputed regions and in the diaspora also came under a hostile spotlight. Profiling of Muslim individuals, desecration of mosques and Muslim-owned properties, and harassment and imprisonment of Muslims happened amidst a growing tide of Islamophobia. Official restrictive policies and societal strictures against 'newer' communities reached their nadir as civil liberties were rolled back in a context of hyped-up patriotism and exclusionary nationalism. The US mass bombing campaign served only to encourage Russia, Israel and India to mount matching campaigns against their restive Muslim communities. The Muslim nations, by contrast, once again stood aloof as four million more Afghans were turned into refugees.[4] The United States had reacted too soon and too vengefully. Yet ironically even after such massive destruction of human communities and natural resources, the US could not even apprehend the two most wanted fugitives: Osama bin Laden and the Taleban's Mullah Muhammad Omar.[5] The year 2002 dawned as 'daisy cutters' and 'cave busters' rained down on Afghanistan, Chechens bled in the ruins of Grozny, Palestinians sought to escape Sharon's mortar and tank attacks, and India and Pakistan stepped nearer the brink of a nuclear war over the disputed territory of Kashmir; whereas partitioned Bosnia remained out on a limb. Preparations were already under way for extending the campaign to Iraq, Somalia, Indonesia, Yemen, the Sudan and possibly even Pakistan. The common opinion of Islam was immensely negative or even hostile. At the year's start, the entire Muslim world looked like a war zone, with Western troops patrolling the deserts and plains from Egypt to Kosovo and from Afghanistan to the southern Philippines,[6] while issues of political marginalisation, economic adversity and warfare in nearly all the Muslim regions continued to be ignored. The Muslim ruling elite – monarchs, dictators and pseudo-democrats – sat aloof, biding their time, while the fundamentalists offered a reductionist palliative to mundane hardships. While pseudo-reformists and fundamentalists in the Muslim world pursued power politics through naked violence, Muslims in the diaspora vacillated between the extreme positions of self-denial and increased religious assertion. In general, a large majority of Muslims, confronted by the severe backlash and disillusioned by pervasive helplessness, has become gravely introvert. Dismay with the contemporary political and religious leadership has become quite apparent, and there is no alternative on the horizon. Consequently, the quest for identity has become more acute, and being a *Muslim* equally problematic.[7]

The tragic and ambiguous nature of the issues confronted by Muslim communities – not always of their own making – stipulates imperatives on a human and global scale. These serious political and economic issues have over the years been exacerbated by external interference. For instance, Bosnia, Palestine, Kashmir, Afghanistan, Somalia and Chechnya are volatile and in turmoil because of foreign invasions, not due to some indigenous Muslim penchant for violence. Focusing solely or primarily on Taleban stragglers, Northern Alliance foot soldiers, Hizbollah fighters, Hamas suicide bombers, Kashmiri insurgents or Chechen guerrillas may lead one to assume that the 1.5 billion-strong Muslim world – despite its inherent diversities – is simply a monolith of bloodthirsty terrorists, as typified by Osama or Omar. Thus, while there is a need to reconstruct Islamic discourse in its civilisational and human context, it is all the more urgent to understand the Muslim predicament and prospects through a more rigorous reflection.[8] For example, on the one hand, political Islam may stipulate resistance to Western hegemony; but at the same time many of its own current forms are equally totalitarian.[9] However, the very term *political Islam* or *Islamism* – as merely a theocracy to be imposed through brutal force – is a misnomer. In this volatile and depressing situation, a number of Muslims, especially in the diaspora, have been struggling to come to grips with these problems. Before one may venture to locate these responses one needs to conceptualise modernity and tradition within their global and specifically their *Muslim* context.

JUXTAPOSING MODERNITY

There is a danger that the current Muslim dilemma may quickly be attributed to some simplistic but dangerous theoretical paradigms, though more clear-sighted scholars have been indicating a more complex relationship.[10] Already, there are three main positions in vogue amongst such intellectuals; firstly, that Islam is totally incompatible with modernity and thus against integration, pluralism, democracy and human rights. According to this view, Muslims will not acquire peace and stability unless they develop a secular position, totally divorced from their Islamic heritage. It is further premised that Islam has not yet encountered modernity in the form of 'upheavals' like the Renaissance and the Reformation, and thus remains locked in a time-warp. This is a Eurocentric opinion which totally ignores the socioeconomic realities on the ground and fails to explain similar challenges confronting other non-Muslim regions in the developing world. The second view – an extreme one like the first – posits that reverting to a pristine Islam is the only way out. This emphasis on back-to-Islam or the reconversion of Muslims through a narrow and literally defined Islamicisation lacks systemic strategies and pathways. In most cases, it is an emotional, introvert and intolerant outburst and is reactive and repressive, as well as hastening fragmentation of the societal clusters. The third position, unlike the other two, is more rational and sustained. It looks at the multiplicity of problems confronted by Muslims and seeks a synthesised strategy for a holistic overhaul. Such a view seeks to incorporate Islamic as well as other human traditions to offer a dynamic solution in the form of universal empowerment, Muslim feminism, Muslim democracy and even Muslim secularism. This kind of wider empowerment, based on innovation – as permitted through *ijtihad* in classical Islam – and benefiting from the positive attributes of Western/Eastern modernity, is still an evolving intellectual paradigm confined to a few individuals or groups; but it holds the promise of a better future.

Obviously, the current ideological debate is not confined to non-Muslim groups; rather it is slowly becoming an intra-Muslim discourse. Muslims in the West are well placed to be the vanguard of this overdue intellectual effort, and despite the various challenges they need to be proactive. By linking Islamic civilisational traditions with the humane values of Western modernity, diasporic Muslim intellectuals and activists can offer linkages between the world of Islam and the West. Their encounter can augur a new era of peace and prosperity and a departure from anguish and conflict. The ongoing polarisation of the various Muslim groups, banking on the primacy of their religious identity over everything else, including national/ethnic/class identity, has been a painful experience. Yet, it is equally important to define modernity in its larger theoretical context before we may proceed to see the nature of the emerging Muslim discourse.

Modernity, modernisation, modernism, Westernisation, Westernism and now postmodernity, describe multiple processes beginning with the explorations, colonialism, industrialisation and capitalism first experienced in Western Europe before being transferred to the

Americas and subsequently to the colonies. The post-Renaissance forces of rationalism, nationalism, secularism, capitalism, socialism, urban professionalism, and more recently of gender equality and social mobility, are some of the powerful imprints of modernisation, which collectively underwrite modernity.[11] The transformation from *traditional* modes of collective socio-political and economic patterns and hierarchies to more professionalised, choice-based and interest-based structures largely accounts for modernisation. Modernity, inclusive of all socio-political and economic forces, has been redefining *traditional* societies in the wake of serious socio-moral dislocations. Not only are traditional social patterns of relationship, such as kinship, clan or extended family systems, giving way to larger ethnic or national communities; newer modes of production, complex management hierarchies and human vulnerabilities to trans-regional influences have also engendered serious uncertainties. Rooted in an unblemished idea of progress, this dominant Western construct received its sustenance from philosophers as diverse as Karl Marx, Emile Durkheim, Charles Darwin and Max Weber. Both Marx and Durkheim believed that 'modernity' was an *essential* stage for any society in its course to development. Their universalisation of the Western model does not deprive it of its significance and relevance to all human societies, including Muslims. While health, education and means of communications have certainly improved in many developing regions, urbanisation, migrations, militarism and consumerism have unleashed several destabilising forces including ethnic, religious and sectarian volatility as well as serious issues of corruption and criminalisation. The ruling elites in the developing world, despite their nationalist pretensions, are mainly motivated by their class-specific interests, but have failed to ameliorate the pervasive anomalies, varying from disempowerment to economic inequity. On the contrary, by using the given state structures to suit their own whims and particular interests, and with the nodding assent of external powers, they have simply exacerbated social conflicts. Their continued dependence on multiple forms of Western largesse has vetoed indigenous regenerative efforts for self-reliance and dented the prevalence of the liberal and egalitarian ethos offered by the first generation of modernists and nationalists. This metamorphosis has not only weakened the morale of vast sections of the populace but has also further marginalised vulnerable groups such as minorities and women.[12]

MODERNITY, COLLECTIVE VIOLENCE AND RACISM

Although modernity has led to numerous positive changes, it has also engendered serious problems of inequity in the form of organised slavery, the persisting forces of racism and a strengthened tradition of warfare. Millions of Africans were shipped to the Western hemisphere in subhuman conditions to run the plantation economies for generations. The 'peculiar institution' uprooted millions of people from traditional societies to suffer from slavery and racism in the modern world. In the same way, the colonial enterprise not only caused the socio-psychological subjugation of vast regions, it equally spawned human, economic and ecological depredations. At another level, imperial warfare and interstate conflicts caused global wars, the Holocaust, ethnic cleansing and a whole range of forces rooted in institutionalised racism.[13] Each form of collective violence – slavery, colonialism, warfare and racism – requires volumes to encapsulate the empirical details, but it is the evolution of modern racism in its scientific form that here demands more serious attention. Not only does racism pose the greatest challenge to pluralism and human rights, it is also the greatest cause of alienation in the Afro-Asian world. While the Western democracies have made significant improvements in recent years, the institutional forms of racism and the indifferent, if not outright hostile, attitude towards the peoples of former colonies as hordes of spongers and barbarians still lurks behind the smokescreen. Of course, racism, in its newer and collective forms, is the most pernicious challenge to a global humanism.

Since the Second World War, many sociologists have been looking at racism both as an ideological construct and a scientific classification based on biological/genetic factors. But the fact remains that the hierarchical categorisation of global communities through such criteria lacks equity and codifies 'the way in which "white" Europeans have historically set out to dominate, exploit and kill "inferior" peoples'.[14] Traditionally, racism in the West has been projected through anti-black and anti-Semitic (that is, hostile to both Jews and Arabs) trajectories, but over the last half century it has become anti-immigrant, especially immigrants from the Afro-Asian world. The hegemonic nature of the Western relationship with the postcolonial world, as reflected in foreign policy, the erection of strict immigration regimes and, more recently, the profiling of several cultural groups, has, in some cases, further regimented this unevenness. Sociologists and anthropologists differ on the historicity and definition of racism as such, which is also a barrier to the total eradication of racism. While racism displayed in pubs, football grounds, streets, factories and markets may appear crude and stereotypical, its subtle forms amongst the educated and well-placed elite are well-entrenched and proportionately more dangerous. That is why institutional racism, as borne out by reports such as *Islamophobia* (1997), or *The Stephen Lawrence Inquiry* (*Macpherson Police Inquiry Report*, 1999), remains defiant and difficult to document. In a powerful way, it is a top-down phenomenon in which the elite formulates and disseminates racism to the grassroots, where it becomes more explicit and violent. For example, the media and politicians throughout Europe and Australia gave out exaggerated accounts of asylum seekers during 2000–03, leading to the sought-after right-wing electoral victories and adding to further strict immigration policies. As reported in a nationwide survey (2000) in Britain, people were subtly led to believe that asylum seekers were a burden on society and the economy.[15] Time and again, 'bogus' asylum seekers were portrayed as the 'new' enemies from 'within'.[16]

The origin of this recent racist legacy is contemporary with modernity, in that the European quest for identity, to a great extent, hinges on racial differentiation.[17] On the Iberian Peninsula, anti-Moorish and anti-Jewish sentiments were defined through a religious idiom that accompanied the Catholic Inquisition from the 1440s. But it was during the eighteenth century that several European scholars started to theorise on racism by developing pseudo-scientific explanations.[18] The enduring biblical attitudes towards Africa, blackness, Jews and Muslims were now combined with so-called scientific and anthropological interpretations. The Swedish scholar, Carolus Linnaeus, in his *Systema Naturae* (1735), divided humanity into four races on the basis of colour: white Europeans, dark Asians, black Africans and red Indians. A little later, Johann Frederich Blumenbach added another category of Caucasians but still subscribed to monogenesis – the theory that the origin of all is from the same human source. Despite this colour-based differentiation, the Enlightenment and the French Revolution stipulated more tolerance. However, from the 1850s onwards, Comte Gobineau and Robert Knox proffered strict boundary-based differentials among the races. Within the context of *fin-de-siècle* Europe, Count Gobineau and other exponents of Eurocentrism reflected the anxieties and tensions of rapidly changing times. In *The Races of Men* (1850), in which he established the modern science of race, Knox dismissed the possibility of any hybrid race. His views also reflected contemporary European fears of miscegenation. Knox seriously considered whites intellectually and physically superior to all other groups and thus departed from the idea of the universality of humankind. Knox also highlighted intra-European racial differences, between Saxon, Nordic, Celtic, Slovenian and Sarmatian groups. Gobineau's ideas of racial superiority of the Europeans – Aryans – achieved immense popularity in Germany, where amidst *Volksgeist* trends racism, combined with extreme nationalism and a growing desire for imperial possessions, assumed pivotal proportions. The myth of Aryan supremacy was strongly advocated in the newly unified Germany, where, earlier, influential Germans such as Richard Wagner had harboured racist sentiments. In France and Britain, influential writers like Ernest Renan and Thomas Carlyle supported theories of the racial superiority of whites over non-whites, and together with the Orientalist and imperialist discourses, the Victorian era was symbolised by the Kiplingesque concept of the 'white man's burden'.[19] From the 1870s, racism in Europe and the United States assumed more sinister forms due to the forces of the new imperialism, jingoistic nationalism, greater social mobility, the evolution of political parties seeking votes, and populist ideologies such as fascism. This phase of scientific racism hinged on biological and qualitative differences between the whites and non-whites. At another level, in addition to the white–black differential, new intra-white and intra-black hierarchies and categories were essentialised. For instance, Jews were defined as biologically different from Aryans and other dominant white groups. This form of reinvigorated anti-Semitism was pervasive in Europe. In the same manner, the new hierarchies proposed for non-whites emphasised the qualitative physical, cultural and intellectual differences between the Africans, Arabs, Indians and East Asians. The scramble for Africa, interstate conflicts in Europe and access to an overreaching media converted racism into a pervasive and institutionalised ideology.

The Ku Klux Klan, Nazis, apartheid, Oswald Mosley's Union Movement, Enoch Powell's tirades, neo-Nazis such as the British National Party, Le Pen's National Front, Austria's Freedom Party and sections within mainstream parties across the Atlantic have been the varying manifestations of similar legacies. However, post-1945 racism, sometimes also called neo-racism, is more complex and is largely directed against immigrants and their descendants, while erstwhile anti-Irish and anti-Jewish sentiments have somewhat subsided. In Western Europe, many immigrant communities are from the former colonies and are predominantly not only non-white but also non-Christian. Muslims, Buddhists, Hindus, Sikhs and other religious identities have usually been viewed as *different* according to the touchstone of colour, culture and class. Despite the outlawing of racist policies and rhetoric through civil legislation, political correctness and legal injunctions, more subtle forms of racism persist.[20] The minorities are further disadvantaged because of their origins in developing, postcolonial regions which, for a long time, have been perceived as 'inferior', 'emotional', 'pre-modern' and 'backward', if not totally barbarian. The modern type of racism – neo-racism – is mostly overt, which, as seen during the Rushdie affair or following the bombing of the World Trade Center, can become covert through selective violence and harassment. Neo-racism is articulated through irresponsible media portrayals, hate-mongering by political parties and by straightforwardly racist groups, and is most dangerous in its institutionalised forms.

FROM REJECTION TO REASSERTION

The forces of political Islam or Hindutva, and projects like Greater Serbia, Greater Croatia and Pan-Slavism, are all societal throwbacks rejecting the erstwhile statist hierarchies, which are collectively perceived as bankrupt and outmoded. They are also the manifestations of modernity gone astray or responses to uneven reformism and Western hegemonism. By posing as ideal alternatives they are simply discretionary, and while using traditional symbols they equally rely on modern means and strategies. Disillusionment with independence, intermittent military takeovers and monopolist monarchies, and disenchantment with nominally democratic orders weak on delivery and strong on promises have also contributed to the wider malaise.[21] Like their opponent regimes, in their pursuit of conformity, these societal activists are equally oppressive, gender-specific and ethnically exclusionary, leaving very little space for moderate and mediatory forces. In most cases, these fundamentalists threaten their own beleaguered civil societies with complete extinction. Although in several instances such groups have declared war on the rulers, in some curious cases, notably in the former Yugoslavia, BJP-led India, Zia-controlled Pakistan and Taleban-led Afghanistan, they have tended to work in tandem with their national

authorities.[22] Though uneven and rather discretionary development
has itself caused serious backlashes in the Muslim world, leading to
desperate acts, again this should not be read as total rejection of modernisation as such. It is curious to note that in critiquing modernity
the postmodernists in the West and the Islamicists share a unique
convergence. Both are opposed to individualism and territorial
nationalism for the perceived dehumanisation that they may entail.[23]

The divergence in handling Westernised modernity has created
deep fissures between the traditionalists and modernising reformists
in all Muslim societies, including Turkey. Traditionalists or revival-
ists like the Ikhwan in Egypt, the Deobandis and Brelvis in British
India,[24] the Salafis in North Africa, the Wahabis on the Arabian
Peninsula, the Mujtahids in Persia and various mystical *silsilahs* saw
in Islamic revival a true, as well as the only, solution to the Muslim
predicament. The reformists, on the contrary, saw no other way out
than accepting the dictates of modern (Western) civilisation through
its manifestations such as the English and French languages,
adoption of Western education and a *national* redefinition of society
as a territory-based, sovereign *political* community. In Muslim India
the early modernising leader was Sir Syed Ahmed Khan (1817–98),
who not only opened a major Western-style academic institution in
Aligarh but also tried to reinterpret Quranic knowledge. The traditionalists were inherently Pan-Islamicists, though in several
exceptional cases such as Jamal-ud-Din Afghani (1839–97) and his
Egyptian student, Muhammad Abduh, or some Young Turks, they
also included elements which, despite their rootedness in Islam, were
willing to coopt some Western values without surrendering Islamic
trans-territoriality – milletism. That is why, in British India, one finds
a powerful trans-regionalism in the works of Sir Muhammad Iqbal
(1875–1938) and among the leaders of the Khilafat Movement (the
movement in India for preservation of the caliphate), for whom
Ottoman Turkey symbolised the last remnant of Islamic milletism.
Iqbal, however, accepted the necessity of territory-based nationalism because of its liberationist premise. In his famous presidential
address to the All-India Muslim League in 1930 at Allahabad, he
envisioned a separate statehood/nationhood for Indian Muslims.
The traditionalist Muslims in South Asia were led by various parties
and personalities including Maulana Abul Kalam Azad[25] and Syed
Abul Ala Mawdudi.[26] These two scholar-politicians both started as
journalists and became the leaders of two powerful religio-political

organisations. To Iqbal, the eventual Muslim fraternity could be achieved following complete independence of the entire colonised Muslim world through nationalist struggle. Thus, to him, nationalism had become a necessary evil – 'one of many new gods' – though its liberationist ideology was inherently 'irreligious' by virtue of idealising secular over sacred and mundane over moral.[27] To Iqbal, as he confided to Halide Edib Khanum, the Turkish republic did not pose any contradiction since Kemal Ataturk's dynamism had saved the sinking boat; but to the traditionalist Maulana Azad, the Khilafat, even in its symbolic sense, was a necessity for the Muslim world. To the Indian Muslims, Turkey, with its sultanate and khilafat, symbolised the last Muslim sovereign entity resisting the Andalusia syndrome. They were initially confused when Kemal himself abolished these institutions but rejoiced with his establishment of a republic through a valiant anti-colonial campaign. It was his anti-Western campaign that brought Indian Muslims back to rally around him, though they were baffled by some of his most radical reforms.[28]

MUSLIM DISCOURSE: A HALF-WAY HOUSE

One may decry the orthodox and fundamentalist elements among Muslims for being overtly aggressive, anti-reformist and solidly intolerant, but looking at the post-independence histories of almost all Muslim countries, it becomes apparent that the monopolistic, arrogant, class-centred and supercilious policies of the ruling elites have not been fair either. Corruption, coercion, centralisation and opportunism have further disempowered vast echelons of society which, in several cases, are subscribing to political Islamism. In its current context, political Islam, sometimes called *Salafiyya* (a return to early Islam), remains undefined. It may vary from place to place but is a reality which Muslims have to deal with. Typical Western denunciation of political Islam as merely barbaric fundamentalism – with reference to the Taleban in Afghanistan, the GIA in Algeria and similar groups in other Muslim polities – adds to the pervasive clerical fury in the midst of which reformers and moderate forces alike lose out. Political Islam at one level is dehegemonising, at another it is utopian since it promises generalist and unresearched deliverance and prosperity. It acts like a soothsayer in the face of Western rejection of Islam and the surrogacy of Westernised elites in the Muslim world. In that sense it has a class dimension, even though it promises to be classless. Ironically, political Islam in its extreme manifestations is becoming more and more introvert, violent and anti-women.[29] It is equally intolerant of pluralism – both ethnic and doctrinal – and thus is becoming a medium for coercive uniformity. Even if it triumphs, as it has in Saudi Arabia, Afghanistan and Iran, its own ambiguous joyriding with the state may preclude any possibility for a new, open, tolerant and forward-looking reformism.[30] Political Islam is modernising yet inherently anti-Western and is keen on obtaining political power to transform society from above. In most cases it is led by the disempowered, literate, intermediate class (*bazaari*) who are retaliating against the state-led forces of monopolisation and corruption. So far, the manifestation of political Islam at governmental level, unlike various intellectual reconstructions, presents half-baked and rather oppressive hierarchies and sadly feeds into the stereotypes of Islam as being authoritarian. On the other hand, the course of intellectual reconstruction of Islam according to the times and exigencies, as initiated by early reformists including al-Afghani, Syed Ahmed Khan, Abduh and Iqbal, has been further enriched by scholars like Shariati, Fazlur Rahman and Abdul Karim Surush. However, such a reformist or even revolutionary activism is still embryonic. These thinker-activists, in their different ways, have stressed the need for understanding Islam within a changing political and scientific context by urging for a reshaping of Islam from within and without. For instance, to them, the *ulama's* single-mindedness, their simplistic emphasis on dogmas, their somewhat strange disregard for human diversity, and their official appropriation of selective Islamic mores for political expediency are evidently hegemonic.[31]

THE DIASPORA: A NEW ANDALUSIA OR A FRESH START?

The projects of both Westernised modernity and political Islam, despite their recent and intertwined histories, are powerful traditions which share commonalities as well as jealousies. Both are transformative and promise better futures. Modernity may be less past-oriented, while political Islam largely receives inspiration from the past and wants to recreate it. Modernity is this-worldly whereas political Islam is largely other-worldly, although both concentrate on this world to achieve their separate goals. Modernity received its impetus from diverse forces such as sceptical reformers and conforming state hierarchies while Islamicists celebrate the primacy of belief and seek political power to impose uniformity. Both are ambitious, energised and have led to further dislocations through violence. Both subscribe to the intricate processes of selection and rejection to suit their own trajectories. Both have mundane and spiritual solace to offer yet both lack holistic solutions. Westernised modernity has the institutional wherewithal, economic power and military clout of global outreach. The globalism promised by political Islam is utopian and encumbered by doctrinal, ethnic, national and class-based loyalties. While postmodernity – a counterweight to modernity – may seek to demolish many of the modern edifices without putting satisfactory substitutes in their place, political Islam banks more and more on fundamentalist backlash. Islamicists enjoy and appropriate modern symbols, means and strategies to gain their objectives, whereas modernists tend selectively to use religious tokenism wherever it may help them form national identities and cultural monoliths.

Political Islam and the West have, both in the past and in the present, continued to see each other merely as religious monoliths. Both exist in each other and are far from being monolithic. West-led globalism is as hegemonic as the concept of *ummah*, though the latter may promise to be non-racial, if still difficult to obtain. The establishment of the Muslim diaspora in recent decades offers a unique opportunity to travel through the labyrinths of past and present within this interesting bilateral encounter. Most of the scholarly works on Islam and the West end up essentialising the differences, or focus only on more recent phases. They also concentrate on one or two case studies and those, too, within the limiting context of immigration, census figures, tables of achievers and non-achievers; or they simply reiterate Eurocentric views. This volume goes beyond these well-worn parameters; it begins, in Chapters 2 and 3, with a reconstruction of Islamic culture in Spain, to establish the historicity and nativity of Islam within the West. It also seeks to trace the evolution of the earliest form of tolerant pluralism on the Continent. These chapters centre on history, arts and the reconstruction of Spanish identity, with reference to a permeating anti-Muslim attitude, as manifested all over the country in yearly festivals – *fiestas* – where the cross overpowers the crescent. Modern-day Spain, Portugal and Italy are more tolerant than they once were, but it may take many years of effort to rediscover their Muslim past and its civilisational heritage, so as to engender greater acceptance for the Muslim minorities who live in their midst today. The decimation of

Muslims and Jews in the once thriving Iberian Peninsula reverberates today as the 'Andalusia syndrome'. Some Muslims fear yet another such total extinction. During the Bosnian crisis, this term was frequently invoked.

Chapters 3 and 4 concentrate on the Islam–UK equation, in which history, literature, Orientalism, colonialism and the postcolonial diaspora offer strong mutualities as well as areas of ambiguity and tension. This portion of the book looks at variables within the Muslim diaspora and goes beyond simple census-centred statistical tables and familiar but societally detached paradigms. Chapter 5 is an overview of Muslims in France, Germany and other European Union (EU) countries. It does not pretend to be comprehensive but locates the evolution of a more comparative outlook in which all the EU countries are seen gradually moving towards similar policies. Of course, the composition of the Muslim diaspora in each European state is quite different, but the regionalisation of Europe may offer more mobility and opportunities to the more recent generations of Muslims in Europe. Apart from language and socioeconomic strictures, immigrants have suffered from lack of organisational and institutional support mechanisms, which demand more cultural activism and concerted institutionalisation away from the routine and restrictive use of mosques. France's secularism needs to be more accommodative to plural needs whereas Germany is gradually moving towards accepting immigrants as new Germans. Chapter 6 may offer a new perspective on the emerging relationship between Muslims and Ireland, which has not been studied before in a volume of this nature. The topic, interestingly, was first discussed by Muslims themselves, offering a unique and comparative outlook. Chapter 7 visits the United States and briefly investigates the evolution and composition of Muslim communities, from the African slaves to present-day professional immigrants. US foreign policy, for example in the Middle East or South Asia, like that of some EU members, still does not reflect Muslim aspirations because of the newness of their Muslim community compared to some well-established counterparts. The situation also displays internal divisions and the lack of those institutional frameworks that could mount sustained and cohesive lobbying for overdue policy alternatives.

The Muslim diaspora in the West is both old and new and, undoubtedly, at the forefront of pluralist debates. How far these Muslims, while benefiting from the democratic processes and holding a position of advantage in the West, are able to construct a substitutive discourse on the larger human interests of Muslim communities elsewhere remains to be seen. How far Western Muslims and their counterparts can learn from one another and develop a better understanding – unlike the Andalusias, ethnic cleansing and militarism of the modern age – poses a great challenge to all.

2   The Saga of Muslim Spain: Pluralism to Elimination

> Do not weep like a woman for what you could not defend like a man. (Aisha to her son, Boabdil, after his surrender of Granada in 1492)

> May Allah render eternal the domination of Islam in this city! (Arabic inscription on a key in Seville Cathedral)

The year 1992 was an exuberant one in Europe and the Americas. The Soviet Union and its communist block had dissolved into pseudo-capitalist entities and the United States was reaffirming its global primacy; Iraq's Saddam Hussein sat licking his wounds after the grievous humiliation that he had largely brought upon himself in the first Gulf War; Palestinians and Israelis were pledging themselves in the Oslo Accords to a new chapter in their otherwise thorny relationship by committing themselves to peace and mutual accommodation; and South Africa heralded a new post-apartheid era under the leadership of Nelson Mandela who had been recently released after over two decades of incarceration under the former white supremacist regime. The European Economic Community had been transformed into a European Union imbued with glowing optimism despite some feeble ideological roadblocks. The West, or better to say North, was ebullient in overcoming economic recession as recovery appeared around the corner. In a self-defining manner, Europe, except for some of its eastern sections, was both integrating and contracting. Within the region, it reinvigorated mutualities and cooperation by deregulating visa restrictions on free movement, while externally it erected the most exclusive and forbidding entry regimes to preclude the possibility of any new migrations from Africa or Asia. Frequent denunciation of Islamic activism, justified in the name of a clash between civilisations, or between civilisation and fundamentalism, reflected through a bullish Islamophobia, was proving immensely opportune for Chetniks in their unmitigated campaign of ethnic cleansing of the Bosnian Muslims. Bosnia was a new Spain – a new Andalusia – where the Serbian conquistadors were pursuing unhindered inquisition in unashamedly full view of millions across the globe. Europe had again closed its eyes on its backyard while Bosnia bled, but only after the Western leaders had callously quarantined Bosnia from any possible external assistance. The Muslim world watched the mayhem in Bosnia helplessly, their leaders kowtowing to Western dictates and safeguarding their own positions. Russia, Greece, Bulgaria and some other traditional Balkan backers kept Serbians well supplied in their offensives, while Turkey, Iran and others simply sat on the sidelines as if relishing the unfolding drama.

The year 1992 also marked the 500th anniversary of the Columbian 'discovery' of the Americas, heralding the emergence of new bastions of European civilisation in the Western hemisphere. But, undoubtedly, for Native Americans, 1492 heralded five centuries of oppression. Similarly, for Muslims 1492 marked the sad and dreadful end to their over 700-year-long existence in Spain. The country's new rulers had turned the tables on people who were not only Spanish by any definition but also had brought glory to their homeland and despite a sustained period in political control had refused to impose Islam on their fellow citizens. Now their descendants at the beginning of the modern era were being made to pay the price for safeguarding and celebrating multiculturalism. Five centuries later, looking back at the demise of Muslim Spain, it appears as a gradual decline that was a long time coming, since the tensions had begun in the Middle Ages. But, in fact, it was rather sudden and traumatic: 'If there was an element of surprise in the entry of Islam into Spain, then there was an element of surprise in its departure, for no nation has disengaged itself from Islam so totally.'[1] The conquistadors were out to reimpose uniformity by an exclusive definition – exactly like their Nazi or Chetnik counterparts five centuries later – by eliminating Jewish and Muslim citizens, a process that had begun a few centuries earlier with the gradual southward expansion of the Christian kingdom of Castile. Now, in the closing quarter of the fifteenth century, Isabella of Castile and Ferdinand of Aragon, having solemnised their marriage vows, led the zealots to impose a 'final solution' on the Judaic–Muslim communities of al-Andalus.[2]

Why the country had turned against its own inhabitants is a question which has baffled many of Spain's own leading thinkers. For instance, Jose Ortega y Gasset wondered: 'I do not understand how something which lasted eight centuries can be called a reconquest.' To Gomez, it was an acute attack of Muslim fever which had taken over Visigothic Spain and had many manifestations. 'The fever – to keep the analogy – had many crises, improvements and relapses; at times it seemed incurable, at other times practically non-existent, only to come back as virulently as before.'[3] Following the conquests of Barcelona, Zaragoza, Toledo, Seville and several other towns across northern and central Spain, the ethnic cleansing had been reactivated with full force. Forcible conversions, murders and expulsions characterised this crusade, which had the support of the papal authorities and regional kingdoms.[4] Spain was to be retrieved and united for Christianity, a religion which had always prided itself in cherishing poverty, tolerance and austerity. The padres, invoking the crusading spirit, joined hands with marauders in a campaign which was made easier by the internecine warfare amongst the various Muslim principalities. Granada was the last one to fall, with Abu Abdallah or Boabdil, the last Nasirid amir, surrendering to the Catholic monarchs on 2 January 1492, though the courageous General Musa, refusing to surrender, rode out of the Elvira gate vowing never to return.[5] Boabdil was allowed to go to the nearby region of the Alpujarras with a handful of followers. Four days later, Ferdinando and Isabella victoriously entered the fabulous palaces of the Alhambra. According to the treaty of surrender, the victors had committed themselves to certain conditions. It was stipulated that the defeated Muslims 'would retain their own customs and religious freedoms and would be held accountable only to their own judges ... [and] Christian women married to Moors and others who had converted to Islam from Christianity would not be reconverted against their will'.[6] However, within less than a decade zealotry resulted in the annulment of this agreement. Soon after the Reconquest, Isabella appointed the notorious Spanish Dominican, Tomas de Torquemada, as Inquisitor-General and on 31 March 1492 signed an edict ordering the expulsion of the Jews. Similar edicts came into force governing official policies towards Muslims. Funds seized from the Muslims and Jews were spent on financing Columbus's four expeditions to the Americas. Subsequently, several Muslims of Granada and the neighbouring towns were either forcibly converted or expelled from their lands. A few of these Moors[7] were, however, retained, mainly to teach settlers from the north in the ways of irrigation and other professions. These Moors were initially characterised as Mudejars. Those who converted to Christianity were defined as Moriscos, and by 1560, were assimilated as fellow Christian Spaniards.

The Moors had been resisting the Catholic onslaught for several centuries and even after the surrender of Granada strove against total annihilation. Various revolts characterised this resistance but all failed due to the absence of a united front and any external support. In 1568, the last major rebellion under the leadership of Maulvi Muhammad ibn Ummayya was justified in self-defence, as he observed: 'We are in Spain and we have ruled this land for nine hundred years ... We are no bands of thieves but a kingdom; nor is Spain less abandoned to vices than was Rome.'[8] The rebellion, legitimated on the grounds of Muslims not being alien and also to preserve long-time pluralism, turned so serious that Phillip II had to seek help from King Don Juan of Austria to quell it. Soon, Spain had not only obliterated almost every possible vestige of its glorious, plural past, it had also triumphantly established itself as the supreme, pioneering imperial power in the Western hemisphere. But this was only after heinous crimes against humanity had been committed, both in Spain and in the newly acquired empire: 'At the beginning of the Columbian era, thousands of books that the Moors had collected over centuries – priceless masterpieces that their geographers, mathematicians, astronomers, scientists, poets, historians and philosophers had written, and tomes their scholars had translated – were committed to bonfires by priests of the Holy Inquisition.' The book-burning, as Jan Carew shows, was part of a massive cleansing programme under which 'an estimated three million Moors and 300,000 Jews were expelled from Spain (and this does not include the thousands forced to convert to Catholicism)'. This was a major catastrophe never seen before in the world on such a massive scale, with so many other annihilative miseries in its wake.

> The burning of the thousands of books and the expulsion of the Moors and Jews was a terrible loss to the Renaissance, although this is seldom acknowledged by Eurocentric scholars. And the glaring irony of it all is that the Renaissance would not have been possible without the seminal cultural infusions of Moorish and Jewish scholarship.[9]

Across the Atlantic, the policy pioneered on the Muslim and Jewish Spaniards was soon to be applied to the Tainos, Caribs and other islanders and, more particularly, on the Native Americans.

Columbus, a Genoan living in Seville, had been in the employ of the royal couple and offered them presents and maps of the new-found India in the Alhambra palace. Cortes, Dias, Pizzaro and several other conquerors of the Americas followed him throughout the sixteenth century to make Spain queen of the seas and the supreme imperial power on earth. Post-1492 Spain was imbued with an aggressive vigour, and hot from its first successful ethnic cleansing, pursued another similar campaign against the Native Americans. Christianity or death were the only two options given to the Indian communities. The Incas and Aztecs were annihilated. Their wealth found its way into the royal *haciendas* of Spain where it was used to build more churches and palaces. Spain had been able to create a new homeland in its own image, both at home and in the Americas, through villainous bloodshed and forcible conversions. The extermination of Muslim and Jewish cultures and communities in Spain and the so-called discovery of the New World are interconnected developments of great historical and socio-psychological significance. Heralding the start of the modern era, they led to other major developments, including the slave trade, within the context of the cultural and ethnic denigration of Africa, and the extermination of Native American and other indigenous communities, which was necessary to justify Spain's claim to have 'discovered' the Americas. In the same manner, the image of Columbus as the greatest hero of our times, imbued with the best of Europe and epitomising personal valour and courage – the essential qualities of latter-day American heroes – was created. He is hailed as the *European* discoverer, with emphasis on his Christian and other human properties, whereas his enslaving and annihilative activities are overlooked. Columbus as the focal point or as a father figure with a pioneering spirit is myth-making which remains at the core of primary education, official propaganda and conventional wisdom in the Atlantic regions. It is only in recent times that a new tradition in revisionism has started to challenge his hitherto indisputable credentials.

In this revisionist tradition, Christopher Columbus caricatured European 'anxiety-ridden perception about Other People', which was itself based 'on fears, fantasies and demons inhabiting the Western mind from Herodotus to Pliny, and from St. Augustine to Columbus ... [and which] had become an integral part of Europe's self-identity'.[10] It is further suggested that the desire to reach the Indies symbolised Europe's urge to confront the Muslim world and reclaim the lost Christian space, as well as to acquire the riches and resources that were promised. It was a psycho-political and religio-economic venture, which received multiple legitimacy through papal bulls,

Crusades and Catholic campaigns against Muslim control of Portugal, Zaragoza, Toledo, Seville, Valencia, Cordoba and Granada. The fall of al-Andalus was part of a process which culminated in the overseas imperial project. The campaign had received great impetus from the Turkish conquest of Constantinople in 1453, which was followed by a papal bull in 1455 crediting the Portuguese king for an effort to circumnavigate Africa in order to make contacts with the Indies so as to reach Prester John. (All through the medieval era, Prester John, a mythical Christian monarch somewhere in the heart of the Muslim world, existed in the contemporary literature and was imagined to have resided in the East.) The Columbian enterprise was possible only after the success of the Iberian campaign:

> The final defeat and expulsion of the Moors, after a protracted and savage racial–religious war of eight centuries and 3,000 battlefields, changed all that. This left enduring scars on the Spanish psyche. The victorious completion of the *Reconquista* left the social order with a vacuum of employment and purpose. The first response to victory over Granada was an initial move to rid Spanish society of its multiplicity, by the expulsion of the Jews. They were simply given an ultimatum either to convert or to go. The date on which this edict came into force was 2 August 1492 – the day before Columbus set sail from the port of Palos. Within a year of the fall of Granada, Spain had acquired a new *conquista*, the vacuum was seamlessly filled, and conquistadors were preparing to set off for *otro mundo*, another world.[11]

Columbus, in the revisionist perspective, is seen 'to have been driven by an overweening personal ambition and a truly monstrous greed, as strange and violent in character as the ends he sought and the adventures he invited'. He is considered 'inseparable' from chattel slavery, rather is perceived as 'the father of the slave trade to the Americas'. And 'this trade, far more than other consequences attached to his name, may be seen – it seems to me without the least manipulating of the evidence – as composing the true and enduring curse of Columbus'.[12] But on St Valentine's Day in 1992, Barcelona's Columbus married the Statue of Liberty – the bride being represented by a 100-foot wedding cake created by Miralda, the Spanish artist, who had worked on the project for ten years. The wedding cake, itself five storeys high, was topped by an Eiffel Tower and went on display in Manhattan's financial district. The extravaganza was sponsored by various US and European multinationals and by Birmingham City Council; the marriage was solemnised under the neon lights of Las Vegas. The festivities, aimed at bringing together artists from both sides of the Atlantic and Japan, took place under an official slogan: 'In 1492 Columbus discovered America. In 1992, America discovers Columbus.' Thus, Columbus remains 'the totemic figure in history',[13] as John Dyson, in his celebratory biography of the great navigator, observes: 'After Jesus Christ, no individual has made a bigger impact upon the Western world than Christopher Columbus.'[14] The transatlantic myth about Columbian discovery obliges millions across the globe to acknowledge its historical dividends. Within the United States and several other countries including Spain, mainstream historiography presents Columbus as the greatest pioneer, though many feel uncomfortable with the myth:

> The manufactured, but widely accepted, myth of Columbus as the brave and noble visionary who set sail on an unknown course and discovered a whole new world belies the real legacy of Columbus: a bloody legacy of rape, pillage and plunder. But, it is a myth which is quite consistent with how most of US history is recounted by mainstream historians – as great deeds by great white men which resulted in great things for all humankind. More specifically, it is a myth which celebrates imperial conquest, male supremacy and the triumph of military might as necessary components of progress and civilisation.[15]

The climactic fall of Granada in 1492 consummated the unification of the country and invigorated the crusading spirit of the Catholic *conquistadors* in the Americas. Sadly, the populace was intent upon removing every vestige – living or dead – of the multiculturalism that interfaced with the Muslim and Jewish past. The ebullient Spaniards, in particular the Castilians, imbued with an extraordinary vigour, did not content themselves with the retrieval of their country but were to carry the Bible and the sword to conquer Native American cultures from the Oregon coast to Patagonia.[16] The fall of the Aztecs in 1519–20, like that of the Andalusian Moors, was, in fact, the herald of a 'reawakened Europe', symbolised by *conquistadors* and monks, and of its expansion westward, eastward and southward, except for those areas administered by three mainland Muslim empires – Ottoman, Mughal and Safwid. Christian Spain established its empire and so-called unity, but at a stupendous expense. Self-denial, self-infliction, social brutalisation and sheer banditry were unable to guarantee an enduring glory and everlasting prosperity. The queen of the seas and explorer of the New World was soon isolated and, at the most, worthy of occasional racist and aggressive rebukes from its northern neighbours. Spain during the next five centuries dismally lacked anything like what it had witnessed before 1492 when it had prized human excellence, rather than depending on booty from the impoverished and debilitated colonies. Spirituality gave way to banditry and criminalisation, the arts almost disappeared from the scene except for the crude conversion of mosques and palaces into cathedrals. Libraries were gutted and the cities of Toledo, Cordova, Seville, Murcia, Granada and Tarifa became deserted, soulless frontier settlements deprived of their urbane past.

> The dizzying successes achieved by Spanish feats of arms during the aggressive expansion of Castile and Aragon consolidated a social structure that was ill-equipped, in the long term, to administer the vast empire that had come under its control. Among its elements were an aristocratic military caste that glorified warfare and spurned trade and commerce; a fanatical and reactionary clergy, hostile to any new ideas that threatened its monolithic ideological grip on Spanish society, and a succession of absolutist rulers who drained the wealth and resources of the empire in ruinous religious wars.[17]

Borrowed time and borrowed wealth brought in by the mercantile economy only added to poverty and social strife. By the mid-sixteenth century, scientific, artistic and philosophical pursuits had already shifted elsewhere to Western Europe as Jesuit fury in the Counter-Reformation and the clerical monopoly that followed almost decimated intellectual tradition. Later, as north-western Europe was industrialising, Spain slumbered on in the feudal age. Its economic and political development was retarded. The forcible evictions and large migrations to the colonies depleted the store of skilled manpower. Some lonely voices in the mid-seventeenth century tried to awaken the imperial hierarchy by suggesting an opening up of the country to inward migrations. Ministers were pressed to utilise the imperial coffers to cultivate the vast underutilised fiefdoms and to re-establish factories rather than waste them on debilitating wars. If Ottoman Turkey was the sick man of the Near East and Balkans,

Spain languished as the sick man of southern Europe. The bridge between Africa, Europe and Asia was gone, disappeared like the deserted and crumbling walls of the Alhambra, which were not rediscovered till the American writer, Washington Irving, reintroduced them to the world (and especially to the Spaniards) with his *Tales of the Alhambra* (1832). The Spaniards themselves exhibited extreme apathy towards their own past.

In the late nineteenth century, a minor skirmish with the United States cost Spain all her remaining possessions in the Americas and the Far East. Throughout the twentieth century, Spain suffered from its chronic problems of a lethargic landowning class, a change-resistant clergy and a factionalist political culture, which eventually led to a bloody civil war and oppression under the military-led dictatorship (1939–75) of General Francisco Franco. Franco tried to revive fascist and jingoistic nationalism by harping on Christian and imperial vainglory. Franco, the conquistador of the twentieth century, tried to retrieve Spain through his espousal of aggressive nationalism, couched in a religious and racial idiom, and sat on Spanish destiny till his death. Under Franco, the Columbian holiday was revived as the day of *Hispanidad* and Seville was selected for a great international exhibition displaying the imperial past. But without democracy and substantial reforms, Spain suffered from domestic turbulence, political suffocation and economic stagnation. Externally, its image remained tarnished even within Europe itself. It was in the 1980s that a pluralist Europe in the form of the European Union re-energised Spain and ended its long era of isolation and desolation. In 1992 a vibrant and changed Spain was well on the way to prosperity. It did not feel any great desire to rewrite its history as it celebrated the Columbian and later colonial campaigns. Ensconced in its newly discovered European identity, it had already protected its southern frontiers against any influx of North African economic migrants. In 2001–03, Spain enthusiastically supported the US-led campaign against terror, and in the process, imposed curbs and surveillance on many of its Muslim inhabitants.

MUSLIM SPAIN: A FORGOTTEN CHAPTER

But why Spain turned against itself as it did 444 years before the civil war of the twentieth century is a question which cannot be easily answered. However we can try to reconstruct pre-1492 Spain with all its strengths and weaknesses. Perhaps that may help us explore the beginnings of the end that came about so tragically in the fifteenth century.

The expansion of Islam outside the Arabian Peninsula was owing to the very universalist nature of the message itself. The Prophet's own austere life yet dynamic strategy to convey the message to non-Arab communities was aimed at presenting Islam as a non-ethnic ideology. To a considerable extent, he was able to achieve that during his lifetime by sending emissaries to the Sassanid and Byzantine emperors as well as to regional powers such as Abyssinia. In addition, he was able to transform and train a whole generation of practitioners around him for whom the demise of the Prophet did not mean halting the process of Islamic propagation. The Pious Caliphate (the reign by four successors to the Prophet), within its tenure of 32 years, had been able to establish Islam as the dominant Middle Eastern and North African religion. Unlike Christianity, Islam intentionally aimed at establishing polities to transform and govern communities. Such an enterprise was not simply a *razzia* – a war for booty – but rather a complex ideology incorporating several factors. Islam was an effective way out of the perennial identity crises experienced by Arabs due to their denigration by external urban Iranian and Roman societies. It was also a rallying cry away from the multifarious ethno-tribal dissensions that had been sapping the energies of both urban and desert Arab communities. Thus, when the Arabs conquered North Africa, the Berbers and several other non-Arab tribes had no hesitation in accepting the new faith. It preserved their social and tribal hierarchies but also gave them a leading role as empire builders.

Spain in the eighth century stood exhausted as its regional kingdoms engaged in terminal internecine warfare. Visigothic Spain of the early medieval era reflected serious discontent among its inhabitants, and the invading Muslims were perceived as liberators.[18] Likewise, Jewish groups in Spain welcomed Muslims as the former had been frequently tormented by their Christian fellow citizens. For the Jews, who were mainly a merchant community, peace under a unifying authority and links with a wider Muslim world provided greater commercial prospects. In addition, Jews were being forcibly converted to Christianity; the advent of Muslims in Spain could give them a breathing space from this.[19] Inner schisms, the persecution of the Jews, a weak economy and a demoralised army – all these made the Visigoth king, Roderick, particularly vulnerable to the Muslim invasion of April 711–12. The invasion followed the establishment of links with important dissidents in Spain such as Count

Julian, who carried a personal grudge against Roderick.[20] The Muslim troops were led by Tariq bin Ziyad, a Berber general, who had been appointed by Musa bin Nusayr, the Arab governor of North Africa. Musa was a close confidant of Walid bin Abdul Malik, the Ummayyid caliph in Damascus. The Ummayyids were a clan of the Quraysh, an important tribe of Hedaz to which the Prophet himself belonged. They had succeeded the Pious Caliphs and were imbued with a great zeal for conquests, for worldly reasons. It was during the time of Caliph Walid that the Ummayyids captured Sindh, Central Asia, parts of North Africa and then Spain. Tariq, the young general, landed with 7,000 troops on the rock, at the southernmost tip of Andalusia, now known as Gibraltar. Named after him, it was called Jablul Tariq (Tariq's Rock) – subsequently anglicised as Gibraltar.[21] Most of his soldiers were Berbers. His advent, like the fall of Boabdil in 1492, has been dramatised in historical and literary accounts. It is said that after landing on the rock, Tariq ordered his men to torch the ships. The shocked soldiers queried the rationale behind this ostensibly lunatic venture, to which he is reported to have replied: 'All those parts of this world, which belong to Almighty Allah, belong to *us*.'[22] It is said that Roderick came forward with a massive force but before the actual hostilities began Tariq was able to enthuse his companions in the name of Jihad – the holy war – and told them that they were left with two choices: either they must fight and be victorious or be defeated and get killed. Tariq, a shrewd commander, was triumphant and started capturing town after town. In July 712, Musa also reached Spain with a fresh army of 18,000 mainly Arab soldiers. He advanced towards Seville and after capturing it moved north to join Tariq at Talavera, near Toledo. In 714, Musa captured Zaragoza while Tariq captured Leon and Astorga; Fortun of Aragon not only submitted before him but also accepted Islam. Both the commanders were moving swiftly and consolidating their hold when, back in Damascus, the caliph died and his brother, Sulayman bin Abdul Malik, ascended the throne. Sulayman, an enigmatic person, halted the Muslim conquests in Spain, India and Central Asia and recalled his generals and governors to the capital. Musa left Spain in the care of his son, Abdal Aziz, and reached Damascus in February 715,[23] while his son kept pressing northwards until he was assassinated in 716. Before his death, Muslims had captured Malaga, Elvira, Murcia and Narbonne (in present-day France). Spain was given the name of al-Andalus and became a province of the Ummayyid caliphate until 750, when the new dynasty of the Abbasids took over. They were also Arab by descent. After defeating the Ummayyids they soon shifted their capital to Iraq, where they founded a new city called Baghdad.

Administratively, the Muslim rulers in Spain largely depended upon the local religious and political leaders, who enjoyed autonomy in their regional affairs but were accountable to the central Muslim authority. In the hierarchical order, the Arabs were the superior class, followed by Berbers. Both ethnic groups mainly pursued the military profession and, in reward, were given official stipends. During the subsequent decades many of them became landowners and the state stopped paying them financial emoluments. The local Christians called Mozarabs were free to practise their religion. In some cases, they were made to pay poll tax in lieu of military service.[24] Initially, Seville was chosen as the Muslim capital of Spain, but subsequently, in 717, Cordoba was selected as the permanent capital owing to its central location. Andalus was controlled by a North African governor based in Qayrawaan (in modern Tunisia) but, given the distances between Damascus, Qayrawaan and Cordoba, Muslim rulers of Spain were largely autonomous. In 732, Muslim armies suffered a major setback at Tours at the hands of French troops led by Charles Martel, which stopped their northward expansion. In 750 they were fighting against King Alfonso I, the Spanish conqueror of Portugal, now out to reclaim Spain.

It was at this critical juncture that a young Ummayyid prince, Abdar Rahman (born 730), began sending his emissaries to Spain. His entire family had been slaughtered by the Abbasids as he escaped to North Africa to seek alliances with the Berbers. His own mother was a Berber, which greatly helped him in forging alliances with the North African tribes. In 756, he entered[25] Spain at the command of a combined Arab and Berber force, and, within a few months, was able to reunify a factional Andalus. In the same year, he was proclaimed emir in the mosque of Cordoba. This was the beginning of the Ummayyid emirate in Spain. Abdar Rahman ruled Spain until his death in 788 and was succeeded by Hisham I (788–96). The next emir was al-Hakam I (796–822), who was followed by Abdar Rahman II (822–52). These emirs tried to unify the diverse Arab, Berber and Spanish Muslim elements so as to preclude any possibility of internal subversion. Tribal rivalries and attacks by northern Christian kings such as Charlemagne of France posed serious threats to the emirate, which needed unity and, above all, an efficient fighting force.

However, from 886 to 912, the Cordovan emirate suffered from an inertia that was rectified with the ascension of Abdar Rahman III in 912 at the youthful age of 21. His long rule (d.961) was characterised by stability, conquests and prosperity. By his time the Abbasid caliphate in Baghdad had become weaker and the Fatimids had established their own dynastic rule in Egypt.

In 929 Abdar Rahman III formally assumed the title of caliph and thus Spain evolved its own caliphate.[26] There may be several reasons for this transformation but, in a significant way, it symbolised Islamic indigenisation in Spain, along with a greater confidence in the sociocultural institutions that the Muslim Ummayyid rule had come to symbolise. A sustained peace, greater interaction among its inhabitants, evolution of the Spanish language, and economic prosperity heralded Spain's entry into its glorious period of intellectual and artistic accomplishments. Muslim Spain developed an agricultural system by introducing efficient means of irrigation. The introduction of new species of fruit and vegetables, such as oranges, sugar cane, rice and cotton, along with a new tradition in building beautiful gardens, added to Spain's prosperity. Islamic culture, with its inherent urban characteristics, developed commerce, higher learning and the arts in Spain, allowing a greater synthesis of various cultural and regional traditions. Spanish citizens took pride in their institutions, which were the envy of contemporary Europe. During the caliphate of al-Hakam II (961–76) a new capital was constructed outside Cordoba, called Madinat al-Zahara. It boasted beautiful palaces, mosques, gardens and castles.

The Spanish Muslims largely belonged to the Malikite *fiqh* (a Muslim legal school) and, initially, it was mainly in areas such as law and jurisprudence that the Spanish Muslims made their scholarly contributions. Various other philosophical traditions were also present among the community, such as the Mutazilites (a rational school) with al-Jahiz (d.828) being one of the pre-eminent jurists. Another philosopher, ibn Masarra (d.931), was influenced by Greek philosophy and is credited with establishing the Andalusian school of mysticism. Other areas of Islamic learning such as exegesis, theology, history and biography received significant patronage from the emirs and caliphs. Despite the assumption of a separate caliphate, Spain did not sever its links with the Muslim world which 'is shown by the fact that a native of Spain, 'Arib (d.c.980), achieved fame as the continuator for the Hijra years 291 to 320 (AD 904–32) of the history of at-Tabari, the greatest of early Arabic histories'.[27] Ahmad al-Razi (d.953), one of the leading Muslim historians of his times, also came from caliphal Spain.

Arabic was the official language of Muslim Spain and Abu Nawas (d.803), a famous classicist in Arabic literature, hailed from Spain. The country's temperate weather and diverse terrain characterised by orchards, brooks, rivers and fragrant air, especially during moonlit nights, reminded Muslims of their ancestral lands. Romantic love, natural beauty, personal valour and heroic narratives provided the subject matter for poets competing for excellence in composition. Scholars, poets and artistes from as far away as Baghdad would congregate in Spain, such as the famous singer, Ziryab (d.857), who was originally an Iraqi Arab, and, after settling in Spain, founded the Andalusian school of music. The most celebrated Andalusian poet during this early period was ibn Hani (d.973), who later went to Egypt to find favour with the Fatimids. Undoubtedly, al-Andalus was a meeting ground for European, African and Asian intellectual and artistic traditions. In fact, as mentioned earlier, scholars attribute the evolution of Spanish itself to Muslim influences. Julian Ribera, in his researches on Muslim Spain, discovered various confluences, especially in the realm of literature. For instance, the development of romantic literature, with special genres such as the *muwashshah*, took place in Muslim Spain. It was

> a marvellous fusion of two literatures and two races in the multi-racial melting pot of Cordoba under the caliphate. It is undoubtedly the most original product of the Ummayyid culture, rising far above the provincial level of its other achievements.[28]

The libraries, scholarly circles and official encouragement for research attracted students and scholars from Christian communities in the north, generating an interaction destined to play a vital role in the subsequent reawakening of Europe:

> At the zenith of Moorish power, al-Andalus, that land of many cities, attracted scholars from England, France, Germany, Italy and the rest of Europe as well as from parts of the Muslim empire. After the Mongol conquests, too, al-Andalus benefitted from the intellectual cross-fertilisation of Muslim scholars fleeing from the wrath of Chengis Khan and his descendants.[29]

During this classical period, a new tradition in Spanish architecture, synthesising Islamic and Christian traditions, emerged in Andalus. Generally known as Moorish architecture, in some cases its achievements even surpassed those of the literary realm. Its earliest and most prominent creation is the Great Mosque (Mesquita) of Cordoba which was originally begun by Abdar Rahman I on a plot purchased from the Christians and subsequently completed by Abdar Rahman II, al-Hakam II and al-Mansur. During the *Reconquista*, the middle section of this unique historic monument was demolished to build a cathedral, but a vast structure dating from the early times is still intact and attracts millions of visitors annually to Cordoba to see the perfection of Moorish art. As mentioned above, al-Hakam also built a separate city outside Cordoba called Madinat al-Zahara – inimitable city – as an unsurpassed specimen of Moorish architecture. This suburban complex included palaces, castles, mosques, gardens, academic institutions and private houses. It reflected a synthesis of Arabic and Byzantine architectural traditions. The glorious monument, like Emperor Akbar's capital of Fatehpur Sikri near Agra, had become uninhabitable by 1013. Like Sikri it suffered from acute water shortage and proved impractical. It subsequently suffered from severe neglect and only recently, due to tourist interest and a new attitude towards the Muslim past, Spanish authorities have started making laudable efforts towards its preservation. Al-Hakam himself was a great scholar and gathered half a million books in his library besides encouraging scholars to pursue research in various disciplines:

> At the height of the Moors' rule, the cities they created – like Seville, Cordoba, Toledo, Granada and others – compared to those in Christian-dominated principalities, were centres of unbelievable enlightenment. At a time when the most insignificant provinces of Moorish Spain contained libraries running into thousands of volumes, the cathedrals, monasteries and palaces of Leon, under Christian rule, numbered books only by the dozen.[30]

Most of the Muslim rulers themselves shared a great taste for intellectual pursuits. It was in Cordoba that the well-known historian, ibn Hayyan, wrote his history of Spain in ten volumes.

After al-Hakam's death, his eleven-year-old son, Hisham II, succeeded him but the young caliph remained under the influence of ibn al-Aamir, who operated as the de facto prime minister with the title of Mansur bil-Allah.[31] Mansur proved to be a capable military general and by carrying out 57 campaigns – mostly waged against the hostile northern kingdoms – he tried to solidify the territorial integrity of the Spanish caliphate. He defeated the rulers of Castile and Barcelona but after his death in 1002 and in the wake of dissension over the succession to Hisham II, the caliphal institution became abysmally weak. Between 1013 and 1027 nine contenders laid claim to the caliphate. By 1030, after several more claimants, the central authority evaporated and, during the age of *fitna* (schism), the caliphate was divided into 30 autonomous principalities, generally known as *taifas*. Possible reasons for this sudden decline, as in Mughal India, are the absence of any clear rules for succession; growing intertribal rivalries; a weak middle class; and external pressures. These small feuding states were like Italian city-states, and were vulnerable to King Alfonso VI.

The divided caliphate subsequently received resuscitation from the Berber emirates, which tried to unify the regional entities by enthusing them with the ideology of Jihad. The credit goes to the dynasty of al-Moravid from North Africa, who themselves were inspired by Sufi Islam and came to be known as al-Murabitun.[32] Their leader, Yusuf bin Tashfin (also known as al-Tashfun), had succeeded in conquering Morocco and Algeria and, on the invitation of Muslim leaders in Spain, entered Spain to fight against the encroaching northern Christian kingdoms. He was able to unify Spain under his Marrakesh-based emirate which he had founded in 1062.[33] In a fierce battle at Zallaqa, Yusuf defeated the combined Christian forces led by King Alfonso VI. Following this grand victory Yusuf went back to Marrakesh but given the sorry state of affairs in Spain he soon decided to come back. In 1091–92, he captured Cordoba, Zaragoza and finally Seville – this last one having been under the control of another Berber emir, al-Muta'mad. Yusuf's successors, Ali (1106–43) and Tashfin (1143–45), strove to weld the dwindling emirate together by defending it from external invasions and internal discord.[34] They were followed by another Berber dynasty called the al-Mohads. They kept the emirate together until the end of their rule in 1223, following which the emirate fell apart, with city after city falling before the northern Christian kingdoms, who were themselves enthused by a crusading spirit.

The Crusaders had inspired the Christian inhabitants of Spain, Portugal, France and Italy to reclaim Spain as well as Palestine for

Christianity. European intellectuals, who two centuries earlier had been praising Muslim Spain for its intellectual and artistic refinement, now turned hostile. The scholastic vitriol of noted thinkers like Dante (1265–1321) and Thomas Aquinas (1225–1274) was couched in a powerful anti-Muslim idiom. The crusading spirit reverberated in the writings of these powerful ideologues of medieval Europe. The al-Mohads defeated Alfonso VIII of Castile in July 1195 at al-Arcos, a town between Toledo and Cordoba. However, the bishop and other priests used their network across the Spanish borders by drumming up support for an anti-Moorish crusade, and in a decisive battle in 1213 defeated the al-Mohad caliph, Muhammad. This battle sealed the fate of Muslim Spain once and for all, all the major towns being lost to advancing Christian armies. The only redeeming factor was the establishment of the Nasirid kingdom of Jaen and Granada in 1231. An Arab by descent, Muhammad ibn Yusuf ibn Nasir (ibn Ahmar) consolidated his power in his small kingdom, resettled the Muslim refugees fleeing from Christian wrath and tried to maintain friendly relations with the victorious northern kingdoms. Muslim Spain had virtually ended with the al-Mohad defeat but the rivalries among the Christian princes gave Granada breathing space. Moreover, a small kingdom of only 240 square miles did not pose any major threat to them. It also served a useful purpose for resettling Muslims uprooted by the Christian rulers in their unrelenting expansion. In addition, the mountainous terrain afforded some natural protection to this last small Muslim kingdom in Spain. Its most splendid phase was the second half of the fourteenth century when the Alhambra palaces were built and the court at Granada, like the erstwhile caliphate at Cordoba, attracted renowned artists, philosophers and poets to cherish its generosity during the vanishing glory of Muslim Spanish culture. It was the twilight hour and the final flicker before the approaching storm. In the 1470s, Ferdinand and Isabella ascended the thrones of Aragon and Castile respectively with an avowed aim of relieving Spain of the last Muslim vestige. Following the fall of Ronda (1485), Malaga (1487) and Almeria (1489) the eyes of the Christian monarchs were set on Granada itself. The attack was launched in 1491 and in the early days of the new year, Abu Abdallah, commonly known as Boabdil, surrendered and departed from Granada with a heavy heart and a few companions.

Curiously, it was during the period of political decline that Muslim Spain once again reactivated its intellectual and artistic activities. The greatest poet of Andalusia was ibn Zaydun (1003–1070), who composed romantic lyrics celebrating the beauty of Wallada, his beloved princess. Ibn Hazm (991–1064) was born in Cordoba, moved to Seville, and wrote *Qasidahs* for Ummayyid princes. He was a theologian and a poet, who pioneered a study of Christian theology and is also known for his famed *Tawq-al-Hamama* or *The Ring of the Dove*. This masterpiece of Spanish Arabic prose has been translated into several languages and as

> a treatise on love, it is the best in Arabic on this theme and can be favourably compared with those of Plato, Ovid, Dante, Stendhal and many others. It is a cornerstone of any discussion about the influence of Arabic poetry in Europe.[35]

Authors like ibn az Zaqqaq (d.1134), ibn Khafaja (1058–1138), ibn Bajja (d.1138) and the latter's student, ibn Quzman – 'one of the best poets of the Middle Ages in any language' – pioneered *zajal*, a variation of *muwashshah,* and excelled in creating romantic Arabic literature which was quite sensuous.[36] Like their contemporary Persian luminaries such as Omar Khayyam, Saadi and Hafiz, they celebrated human attributes and virtues; wrote of drinking parties by the rivers and fountains; and idealised the physical attributes of their beloved girls dancing in the moonlit nights and hiding among winding paths in gardens emitting the fragrance of jasmine and roses. The pre-eminent philosophers, such as ibn Rushd (1126–1198), known in the West as Averroes, represented the culmination of Islamic rationalism deeply steeped in faith. Undoubtedly, ibn Rushd was the most eminent intellectual of the medieval period and was duly acknowledged both in Europe and the Muslim world. Born in Cordoba in 1126 at the time of the Almoravids, he spent his youth in this town of universities and libraries. He translated Aristotle and his name became closely linked with the Greek philosopher. He attained such an international acclaim that special schools were opened in Paris, Padua and Bologna to study and propagate Averroism. In addition to pursuing philosophy, ibn Rushd was also an eminent physician: 'In fact, Averroes was a renaissance scholar long before the renaissance; he was a poet, scientist, philosopher, historian and mathematician.'[37] He had received the patronage of the Moorish ruler, Abi Yaqub Yusuf, and due recognition from the most famous Jewish philosopher, Musa ibn Maymun (1135–1204), also known as Maimonides.[38] It was largely through the efforts of Maimonides that Averroes' works were published, in 38 volumes.

Ibn Khaldun (1332–1406), the well-known historian and sociologist, was another contemporary luminary, of African origin, whose voluminous *Muqqadimah* – an introduction to history or 'Prolegomena' – remains one of the celebrated interpretive works on the origin and decline of civilisations. Through Muslim Spain, his influence was deeply felt all over Europe. A great North African thinker, he first came to Seville and then settled in Granada before moving on to Egypt. The well-known mystic, ibn Arabi (1165–1240), was a native of Murcia and later on travelled to the Middle East. A pre-eminent intellectual and prolific writer, he developed a mystical philosophy of Wahdat al-Wajud (all entities are one in the One), which influenced several generations of Sufis across the Muslim world. The last famous poet of Andalusia during this closing phase was ibn Zamrak (1333–1393), who was a renegade pupil of ibn Khatima (d.1369), whom he also succeeded as a cabinet minister after his assassination. Ibn Zamrak, despite his fame and power, evident even today from his numerous poetic inscriptions on the monuments in Alhambra, was also killed by the palace guards. Abu Hayyan (1257–1344) and ibn Malik (1208–1274) were the most prominent grammarians of the time, when a number of scholars had started leaving Spain for the Middle East. All through the history of Muslim Spain, Jews made quite significant intellectual, cultural and economic contributions. In Spain, under the Muslims, they found a secure and peaceful place and actively participated in diverse activities. The best-known Jewish philosopher and scholar of the later period was, as mentioned earlier, Maimonides (1135–1204), who lived in Cordoba and was widely respected for his scholarship. He wrote both in Hebrew and Arabic. Other famous Jewish luminaries included ibn Gabirol (1021–1051) and Ben Jacob (d.1283), whose works underwrote the evolution of Jewish intellectual renaissance in Andalusia and North Africa.

The end of Muslim rule in Spain signalled the end of a plural and versatile phase in Spanish arts and literature. The sad demise of pluralism coincided with an ethnic cleansing campaign in the Americas by both Spaniards and Portuguese and a big increase in transatlantic slave trading. However, the beginning of the end of the Muslim era in Spain marks the start of the modern era in international history and intercultural relationship. Before one can understand the extermination of the Muslim and Jewish communities in the Iberian peninsula – the former being the earliest and the largest Muslim community in Europe – one needs to have an overview of their surviving cultural and architectural edifices, which stand silently all over Spain and are visited by millions of tourists every year. The original Muslims of Spain may be long gone, yet Moorish Spain lives through the names of its cities and people, its cuisine, music, literary genres, and hundreds of architectural monuments, despite their mutilation; and, most of all, through a very living Spanish language. As will be seen in the next chapter, in cities such as Seville, Cordoba, Granada and other places across the country the Muslim historical and cultural imprint remains indelible.

3 Muslims in Spain: Beginning of an End

> Had I known what this was, I would not have allowed it to reach the ancient part, as what you are doing is already done elsewhere, but you have undone what is unique in the world. (Charles V on seeing the wide-ranging destruction of the Cordoba mosque by Christian clergy)

> *La ghalib illal Allah* (Nobody is all-powerful except for Allah). (A calligraphic inscription in the Alhambra)

The Spanish Muslims have been long gone from the Iberian Peninsula but their cultural, artistic and literary imprints are an integral part of the Spanish heritage. The celebration of Moorish architecture, especially in recent years, is due not simply to its financial and tourist implications but also to its historical and artistic significance. With a growing recognition of the Muslim past as the *Spanish* past, the Muslim manuscripts, various artifacts and architectural remnants have attained a new salience. This literary and cultural nostalgia, ironically, coexists with an enduring anti-Muslim sentiment displayed through mock fights and fiestas all over Spain.

It is pertinent to study Spanish Muslim architecture in order to reconstruct the richness and nativity of Muslim artistic experience and also to historicise Islam in the West. The best way to do this is by visiting Muslim buildings – both those that remain intact and those that have been transformed – all over Spain; and there is no better place to start the journey than in Andalusia itself, the southernmost province and the last abode of the Spanish Muslims. This will also help the historian to comprehend the sense of loss among Muslim scholars worldwide over the extinction of a rich culture in Spain, especially at a time when Europe was revitalising itself through significant commercial, intellectual and geographic innovations. These parallel processes of extinction and regeneration, viewed nostalgically by South Asian Muslim intellectuals such as Muhammad Iqbal, Abdul Haleem Sharrar and Nasim Hejazi and by Arab writers such as Nisar Kabbani, as well as by contemporary Muslim intellectuals in the diaspora, spawned a permanent fear of the total elimination of a Muslim community, generally known as the 'Andalusia syndrome'.[1] It is in cities such as Seville, Cordoba, Granada and countless other towns across Spain that one encounters a 'lost' past in the country's plural history. While Muslim intellectuals may remember this past with nostalgia and sorrow, the Spanish seasonal fiestas posit it as a triumph of cross over crescent.

Seville, during the colonial period, emerged as the main channel in the tobacco trade with the Americas. Here the Muslim and Mudejar arts developed at their best, though subsequently the focus shifted to a neo-Gothic style. The three major landmarks in Seville – the Giralda Tower, the cathedral and the Alcazar – are within easy access of the winding and intersecting alleys of Barrio Santa Cruz and the medieval Jewish quarter. Despite the Muslim caliphate shifting to Cordoba a few years after the Muslim conquest of Andalusia, Seville retained its cultural and political primacy. During the caliphal decline in the eleventh century it re-emerged as the capital of the most powerful independent state, which included Murcia, Cordoba and Jaen. The ruling Abbadids, especially during their heyday (1023–91), led Seville to a golden age in literature and the arts. Especially under the last ruler, al-Muta'mad – generally known as the 'poet king' – Seville's court became unrivalled in literary excellence. Following the Almoravids, Seville became the capital of the last major Muslim empire under the Almohads, another Berber dynasty. Until their defeat in 1212 by the combined northern Christian powers at Las Navas de Tolosa, the Almohads rebuilt the Alcazar, further enlarged the main mosque and built a 100-metre tower capped with four copper spheres. The tower could be seen from miles around and symbolised Islamic power, besides being used as the minaret for calling the faithful to prayer. In addition, it functioned as an observatory. Because it was such a symbol of religio-political power, the fleeing Muslims tried to destroy it before the Christian conquest of Seville. An ultimatum by King Alfonso X, however, stopped them from demolishing it and the minaret was renamed in the sixteenth century as the Giralda, literally meaning the weather vane. Now it serves as the bell tower for the cathedral built beside it. The 35 gently inclined ramps, wide enough for two mounted *muezzins* to negotiate its bends, take visitors to the top to glimpse the old town, the cathedral's Gothic roof tops and buttresses, and the river. It took the Muslims twelve years (1184–96) to build the tower – a structure made entirely of brick, with arched niches and successions of windows. Latter-day additions, such as the balconies and a belfry in four diminishing storeys, were built during the Renaissance period as Christian symbols, but they have only spoiled the original simplicity and harmony. Despite the replacement of the original copper spheres this is still one of the most magnificent historical monuments from the Muslim past.

The present-day entrance to the Giralda was, in fact, the original entry to the mosque site; its exit was somewhere in the left-hand corner of the cathedral. After the reconquest of Seville by Ferdinand III in 1248, the mosque, enlarged by the Almohads, was consecrated to the Virgin Mary and converted into the cathedral. The original structure of the mosque survived until 1402, when a project for an 'unrivalled cathedral' was started. Only the Giralda, an arch near the entrance, and the main courtyard, the Patio de los Naranjos, with its Arabian fountain in the middle, remain of the old mosque.[2] In one of the cathedral's rooms, used as the treasury, amidst the silverware and other tokens of colonial wealth, lie the keys presented to Ferdinand by the Jewish and Muslim communities of Seville following the surrender of the city. An Arabic prayer – 'May Allah render eternal the domination of Islam in this city!' – ironically adorns one of the keys. Nearby, stands a massive monument to honour Columbus: four allegorical figures representing the kingdoms of Leon, Castile, Aragon and Navarra bear the hero's coffin. The lance of Castile is shown piercing a pomegranate, symbol of the emirate of Granada.[3]

Facing the cathedral and across the Plaza del Triunfo – marking the Christian reconquest through a statue of the Virgin and a large cross – lies the Alcazar, the most beautiful and sensuous building in Seville. Still used today as a royal residence during the ruling family's visits to Andalusia, the Alcazar was originally built as a palace by the Arab rulers, though for a time, under the Almohads, it was turned into a citadel. During the reign of Abdar Rahman III, the first gubernatorial residence was built on the present site of the Alcazar. The residence-cum-fortress, of which only the parade ground still exists, is presently known as the Flag Court and was designed by the Syrian architect, Abdallah bin Sannan. In its early heyday, the Alcazar covered a huge expanse of land all the way to Torre del Oro on the banks of the Guadalquivir. The emergence of the cathedral, Lonja and several more recent buildings have gradually circumscribed the complex, which represents Arabian, Berber, Mudejar, Renaissance and modern architectural traditions. Portions of the early walls and various other arches of the original buildings do, however, survive here and there amongst the various additions and changes. The gateway called the Lion's Gate is built in the original, massive Almohad wall and opens into a courtyard where Pedro the Cruel (1234–1269) used to issue his hasty judgements. The entrance got its name from the portrait of a crowned lion on a tile positioned in the red wall right above the main entrance. This is believed to have replaced an original tile which carried the Arabic name of the complex – *al-Qasar al-Mubarrak* – the blessed palace. The main palace stands within the courtyard flanked by several buildings attributed to Isabella and her grandson, Charles V. The facade represents Mudejar art, and its marble-columned windows and overhanging roof are the finest of their type in the entire complex. Inside the palace there are several small rooms built of marble, with intricate *jalli* works and mosaics. Small pillars support the decorated arches, whose borders, like the main walls, bear exquisite Quranic calligraphy. The Patio of the Maidens, reserved for women, has elaborate tilework on the walls and doors, attributed to Granadan craftsmen. Nearby is the bedroom of the emirs, with similar tilework and a small fountain in the middle.

The most splendid room in the Alcazar, called the Salon de Embajadores (Salon of the Ambassadors), is capped by a half-domed wooden ceiling. It is decorated with red, green and golden cells and horseshoe arcades originally inspired by Madinat al-Zahara, the new capital built by Caliph Hakam II, outside Cordoba. The Salon de Embajadores was, in fact, the throne hall, where literary meetings attended by well-known poets of the time used to be convened. In this room, al-Muta'did, the Abbadian emir, himself a known poet, would occasionally sing his passionate, romantic love songs for his beloved Rumaykyya.[4] Further down is the third most beautiful room of the Alcazar, ironically known as the Patio de las Munecas (Patio of the Dolls), originally a living room meant for women, where Pedro the Cruel killed his own brother in 1358. Another royal guest, an emir of Granada, was killed by Pedro here for his jewels. One of those jewels, the 'Black Prince', was subsequently given by Pedro to Edward the Black Prince and is held by the British crown. Charles V built several other rooms adjacent to the old Alcazar and decorated their walls with massive tapestries of orange, pink and green patchwork showing various battle scenes. Behind the palace itself are the Alcazar gardens, characterised by meandering streams and exotic plants. Lacking a uniform pattern owing to various subsequent additions, the gardens appear asymmetrical. The vaulted baths, rebuilt several centuries later, figure in a number of stories of royal conspiracies and romances.[5]

Cordoba[6] sits by the river Guadalquivir with the Sierra Morena marking its northern hemline. The town became famous with its conquest by Abdar Rahman, the Entrant, in 756. The emir chose it as his capital and after purchasing land adjacent to the central church of St Vincent, for 100,000 dinars, he began construction of the mosque – now known in Spanish as La Mezquita. As well as paying this huge sum to the Cordovan Christians, he allowed them to construct new churches in the town. Work started on the mosque on 31 August 786 but Abdar Rahman died before its completion, which was carried out by his son, Hisham I. The first mosque, completed by 797, consisted of one-fifth of the present structure and, despite subsequent neglect and crude mutilation, remains the oldest part of the grand monument, which for so many centuries was the most beautiful mosque in the entire Muslim world. It was divided into two parts: an open courtyard used for ablution and a prayer hall with the capacity for 10,600 faithful. The rectangular covered area was made up of twelve transversal and eleven longitudinal naves. Five naves faced the ablution courtyard, each with an arcaded opening. Behind the naves are the lines of horseshoe and semi-circular arches, which not only supported the roof but also added height so as to let in more light from the courtyard. The roof-top ends of these arches provide a series of aqueducts channelling rain water towards the courtyard and side streets. The aerial view of the mosque highlights a geometrical symmetry among the rectangular rooftops, though the cathedral subsequently built in the centre of the mosque has greatly disrupted it. Inside the mosque itself, the red and white arches – unique in their character and style and made of brick and limestone – stand on round marble columns, which display a geometrical evenness from every possible angle. Hisham used local pine, found by the banks of the Guadalquivir, to build the mosque's ceilings and surprisingly they survived until very recently, when several had to be replaced. Hisham finished the courtyard and built a minaret which was later dismantled by Abdar Rahman III.

Independently of the Abbasid caliphate in Baghdad, the Cordovan emirate, under Amir Abdar Rahman II (822–52), initiated sophisticated irrigation schemes and built its own institutions of learning, science and industry. Besides consolidating his expanding empire, Abdar Rahman developed diplomatic relations with other European rulers and received envoys from Byzantine rulers. He devoted his energies to expanding and beautifying the mosque, which became a religious and cultural centre of Spanish Islam. After the Holy Kaaba and the al-Aqsa Mosque, it emerged as the pre-eminent religious centre in the Muslim world. Eight new naves were added to the original structure, with a greater emphasis on interior beautification reflective of contemporary Cordovan art. The extension and restoration work of the original building was carried on by his son and successor, Muhammad I. Under Amir Abdar Rahman III (912–967), who assumed the title of caliph, Cordoba surpassed its counterparts in Europe and Asia in intellectual and artistic accomplishments. Himself a great administrator and an erudite scholar, Abdar Rahman III built schools, libraries and hospitals. In the late tenth century Cordoba had 27 schools, 50 hospitals, including pioneering separate facilities for lepers and the insane, 900 public baths and more than 60,000 noble mansions. In addition, the city boasted 214,000 houses and 80,000 shops, making it the most resplendent city on earth, outshining even Baghdad, the proud capital of Caliph Harun Rashid and his son, Mamun Rashid. It also excelled Cairo, the Mamluk capital and a metropolis of historic and academic monuments. Cordoba was more prosperous than Rome and its houses reflected a beautiful mixture of Arabian, North African and Roman architecture. The central library housed thousands of books and the Cordovan schools attracted scholars and artists from many regions. Cordoba had undoubtedly emerged as the new focal point between East and West, and between North and South, overshadowing even Seville and Toledo.

Caliph Abdar Rahman expanded and adorned the mosque with the utmost zeal and built an 80-metre minaret topped by three pomegranate-shaped spheres, one made of gold and two of silver and each one weighing a ton. The minaret has not survived. Following the Reconquest, the cathedral belfry, near the Puerta del Perdon, was built to replace it. However, one can still see the remnants of the old minaret; the reddish tower reminds one of the Giralda in Seville. The caliph enlarged the ablution courtyard and enclosed it by another facade. These works were completed by 951, though seven years later he had to repair a portion of boundary wall which had collapsed over the courtyard. A new enclosure buttressed by massive arched gates replaced the fallen one.

It was his son, Caliph al-Hakam II (971–976), who made the most brilliant additions in the mosque – generally known as the Second Extension – by adding twelve new naves, numerous columns and niches, and, most of all, by building a magnificent *mihrab* or prayer niche. At the entrance to this new extension, over the central aisle, a beautiful dome was erected both for beautification and to allow more light into the enlarged structure. Similar smaller domes were placed above the *mihrab*, supported by stone cross-ribs. The *mihrab*, with its calligraphic and floral mosaics – of Islamic and Byzantine origins – has survived the vagaries of time and presents the most splendid piece of early Islamic architecture in Spain. The inner vestibule of the niche has been roped off to tourists; behind it are the chambers where the caliphs used to pray. The *mihrab* consists of three oratories each with its own lantern. The central dome is criss-crossed by eight arches of exquisite beauty which support an immense single block of marble shell itself forming the cupola of the *mihrab*. Its mosaic decoration is bordered with glazed ceramics and Quranic inscriptions in Kufic style. A huge engraved silver chandelier hanging from the cupola holding 1,454 perfumed oil lamps used to illumine the *mihrab*. Within the *mihrab*, the niche is a small octagonal room whose floor is of marble and the frieze of alabaster. Nearby is the door of the treasury – *Bait ul Mal* – made of copper with *mihrab*-like arched decorative mosaics and calligraphy carved on it. Al-Hakam had enlarged the mosque to its farthest extent; beyond it lay the river, so any future extension could only have been to the east. A stone plaque with Kufic characters is inserted into the wall by the main entrance to Abdar Rahman's portion, testifying to al-Hakam's extension.

The third major extension of the mosque took place under the powerful chamberlain, ibn-i-Aamir (977–1002), who added seven rows of columns to the eastern side. As regent to the juvenile Hisham II, the son and heir of al-Hakam II, ibn-i-Aamir was the de facto ruler. Since the *mihrab* was in the centre of the early structure, the new eastern expansion, consisting of eight new naves, seemed asymmetrical. But it did not spoil the original style or structure and given a huge Muslim population of almost one million, the expansion was widely welcomed. The old eastern wall was opened up by new arches and some of the ancient doors were re-erected on the site of the new outer wall. The mosque – the largest in the Muslim world – now included 1,264 marble columns, 280 chandeliers and 1,445 lamps. After the reconquest of Cordoba in 1236 by Ferdinand III, also known as the Saint, construction of a cathedral was begun in the very centre of the mosque. This superimposition, amidst columns, double arches and spotless serenity, ruined this magnificent monument. The new buildings aimed at symbolising the Christian victory; they are largely situated in the section built by Abdar Rahman II, though a portion of al-Mansur's extension has also been affected. The mosque was mutilated not only by the construction of the cathedral but also through the displacement of niches by altars and the hasty blocking up of various entrances during the Inquisition and afterwards. Outside, the main courtyard, the Patio de los Naranjos, with its rows of orange trees, also underwent frequent extensions and in its present state covers a vast area. Almost in the middle is a fountain bordered by orange groves. Nearby stands a solitary olive tree which, over the centuries, seems to have radically twisted its trunk and lost most of its vigour. Centuries ago, this was the place used for ablution by the faithful.[7]

Soon after the fall of Cordoba[8] on 29 June 1236 before the armies of Ferdinand III, the Muslims of the city were forcibly expelled and on 6 July the bishop of Osuna, Don Juan, renamed the mosque Santa Maria la Mayor. Services were conducted within the centre of the mosque until, in 1275, the area occupied by al-Hakam's extension was converted into a chapel and the great caliphal arcade disappeared. More than two centuries of massive, fanatically zealous construction in the mosque continued to devastate this great heritage until King Charles V, himself a great defender of the Christian faith and no particular friend of Muslims, on seeing the destruction, could not restrain himself. In disgust, he told his fellow Christians: 'Had I known what this was, I would not have allowed it to reach the ancient part, as what you are doing is already done elsewhere, but you have undone what is unique in the world.'[9]

The mosque, the Alcazar, the Jewish quarters and a few other early monuments lie in the old Cordoba. The mosque is the central landmark, whose tower is visible from a distance. The alleys around the mosque are quite narrow and winding and remind one of those in Seville. Right behind the massive, southern wall is the old bridge used in Muslim times. At both ends of the bridge are massive buttresses and arched structures. This was the site of an old Roman bridge. Just a few yards downstream is a huge wooden structure which looks like a giant version of a Persian well. This wooden wheel, like several others of its type, was once used to draw water from the river for the Alcazar and other royal buildings as well as the gardens. Above the water wheel, on the right bank of the river, once stood the original Alcazar, whose gardens, fountains and flour mills received water channelled through aqueducts. This Alcazar was located next to the mosque on the site where the Episcopal Palace stands today.[10] The north-western section of the town is known as Juderia, or the old Jewish quarter, and was once home to Averroes and Maimonides and, unlike its counterpart in Seville, is still very traditional.[11]

In 1931 Muhammad Iqbal (1876–1938) undertook a journey to southern Spain and Sicily and stopped first in Cordoba. The mosque had been closed for centuries and praying there was unthinkable, as it is today. A sensitive Muslim from a distant land reached the town and absorbed its past. Not many tourists came this way and Iqbal was able to persuade the guard to let him pray. An emotion-ridden Iqbal prostrated before God in this huge, desolate, almost derelict building which once was the pride of Muslim glory and wrote his masterpiece. 'Masjid-i-Kartaba' is a moving poem in Urdu which recaptures the Muslim past, celebrates love and dynamism and takes the community to task for its ultimate laziness resulting in complete annihilation. Iqbal's rationale for the longevity of the mosque, despite all the intentions and actions to the contrary, was the primacy of eternal love for God, which had rendered it an everlasting existence. Iqbal's vision accepts no pessimism and lethargy. Everything is attainable only if the motive is pure and is rooted in genuine love:

> Shrine of Cordoba! from Love all your existence is sprung,
> Love that can know no end, stranger to Then-and-Now.
> Colour or stone and brick, music and song or speech,
> Only the heart's warm blood feeds such marvels of craft:
> ...
> Shrine of the lovers of art! Visible power of the Faith!
> Sacred as Mecca you made, once, Andalusia's soil.
> If there is under these skies loveliness equal to yours,
> Only in Muslim hearts, nowhere else can it be.[12]

Visiting Cordoba and not thinking of Iqbal is like visiting this historic town without ever venturing into the mosque, which is itself perhaps the unique and enduring monument symbolising an age, an epoch, a glorious tradition, a vanquished civilisation and a great tragedy.[13] To see the vestibule and *mihrab*, one has to be part of a guided tour; the guard[14] will not let any one else in, an attitude which is quite discriminatory.[15] When Iqbal visited Andalus a century ago there would presumably have been no tourists and officious guides and the Spanish guards would have been friendlier to a traveller from a distant land. But this is conjectural.[16]

Any account of Muslim buildings in Cordoba remains incomplete without an overview of Madinat al-Zahara, a whole capital built by Abdar Rahman III about 5 kilometres outside Cordoba. Like Shah Jahan's Mumtaz Mahal, he named it after his beloved, al-Zahara, the radiant, and spent a huge amount on its construction. Started in 936, it proved an unnecessary extravaganza claiming massive funds and was not completed until 961. Ten thousand workers and hundreds of mules, horses and camels were employed to build the project, which was intended primarily as a palace. It was 2,000 metres long by 1,000 metres wide and was located on three terraces overlooking the foothills of the Sierra. In addition to the palace, it consisted of a zoo, an aviary, four fish ponds, 300 baths, 400 houses, weapons factories and two barracks for the royal guards. It was a suburban capital and its visitors were stunned by its wealth and exquisite beauty. One conference room was illumined by pure crystals, which in the sunshine created a rainbow across the hall. The complex was used as his capital by al-Hakam II, who added to its decorations. However, after his death, his son, Hisham II, became a virtual captive of ibn-i-Aamir, the wily chamberlain. We should perhaps not be too hard on ibn-i-Aamir, though he was, of course, a dictator. He kept the caliphate together: given his raw age of 11, Hisham would not have been able to shoulder the administrative responsibilities of a huge caliphate, always vulnerable to invasions from the north. Palatial intrigues also threatened the caliphate from within and 'the Protector', also known as al-Mansur, kept it intact. He was able to extend caliphal political influence as far as Barcelona by conquering Catalonia and Galicia. His death in 1002 left a vacuum as his two sons squabbled for power and tried to influence the caliph, who now spent most of his time at Zahara palace, which itself suffered grievously from the strife. Within a hundred years, the town had become a deserted place as its precious bricks, marble, tiles, chandeliers, fountains and other expensive materials were continuously plundered by marauders. Especially after the downfall of Cordoba, the palace, royal house and mosque of al-Zahara, like all other Muslim monuments, fell into ruin. Excavations after the Second World War succeeded in unearthing remnants of these beautiful buildings. Like Akbar's Fatehpur Sikri or Delhi's Qutb Minar, it looks like a ghost town.

The survival of the small Granadan emirate for two hundred years during the Inquisition, with expulsions in full spate, in contrast with the maturing of its Moorish culture and its tragic end, recapitulates the entire Muslim saga in Spain. Though an ancient Roman town, Granada (Gharnata in Arabic) was one of the early provinces of the caliphate which, during the twilight years of the schisms – *Tawaif al-Maluki* – came under the control of one of the viceroys, Zawi bin Ziri. He selected the hilltop as his capital but, in 1013, brought it down to the site of the present-day city. Granada flourished under the al-Movarids, who captured it from the Ziris; the al-Mohads equally added to its significance. But the most splendid period of Granadan history began in 1236 after the fall of Cordoba, when Granada emerged as the last bastion of Muslim Spain. In 1238 it was established as an independent kingdom by Muhammad ibn Ahmar, a prince of the Nasirid tribe who had been driven south from Zaragoza. The hero of Nasim Hejazi's Urdu fiction, ibn Ahmar – a survivor against the odds – proved to be a just and successful ruler. Following the fall of Toledo, Cordoba, Jaen and other towns before the approaching Christian power, this was a difficult time for Muslims, who were being expelled from their homes in the north and were forced to move southwards. Granada emerged as a last haven for displaced Spanish Muslim and Jewish families. It was by paying tribute to the Christian kingdom of Ferdinand III of Castile that ibn Ahmar ensured his own survival. He even helped the Spanish king in his conquest of Muslim Seville, rather than putting up a united front with the Muslim principality. By his death in 1275, Granada was the only surviving Spanish Muslim kingdom. Including coastal towns like Almeria and Tarifa, it benefitted from the presence of migrant Muslim artisans and traders. Industry, art, agriculture, literature and architecture reached their zenith in the small Nasirid kingdom, which survived for over two centuries by giving allegiance to the Christian rulers of Castile and Aragon, who had their own reasons for letting it survive. The city-state flourished under Yusuf I (1334–54) and Mohammad V (1354–91), the two sultans credited for most of the buildings of the Alhambra palace.

By the mid-fifteenth century, history was repeating itself and the internecine palatial and intertribal intrigues and warfare unleashed several wars of succession. The Spanish kingdoms of Aragon and Castile were united in 1479 as a result of the marriage of their respective rulers, Ferdinand and Isabella. These two were enthused by a great expansionist zeal, and by exploiting the divisiveness of the Nasirids through building up a network of spies, were able to conquer Ronda, Malaga and Almeria within a decade. Thus, by 1490, the city of Granada stood all alone, totally unprepared to confront the approaching armies. Its ruling hierarchy was torn apart by a civil war between the supporters of the Sultan Abul Hasan's two favourite wives. The Catholic monarchs stepped up their pressure until the war broke out in 1490. Boabdil, the last Moorish sultan, appealed in vain to Ottoman Turkey and the rulers of Morocco and Egypt to come to his assistance, but it was already too late. In 1491, at the head of an army of 150,000 troops, Ferdinand and Isabella attacked Granada and laid siege to it for seven months. Finding himself quite helpless and unwilling to fight, on 2 January 1492 Boabdil formally surrendered the keys and was allowed to proceed further south with his family and supporters. After more than 700 years, Muslim Spain had come to a tragic end.

The city of Granada today can be considered as three sections: firstly the Alhambra, the Alcazaba and the Generalife; secondly the old town itself, consisting of the Moorish portion called Albaicin and the post-1492 Christian township; and, thirdly, the modern town of high-rise blocks, open boulevards and suburbia. It is the first two sections which incorporate the historical monuments that give Granada its unique character. 'Alhambra' literally means red, and the name may have been due to the red stone used in the palace, fortress and other buildings constructed during the caliphal or subsequent emirate times. The Casa Real or the Royal Palace, the Alcazaba and the Generalife – the gardens – are the main features of the site, besides the palace of Charles V. Ibn-i-Ahmar[17] rebuilt the old eleventh-century town of the Ziridians and added huge towers and a boundary wall around the structure. He diverted the waters of the River Darro eight kilometres upstream to supply the complex. The royal palace – the central feature of the Alhambra – was further expanded and redecorated by his successors. After conquering Granada, Ferdinand and Isabella lived in the palace for a while and converted the adjacent mosque into a church. Their grandson, Charles V, went further and demolished several rooms and the boundary wall of the palace to build his own circular palace. In his zeal to forge a link with Roman antiquity, he selected the design of an amphitheatre. His irreverence towards the Nasirid palace and other buildings resulted in further demolitions and an enduring legacy of indifference towards this notable heritage site.

For a long time, the Alhambra was totally ignored and was used as a prison until Napoleon invaded Spain. His troops greatly damaged and looted the palace and on their departure from Granada even attempted to blow up the entire complex. Their efforts were foiled largely owing to a crippled soldier who was left behind and took the initiative of removing the fuses from the explosives. The Spaniards continued to neglect the Alhambra until the noted American author, Washington Irving, set up his study in the empty rooms of the palace to write his *Tales of the Alhambra*. This publication drew attention to the significance and grandeur of the palace and the neighbouring gardens of the Generalife, resulting in its appropriation as a national monument. Recent restoration work has allowed the Moorish buildings and their decorative art to be seen in their original forms.

Most of the buildings in this part of the Alhambra, once inhabited by courtiers and other citizens, are now in ruins, except for the tower-like structures at each end. The extreme southern tower overlooking the sprawling city of present-day Granada, is called Torre de la Vela, named after its huge bell, which until recent years was chimed to alert the workers about irrigation hours. It was from this tower, at 3 p.m. on 2 January 1492, that the cross was first displayed above the city of Granada and the bell was chimed to inform everybody of final victory over the Muslims. Amidst exuberance and celebrations, the Christian banners were unfurled. A defeated Boabdil looked back at Granada and cried; to which his mother, Aa'isha, made the oft-quoted response: 'Do not weep like a woman for what you could not defend like a man.'

Unlike the Alcazaba, the royal palace – the jewel of the Alhambra – is a delicate, exquisitely designed complex of various rooms, private quarters, gardens, water tanks and famous fountains. It is divided into three main portions: the Mexuar, the Serallo and the Harem or living quarters. The decorative patterns on the walls and ceilings – of wood, marble or alabaster – are interwoven into simple but extremely well-proportioned designs and motifs. They seem to testify to the oneness of God and praise His power and majesty. The inscriptions are taken from the Quran along with some of the poetic eulogies composed by court luminaries like the famed ibn Zamrak. The phrase *Wala Ghalib Ilal Allah* (There is no Conqueror but Allah!) appears repeatedly everywhere on the walls, pillars and ceilings of the royal palace. It is said to have been the battle cry of ibn-i-Ahmar, the founder of the Nasirid kingdom, against a similar slogan (Allah the only Victor! Or Allah, the only Helper!) of Mansur and the Sevillian Muslims.

The Nasirid sultans used the Mexuar, the initial part of the palace, for court purposes; here they would deal with administrative and judicial matters. The main room of this section has a raised floor and decorated wooden ceilings, and was eulogised as a 'haven of counsel, mercy and favour' by ibn Zamrak. Opening into several smaller adjacent rooms, it has an arched balcony.[18] It is through a patio that one enters the Serallo, the royal residence, that was built mainly by Yusuf I, a romantic and scholarly sultan. He himself was murdered by a madman while praying at the mosque. After negotiating one's way through rooms and arched columnades, one saunters into the Court of the Arraynes (Myrtles). This is an area of splendid beauty and incomparable decorative art. The oblong water tank made of marble is bordered at both ends by small running fountains, while the arched slender columns, with intricate *jalli* and decorative work, usher one into some of the most beautiful rooms of the entire palace. The water tank with its gold fish is bordered by myrtle bushes beyond which stand the boundary walls. On the northern side is the Salon de Embajadores or the Hall of the Ambassadors. From the Mexuar, access to this magnificent room is oblique, via a columned corridor, so as not to afford direct and abrupt access to the sultan. Eight slim columns of marble support the arches that support the wooden ceiling. At both ends of this corridor are arcaded entrances into side rooms. Right in the centre of the corridor, the huge wooden gate, with two great doors displaying complex carving, opens into the ambassadorial hall, the biggest room of the entire complex, where Boabdil signed his surrender and handed over the keys to his Christian conquerors. Later on, well supplied with the treasures of Muslims and Jews, Ferdinand conferred here with Columbus to underwrite his campaign to discover a new route to India. The tiled margin of this gorgeous room is quite geometrical, with the dome-like ceiling consisting of several intertwined knots. The dome supposedly combines the philosophical and the spiritual, symbolising the Muslim belief in the seven heavens. It was built by Yusuf I as the throne room – *divan* – and was the hub of political and diplomatic activities. The Salon de Embajadores is a square structure measuring 11.3 metres on each side and is 18.2 meters in height. The name *Comares* is derived from its Arabic origin, *qamariyyas*, meaning colourful windows. A number of doors, openings and balconies attached to this room display an impressive amount of decoration and minute tile work. The ornamental motifs are done through characteristic epigraphs and the inlaid jalli work embodies a symmetrical precision. At present, just two solitary chairs sit in two corners, though during its heyday the room must have been furnished in elaborate style. Charles V, true to his frenzied temperament, destroyed the rooms at the southern end and only a portion of latticed balcony or gallery remains, since the space has been taken by his palace right behind these splendid buildings. The second floor between the Mexuar and this part of the palace, unfortunately inaccessible to visitors, is characterised by arched windows and wooden screens; it overlooks the courtyard, which is largely occupied by the tank and its two bordering rows of evergreen myrtle bushes.

Away from this central portion of the palace a corridor connects the Patio de los Arrayanes with the Patio de los Leones – the Court of the Lions – which has become the archetype of the Alhambra. This area, in the past, was the private quarters or harem of the sultans. The fountain in the courtyard is borne upon the heads of a dozen lions – symbolically meant to show the power of the kingdom – and gave its name to this section of the palace. A poem, attributed to ibn Zamrak and inscribed on the bowl of the fountain, tells of the fierceness of these twelve lions, who are restrained out of their respect for the sultan (Muhammad V).

The courtyard is surrounded by 124 extremely beautiful and fragile-looking slender columns made of marble, and consists of three main rooms, each with its own fabled past. At the northern end is the Hall of the Kings or Sala de los Reyes, whose alcoves preserve a number of early paintings on leather. The paintings are rare in their portrayal of humans and were done on several hides sewn together. One painting decorating the ceiling consists of ten Nasirid sultans, young and old, wearing robes and holding swords. Each one has his hand up as if expecting divine help. Sitting on a rug, one of these turbaned figures, apparently ibn-i-Ahmar, seems to be the centre of attention, but he too has his fist directed upward. Interestingly, all of them have a Caucasian complexion though their dresses are Arabian or North African. Entrance to the room is through three porches characterised by triple arches which are themselves anchored on slim columns. The Sala de los Reyes is a rectangular structure divided into three sections by half a dozen arcades. The arches display quite complex work in ornamentation and geometrical designs, while the borders display arrangements of small, square and circular tiles of various colours. The floor is also decorated with brown, blue and white tiles forming exquisite geometrical designs. Near the ceiling the arched decorative alcoves of similar intricate inlaid work give the impression of another upstairs floor.[19]

The Hall of the Two Sisters or Sala de las Dos Hermanas is named after two marble slabs on the floor and was built by Muhammad V. Built to a square plan measuring eight metres on each side, the room is splendidly decorated with 5,000 honeycombs which seem to hang from the ceiling in defiance of the forces of gravity. This was the residence of the sultana, the favourite queen, and opened into another inner apartment and a balcony called Mirador de Daraxa, known in English as the Eyes of the Sultana. From here she could see the festivities down in the main room and in the rear gardens. The windows in this room are not very high, but the location of the palace on the hills overlooking the valley and the town below would have given the sultan and sultana extensive views across the river Darro and the Albaicin. The balcony walls and the adjacent room are covered by plasterwork highlighting Quranic inscriptions. Passing through the various apartments, many of them redecorated by Charles V and subsequently used by the American author Washington Irving, one enters the Peinador, or Queen's Tower, an oratory used by the sultanas and later by the Catholic queens. Further below are the royal baths, with plain walls, marble floors, smooth arches and vaults for hanging the chandeliers.

Outside the palace, one enters the Partal, the big tank surrounded by well-designed gardens and a tall watchtower overlooking the town and the river Darro. It is called the Torre de las Damas and has several arched windows opening in all four directions. The ornamented wooden ceiling still retains its original decoration and the central cupola is adorned with stars and smaller domes. The oblong pool is guarded by two stone lions facing the tower, which has an arched, open-air structure underneath it; this seems to have been a mosque. The entrance to the mosque is through five high horseshoe arches, of which the middle one is the tallest. There are several other pools with lilies, surrounded by cypresses and various other types of trees. They are fed by water channelled from the Darro.[20]

The Generalife[21] is a huge complex of several gardens, patios and summer residences of the sultans and sultanas. The sculpted junipers, cypresses, terraced flower beds, several rows of fountains and secluded walks affording privacy to the lovers make this garden a unique experience. It has a staircase with water flowing down its balustrades, called Camino de las Cascades, and above it is the summer palace, called the Patio de las Acequia. This is an airy building like the royal palace, with decorated arches, arcades, wooden doors, ornate ceilings and latticed windows. Quranic inscriptions decorate the arches along with the usual Nasirid slogan: *La Ghalib Ilal Allah!* Across the palace is an oblong garden divided into two halves by a stream fed by dozens of fountains pouring water into it. Looking at the marble columns, arches, calligraphic inscriptions and, above all, the design of the gardens and fountains, one immediately thinks of the trans-regional aesthetic affinity amongst Muslims from India to Spain.[22]

The fist-shaped Albaicin further up from the Darro is another historic place embodying Moorish characteristics. It is the Old Granada, a city of romance, love, hope and despair, where once pluralism worked triumphantly before humanity succumbed to ferocious encroachment. Surrounded by the river, the Sacromonte hill, the old wall and the winding Call de Elvira, Albaicin sits across the Gran Via de Colon, which separates it from the post-1492 sections of the modern town. There are still some old Arabian buildings left on the other side of the Gran Via in the post-Reconquest portion of Granada. Just behind the Reyes Catolicos, in a small alley, stands the Corral del Carbon, a caravanserai used by Arab and North African traders. The entrance to this square building is through a horseshoe archway which still bears traces of the original Quranic calligraphy.

The two grandest commemorative buildings erected after the Reconquest are the Capilla Real (Royal Chapel) and the cathedral, massive Renaissance structures, the first the final burial place for the Conquering Couple and the second the largest church in the area. Right across from the Capilla Real is an immensely beautiful Muslim building called the Palacio Madraza, or *madrassa*. A remnant of the central mosque, this was once part of a large Islamic college, but only the prayer hall and *mihrab* remain. The prayer hall consists of a courtyard with a fountain in the middle, while the beautiful *mihrab* itself is a smaller version of its more magnificent counterpart in the Cordoba mosque. The facade of the *madrassa* is rather curiously painted, and its patios are closed to the public. The oratory is bordered by several arches supported by slim marble pillars, all in the same Granadan style as that used in the royal palace. While the lower border is decorated by geometrical, ornate tiles, the upper walls, ceilings and decorative arches are all done in the honeycomb style. Elaborate Quranic calligraphy decorates the pink and white *mihrab*, while its ceilings represent an intricate wooden arrangement with a contrasting centre made of pebbles, pieces of marble and glass arranged in angular designs. The honeycombs, slender pillars, wooden ceilings and overall layout are reminiscent of the Room of Banu Cerraj in the royal palace. The *madrassa* was built in the thirteenth century and, as suggested earlier, only a small portion of the main mosque survives. The flooring is of white marble while the bigger columns supporting the upper storey are of red stone, native to Granada.[23]

Four months after the Reconquest the first major cathedral in Granada was established in the mosque of the Alhambra itself. Later this was shifted to the Monastery of San Francisco,[24] now called the *Parador*, until it was decided to construct a huge cathedral near the great mosque in Granada, of which only a proportion now remains in the form of the *madrassa*. By the cathedral's entrance, one can see the famous painting by Pradilla entitled 'The Surrender of Granada'. The painting, with its background of the Alhambra, shows Christian and Muslim armies meeting on a mud road with Boabdil riding a black horse. He is followed by his Muslim companions, all on foot, anger and anguish writ large on their faces. They are confronted by a garlanded brown horse ridden by a red-clad Ferdinand with a green-robed Isabella on a white horse proudly flaunting a crown. The Christian army, including women, looks triumphal and jubilant, whereas the austerely clothed Boabdil is surrendering his sword to Ferdinand, who is extending his hand to receive it. The trees on the Muslim side are all bereft of leaves while on the Christian side there are green cypresses. Further down towards the Alhambra, the painting shows a few more horses and men, largely indistinguishable but most probably from Boabdil's camp, exiting from their fortress. This powerful contemporary painting shows crosses and banners on the Christian side while the Muslim side is lacking banners. Much space has been given to the victors and their elaborate regalia; the defeated Muslims are confined to one corner. Ironically, the hills behind the Alhambra all appear barren.[25] Another place to see in this part of the town, right next to the Corral del Carbon, is the City Hall, or Ayuntamiento. Reputedly, it is housed in a former monastery. Within the building there is a history museum which contains the original two-page treaty of surrender of Granada.[26]

Despite its indigenisation, Muslim rule over the Iberian Peninsula and various Mediterranean islands was viewed as an external imperial enterprise by several sections of these societies. Such a contrived perception of its externality, especially during the Crusades and the Inquisition, was greatly emphasised by religious and localist elements. The clash of religions, in particular, was used by the Catholic kings as a justification for winding up Muslim rule; they began to zero in on the Muslim community, which, after the fall of the upper provinces of Spain, had been confined to Andalusia. Although in recent years there seems to be a healthier recognition of Spain's Muslim past, even now there is a common assumption that Muslim rule was confined to Andalusia. This may be partly due to the fact that Muslim Spain is still an unresearched and unrecognised area within European historiography.[27] Despite the physical and demographic transformation of the reconquered towns and the expulsion of Muslim traces over the centuries, there is a multiple cross-regional affinity in the retention of several Muslim imprints.[28]

Toledo is a microcosm of the Spanish historical past and a miniature of Christian, Jewish and Muslim cultures. Surrounded by the river Tajo (Tagus) on three sides, Toledo sits on a rocky mound and, given the shortage of space, remains quite congested. Known as the city of El Greco, it was originally a Roman town called Toletum, which was under the Visigoths when Tariq captured it in 712. Comprising Muslims, Jews, and Mozarabs (Christians living under a Muslim government), Toledo became the most important town in the caliphate in its wars against northern attack. Known for its schools and buildings, it was a dynamic city of culture and trade. The Christian king, Alfonso VI, captured it from the Muslims in 1085. Even long after the conquest, Muslim cultural and architectural influence remained very strong, though gradually Muslim monuments were displaced or disfigured by new construction. Now only a small mosque remains from that era, though several buildings inadvertently display persistent Muslim influences. In several cases, these buildings were constructed by Muslim artisans employed by the new Christian rulers, examples of the well-known Mudejar art. Toledo was also a great centre of Jewish culture with seven synagogues, of which only two, Santa Maria la Blanca and the Transito, survive today. For quite some time, Spanish Jews occupied prominent positions both in the Muslim and in the subsequent Christian periods.[29]

To the west of Madrid on the way to Portugal is the beautiful city of Salamanca, an important centre in old Castile. Its houses and cathedrals are all made of golden sandstone and give it a unique appearance, making it perhaps the most beautiful city in Spain. As is obvious from its name, it was an Arab city, though it has lost almost all physical trace of its Muslim past. Besides its two prominent cathedrals and several churches, it is Salamanca's pride to house one of Europe's oldest universities, which in its heyday equalled its counterparts in Bologna and Oxford. Centuries ago this university used to teach 7,000 students, though its significance has gradually decreased.[30] To the north of Salamanca is another town with an Arabian name, Zamora, known for its churches and for providing foot soldiers to the Catholic kings in their campaigns against the Muslims. Further north-west of Madrid one eventually reaches Leon, the capital of the province of Leon, which at one time was part of the Cordovan emirate and caliphate until it was lost to the Christian monarchs. It was recaptured by Mansur only to be lost again during the internecine wars among his successors.

To understand the inquisitional fervour which eventually resulted in the expulsion and elimination of Jews and Muslims, the present-day researcher has to read through the pages of history; visit all the monuments and cathedrals which, in several cases, were once mosques and synagogues; and, above all, attempt to recapture the total and systematic ethnic cleansing. But there are two regions in Spain, other than Andalusia, which are living illustrations of an anti-Muslim venom created by the enduring ideology of Crusades, Reconquest, conversion, expulsion and transformation. These two regions, in opposite directions from Madrid, are Galicia and the Levante; brief visits to them may help determine the origin and spread of an anti-Muslim crusading ideology. It must be remembered, however, that within the context of the Spanish historical perspective this ideology played a crucial role in fusing the diverse regions and peoples into a single exclusivist nationhood.

Quite distinct from the rest of Spain, bordered by the Atlantic to the north and west and Portugal to the south, Galicia is a wooded land of rivers, beaches and waterways. Its terrain, culture, economy and even climate resemble those of Ireland. It is the north-west region of Spain, a land of hardy fishermen, farmers and navigators; and, most of all, it marks the end of a well-known Christian pilgrimage route which played a crucial role in the evolution of anti-Muslim ideology.[31] It was in Galicia during the Muslim conquest of the Iberian Peninsula that the early Christian kingdom of Asturias came into being, where a close collaboration was developed between the clergy and other trans-regional allies to begin the Reconquest. This mountainous territory, enjoying close links with France and the rest of the Christian world, became the stronghold of the anti-Muslim Crusades in Spain and elsewhere. The Camino de Santiago, the symbolic Christian pilgrims' route, the longest of its type, terminated here in the city of Santiago. Millions have visited the holy shrine of St James, whose body, along with that of his two companions, is believed to have been buried here. St James the Apostle, known in the Spanish-speaking world as Santiago and as St Jacques to the French, was a cousin of Jesus who visited Zaragoza before going back to the Holy Land. He was killed by the Egyptians and his body taken to Jaffa by two of his disciples. According to general belief not substantiated by the Bible, a sail-less and crewless boat appeared from nowhere and took the body of St James and his two followers to the Atlantic coast of Spain. According to commonly held belief it took the boat only seven days from Palestine to reach Padron, 20 kilometres south of Santiago. According to legend, the saint's body was buried at Santiago, though over the next 750 years people seem to have forgotten the location of the burial place. It was 'rediscovered' at Compostela in 813 at an opportune moment, when the Moors had captured almost the entire peninsula and carried out their campaign against the Christian kings of Asturias. The Muslims waged Jihad against these enemies, who felt a need to counter this formidable ideology with a similar one. By that time, Cordoba had become the political, cultural and intellectual centre of the Muslims and its mosque had emerged as the third most respected Muslim place of worship after the Kaaba and al-Aqsa. The discovery of the bones of St James, under the altar of a site traditionally attributed to him, proved timely. A hermit is reported to have been guided to the hill-site known as Compostela, or field of stars.

News of the discovery flashed like wildfire all over the Christian world. The king of Asturias, Alfonso II, came to pay his respects and built a chapel to the memory of the saint, who then assumed a position as a beacon in the fight against the Muslims. All kinds of stories began to circulate about his numerous appearances – at least forty of them – during battles with the Muslims. Christian propagandists gave out stories of his hand-to-hand fights with the bearded Arabs, killing hundreds of them with a single blow of his sword. Alfonso's successor, Ramiro I, swore that in a battle in 844 he had personally seen St James fighting against the Muslims and killing 60,000 of them. The saint was named Santiago Matamoros or St James the Moor-killer. (It is interesting to note that, later, the saint was rumoured to have been seen fighting against Native Americans as well.) Thus the cult of Santiago became a major motivational force behind the Crusades and the *Reconquista*.

Soon after the discovery of the bones and the stories of his physical participation in anti-Muslim battles, streams of Christian pilgrims started visiting Santiago, and the pilgrim way, the Camino de Santiago, came into being. Many people on the pilgrimage established monasteries and almshouses to feed other pilgrims. People, such as Chaucer's Wife of Bath, who had 'been in Galicia of Seyent James', came for a variety of reasons: some came for the remission of their sins or for meeting possible suitors, while to others it was an adventure worth trying.[32] After Jerusalem and Rome, Santiago became the third-holiest place in the Christian world. During the Reformation, however, it lost some of its popularity due to the Lutheran revolt. Catholic rulers such as Ferdinand, Isabella and Carlos V, Francis of Assisi, generals Franco and de Gaulle, Pope John Paul II and other Western notables have visited Santiago, further authenticating its significance in the Christian legends.[33]

It is the Romanesque cathedral in the town which is the centrepiece for the pilgrimage. In 977, Mansur, the regent in Cordoba, not believing in these legends, led an attack on the site. He wanted to expose the hollowness of the claims. His excavations, however, failed to find the body of the saint. In punishment, he ordered the citizens of the town to carry the bells from the belfry all the way to Cordoba. Eventually, after the fall of Cordoba, these bells were brought back to Santiago. The original shrine is now inside the cathedral and contains sculptures of the saints, with St James sitting beneath Jesus. By tradition, pilgrims usually pray with the fingers of one hand pressed into the tree below the saint's statuesque profile. For further spiritual elevation the pilgrims also embrace the Most Sacred Image of the saint behind the altar and kiss his bejewelled cape. During this sojourn they are handed a Latin document called a *Compostela,* guaranteeing a remission. The saint's bones are in the crypt underneath the altar. They were lost in 1700 just before an English invasion but were rediscovered in 1879. They form three skeletons believed to be of St James and his two disciples. Initially, the skeleton of St James was headless, but after a skull that fitted the gap was found in a church in Tuscany, the skeleton achieved completion. Its identity was authenticated by Pope Leo XIII in 1884, with a further affirmation by Pope John Paul II a century later.

Archbishop Gelmeriz was a well-known local priest in Santiago who rebuilt the cathedral in the twelfth century and claimed to have 'discovered' a ninth-century letter asking for annual dues for St James's shrine. The donations were to be one bushel of corn from each acre of land reconquered from the Muslims. For several centuries these donations were made, until the order was repealed in 1834. The archbishop's splendid and rather luxurious palace forms the northern section of the cathedral and shows a generous use of all these proceeds. The Catholic kings, deeply helped by this ideology, reciprocated by building more parishes and hostels for the pilgrims in the town. During the Reconquest, the conquered lands were distributed among supporters so as to provide a ready supply of soldiers. Consequently many of these huge tracts of land supported a feudal class. Interestingly, centuries later, much of the land in rural Spain is still owned by the descendants of these feudalist lords, several of whom, as satirised by Cervantes in *Don Quixote*, were quite uncouth or simply stupid.

Valencia in south-eastern Spain is one of the largest cities in Spain. It was captured by the Arabs from the Visigoths and remained an important commercial and military centre until 1238, when James I of Aragon conquered it. In Valencia and the adjoining countryside, the Reconquest is recreated regularly in the form of well-organised fiestas, where Christians wage mock battles with Moors (*Cristianos y Moros*). Such wars, characterised by Muslim defeats, are an important part of folk culture and general memory. They always end up with bonfires and great feasts. Each year, from 2 to 5 February, a battle for the castle at Bocariente is followed with a firework display at night. On 22 to 24 April, following a colourful procession, the two armies battle each other in Alcoy. Sixty kilometres from Alicante, the second largest town on the Valencian coast, Alcoy makes elaborate arrangements to celebrate its *Fiesta de Moros y Cristianos*. Around St George's Day processions and mock battles for the castle take place until the saint himself appears, to help the Christians. This legend of his personal appearance evolved out of the Battle of Alcoy in 1276 during the town's siege by the Muslims. Each year, new elaborate costumes are prepared and prizes distributed for the best in design and symbolism. The costumes then go on public display in the local museum. On the first day of the festival itself, the Christians enter the castle, followed by the Muslims in the afternoon. The second day is devoted to religious processions. On the third day, the gunpowder battle takes place, culminating in the appearance of the saint on the battle ground.

On 1 to 5 May, Caravaca de la Cruz enacts more battles and festivities. Early July witnesses similar street battles and music parties in Denia, while a five-day-long fiesta in Orihuela is characterised by mock battles and jubilant victories. From 25 to 31 July, Muslims and Christians arrive by land and sea in Villajoyosa, followed by a two-week-long battle between the two enemies in Sagunto. This town has an interesting old section of cobbled alleyways with medieval houses originally belonging to the Muslims and Jews. In Bunol, a similar event is followed by a tomato-throwing festival. All through the summer and early autumn such fiestas continue to commemorate the bygone polarity, with all kinds of demerits heaped on Muslims. In the third week of December, in Petrel, for four days Muslims and Christians battle each other, followed by victory celebration. Such fiestas naturally warmed anti-Muslim sentiments during the Expulsion and are still very effective in maintaining an anti-Muslim animus, though there are no Muslims at all in many of these townships. Like bullfights, these festivals serve only to invoke bitter memories and add to aggressive pride.

Murcia was founded by the Muslims in the ninth century as a regional capital on the banks of the river Segura and soon it became a major commercial centre. Most of its old buildings remain intact and not many visitors head this way, leaving the birthplace of Mohy ud Din ibn al-Arabi, a famous Sufi, much to itself. Murcia's main cathedral, started in the fourteenth century and completed four centuries later, stands in the heart of the town, having displaced the central mosque and other old Muslim buildings.

The Spanish islands known as the Balearic Islands comprising Ibiza, Formentera, Mallorca (Majorca), Meinorca and Palma, accessible from the Levant, were also once under Muslim influence, but were gradually captured by Aragon.[34] On these islands, with millions of European tourists milling around, every few months there are fiestas characterised by mock battles between Christians and Muslims, with Spanish heroism symbolically fighting against Moorish barbarism. For instance, the big fiesta on 17 January in Ibiza commemorates the victory of Alfonso III over the Muslims in 1287 and features mock battles. Palma, the hub of Mallorca, is characterised by several grand mansions in the twisting alleyways in the old town. Within the remnants of the old city wall, there is a huge cathedral on the site of a Muslim great mosque taken after the Reconquest in fulfilment of a vow by Jaume I. The Banys Arabs is the hamam with horseshoe arches and arcaded chamber which, somehow, has survived the wrath of ages.

To study some of the earliest Muslim and subsequent Mudejar monuments now part of Spanish heritage one may visit Aragon, a province active in the *Reconquista*, which lies between France and Madrid. A mountainous land of the picturesque Pyrenees, Aragon is hemmed in between Castile and Catalonia. Its capital, Zaragoza, with a population of a million people, accounts for half the province's population, and can be reached en route to or from Barcelona. Towns like Tarazona, Calatayud, Daroca, Alcaniz, Hijar, Ainsa, Sadaba and Torla not only maintain their Arab names but also house a number of early Muslim or Mudejar monuments.[35]

Hedged between the Ebro and Huerva rivers, the old town of Zaragoza (Saragossa) is a city of churches and plazas. Its best-known monument, the Aljaferia – the Arabian Palace – is still in use and is situated on the Avenida de Madrid, outside the old town itself. It was built by the Bani Kasim dynasty which ruled this part of Spain after the death of Mansur and during the decline of the Cordovan caliphate. Zaragoza was their capital during the tenth and eleventh centuries and the palace was built in the middle of the eleventh century. Thus, it is older than the Alhambra and Seville's Alcazar. However, following the Reconquest, several new additions were made to the palace.[36] Close to its entrance lies an extremely beautiful mosque which is still quite intact. Nearby is an original and dexterously decorated court, renamed the Patio Santa Isabella. A staircase leads to several rooms with carved ceilings built in the thirteenth century, the most beautiful of which is the Throne Room. The palace was used by the subsequent ruling dynasties, including the Nasirids, whose leader, ibn Ahmar, finally sought refuge in Granada.

In the plains of Aragon various towns and villages retain Moorish monuments such as castles, caravanserais, remnants of mosques and palaces. The old town of Tarazona is such a place; standing on a hilly site by a river, it is a maze of alleys, medieval houses and church towers mostly built in Mudejar style. Daroca is another small village with an impressive series of ancient walls with 114 towers, now in need of repair. Mudejar art is prominent in Teruel, especially in the cathedral, which was built by Muslim craftsmen. Barcelona is not only the last major Spanish city to the north-east, but is also the capital of Catalonia. It is the most cosmopolitan city in the country, a crossroads for various regional and international influences. The most prosperous and the third largest city of Spain – very confident of its own distinct Catalonian identity – Barcelona is known for its Gothic and especially *modernista* architecture. It is the city of Antoni Gaudi (1852–1926), founder of the Modernist movement, which combines Gothic and Moorish characteristics.[37]

The historical awareness of Muslim Spain and its cultural and artistic heritage is crucial in safeguarding present-day plural societies. It is certain that the shadows cast by the post-11 September campaign in North America and Western Europe, with its stringent internment rules and other restrictive practices, have once again generated apprehensions among Muslims in the diaspora, including Spain. Arrests of individuals on suspicion of involvement in terror – in most cases unsubstantiated – have increased the general fear of an anti-Muslim backlash. Such discretionary policies and antagonistic attitudes do not help a successful plural polity and there is a need for civil society in Spain and elsewhere to rise to the occasion. Efforts on all sides, especially by intellectuals, will strengthen the multicultural prerogatives guaranteeing a better future for all.

4 Islam and Britain: Old Cultures, Odd Encounters

... where's the Turkish Alcoran
And all the heaps of superstitious books
Found in the temples of Mahomet
Whom I thought a god? They shall be burnt ...
(Christopher Marlowe, *Tamburlaine*, Part II)

The interaction between Britain and Islam is the most complex of all such encounters, characterised by multiple channels, diverse responses and varied imprints. The internationalisation of Britain through powerful political, cultural and intellectual instruments curiously concurs with the trans-regionality of Islam to germinate several mutualities as well as divergences. Though there has been an inherent unevenness between the two cultural trajectories, their encounters are of enduring consequence. To Muslims at large, Britain has mainly symbolised a predominantly *Christian* and rather imperious culture but it is seen to have taken substantive strides towards a greater degree of operational multiculturalism. While it is customary to study Muslim experience in Britain with reference to post-Second World War immigration, the early phases of the Crusades, colonialism, Orientalism, religio-economic interchanges, the slave trade and the recent emergence of a Muslim diaspora in Britain are all interrelated when one looks at the permeating nature of mutual perceptions and dissensions governing every aspect of this bilateralism. Whereas one is intrigued by the centrality of Britain in establishing the Orientalist traditions in her reconstruction of *Muslim discourse*, one cannot, however, ignore the reality of a creative and regenerative debate among certain sections of the Muslim diaspora. The universality of the English language, the intermingling of various intra-Muslim opinion groups, and their vanguard role in multicultural relationships with politically and economically powerful societies in the West make Britain a focal point in understanding Muslim encounters with modernity.

Most of the recent Muslims migrants who came to Britain for economic reasons as 'pioneers' have spent their time and energies in settling down. The second generation – accounting for an over-whelming proportion – is largely 'home grown' and has been attempting to mediate between two identities.[1] Their own commun-itarian imperatives are making the contemporary Islamic experience in the West extremely vital and productive, though it still suffers from numerous pains and pangs owing to the obvious forces of racism accruing from culture, colour or class-based denominators. At the same time, it would be quite fair to acknowledge the greater amount of freedom, mobility and economic stability that Western societies such as Britain have offered to Muslims so as to herald the desired debate and rethink, which is still not possible 'back home' due to various political, economic, societal and sectarian impediments. Britain is home to Muslim dissidents varying from Muhammad al-Mass'ari of Saudi Arabia to Altaf Hussain of Pakistan, in addition to Kurdish and Iraqi opposition groups.[2] Benefiting through largely conducive democratic traditions and efficient communication systems, such elements play vanguard roles in oppositional politics back home.[3] Some of them eventually return to assume significant positions. A relatively recent example is that of Benazir Bhutto who, after her father's execution by General Zia ul-Haq in 1979, lived as a political exile in Britain where she maintained a high-profile struggle against the military regime. On her arrival in Pakistan in 1986 she was received quite enthusiastically and two years later became the first woman prime minister of a Muslim country.[4]

Muslim diasporic society and European converts to Islam are still not situated totally within the mainstream *Western* cultures and, despite several handicaps, are striving to obtain greater opportunities at local, national and even global levels. These often rather margin-alised and ghettoised communities have been resisting this multiple peripheralisation as well as unrestrained assimilation. The individual 'pioneer' immigrants or settlers, when joined by their families in the 1970s, began their early localist efforts to establish initial religio-cultural institutions such as one-room mosques, which by the next decade had come of age. Since the 1980s demands for better schooling, housing and job opportunities have coincided with anger over the Rushdie affair. The dissolution of the Soviet Union, the bru-talisation of Bosnia, the evolution of Islamophobia and the terrorist attacks in New York and Washington in September 2001, and the subsequent multiple campaigns against Afghanistan and Iraq in particular and others in general have served to stimulate the otherwise slackening quest for a proper niche in the West.

Consequently, educated and concerned Muslims rejected and openly criticised the usually derogatory portrayal of Muslims as terrorists and anti-intellectual mobs and – though haphazardly – began to reorganise themselves into some kind of a *Jewish* model of identity which will allow a loose and inclusive definition of being *Muslim*. Such a development may have its own future ramifications yet it has affirmed the indiginisation of Islam once again in the West.

The British Muslim experience and Islam in Britain need to be revisited within the context of history, image makers and the realities of colonialism and postcolonial migrations. Politico-economic domination and long-held images on both sides, especially following Western evangelical activities and a continuum of cultural, intellectual, military and economic hegemony, have collectively given weight to the British factor relative to its Muslim counterpart. Despite the fact that France began institutionalised interaction with Muslims earlier, especially during the Napoleonic era, followed by a sustained control of the Maghreb and other African and Middle Eastern territories, British influence in the Muslim world seems to be more diverse and far-reaching than the French. This becomes more apparent when we look at Anglo-American mutualities and the assumption of specific attitudes by North Americans treading in the footsteps of their British counterparts. The salience of the English language, British global supremacy until the 1940s, and the 'special relationship' between Britain and the United States have allowed the British an edge over the French. The popularisation of American culture is, of course, a latent form of globalisation, yet the prevalence of British literary, political and even elite traditions such as cricket and private schooling continue to play a crucial role in the former colonies. The British media, symbolised by the BBC among others, academic and training exchanges through the British Council, and the internationalisation of British literary and intellectual traditions by a faithful, international Oxbridge elite in the developing world, assign Britain a pre-eminent role in these societies.[5]

This chapter looks at the phases of British–Muslim interaction from the Crusades to the eighteenth century, when the traditions of colonialism, Orientalism and the slave trade began to establish an enduring British hegemony over the Muslim world. The next section concentrates on Muslim immigration into Britain and the establishment of various communitarian institutions in recent decades. The unequal nature of a relationship based on a minority–majority paradigm or other similar theoretical frameworks provides the remaining themes of this chapter.

THE HISTORICAL PERSPECTIVE

During the early phase of the British–Muslim relationship, conflictive patterns based on the religious divide were quite apparent. During the medieval period, Islam was perceived as a potential threat banishing Christianity from its Middle Eastern heartland.[6] The Muslim conquest of the Iberian Peninsula, Cyprus, southern Italy, and other such territories in the Near East previously held by Christian rulers, created an immense amount of anxiety and anger towards Muslims. The Crusades were largely the result of a widespread wish to wrest control of the Holy Land from Muslims, though intra-European strife mingled with strong economic incentives equally spawned these centuries-long campaigns. The tussle between various European monarchs, the feudalist nomenclature and the reassertion of the papal establishment against a backdrop of jealousy and hatred towards Muslims and Eastern Orthodox Christianity collectively activated the crusading spirit. Ironically, the Crusades were initially targeted against neither Turks nor Arabs but against the Jews, who were mercilessly murdered by the Crusaders in their long marches to Palestine. Concurrently, the Crusaders carried out equally frenzied attacks on fellow Christians of the Orthodox Church and other non-Catholic denominations, and in the process destroyed their townships and properties, including the tragic decimation of Constantinople. The Crusades are believed to have 'both initiated and perpetuated the representation of Muslims as evil and depraved, licentious and barbaric, ignorant and stupid, unclean and inferior, monstrous and ugly, fanatical and violent'.[7] Pope Urban made a famous speech on 27 November 1096 announcing his mission to expel the Seljuk Turks from the Near East and to wrest back Jerusalem from the Muslims. In an emotion-ridden voice, using misleading terms about the Seljuks, the Pope thus spoke before a massive audience:

> They have circumcised the Christians, either spreading the blood from the circumcisions on the altars or pouring it into the baptismal fonts. And they cut open the navels of those whom they choose to torment with a loathsome death, tear out their most vital organs and tie them to a stake, drag them around and flog

them, before killing them as they lie prone on the ground with all their entrails out. They tie some to posts and shoot at them with arrows, they order others to bare their necks and they attack them with drawn swords, trying to see whether they can cut off their heads with a single stroke.[8]

Five years after the papal decree, on 15 July 1099, the Crusaders, led by a 21-year-old Norman commander, attacked the Dome of the Rock on the Temple Mount. This was a Friday and thousands of Muslims were offering prayers at the holy place from which the Prophet Muhammad is believed to have undertaken a miraculous flight to heaven. Following the attack Muslims withdrew to the al-Aqsa Mosque and that is where, contrary to early assurances, the entire Muslim populace of Jerusalem was massacred:

The following morning the Crusaders re-entered the al-Aqsa Mosque and slaughtered every Moslem sheltering there. No one knows how many died; the Moslem chronicler reports seventy thousand. One of the Crusaders reports picking his way through a mess of blood and bodies more than knee-deep.[9]

The European counts, priests and fortune seekers eliminated the entire Muslim population, as was recorded by Fulcher of Chartres:

Our squires and footmen ... split open the bellies of those they had just slain in order to extract from the intestines the gold coins which the Saracens had gulped down their loathsome throats while alive ... With drawn swords our men ran through the city not sparing anyone, even those begging for mercy ... They entered the houses of the citizens, seizing whatever they found in them ... Whoever first entered a house, whether he was rich or poor ... was to occupy and own the house or palace and whatever he found in it as if it were entirely his own ... In this way many poor people became wealthy.[10]

Knowledge of contemporary Islam in medieval Europe, including the British Isles, stayed largely confined to ecclesiastic groups, and was both scanty and stereotypic.[11] At one level, it displayed elements of curiosity and envy for this new religio-political culture, but at the same time it was grounded in misperceptions of bloodthirsty, warring barbarians out to destroy the Christian cultural edifice. Islam was both an exotic attraction and a formidable enemy in contemporary European thought. Muslim intellectual and scientific achievements in plural societies like Spain, Portugal, Italy and the Balkans invoked respect as well as contempt. Thus, while translations of the Quran and commentaries in Latin allowed Europeans to hold diverse opinions on the origins, beliefs and rituals of Islam, they equally helped them to generalise on the similarities and differences between Islam and the Judaic–Christian ethos. The Prophet Muhammad was deemed both an innovator and an impostor. Dante's *Inferno* (c.1300) allocated the ninth circle in hell for the Prophet and Ali, his son-in-law, whereas Saladin, Avicenna and Averroes stay in Limbo in the company of Virgil and Aristotle. Inadvertently, the Crusades had alerted educated Europeans from both secular and ecclesiastic groups to take Islam rather more seriously without persuading them to abandon their stereotypic and exaggerated images. The Prophet's pivotal position within Islamic civilisation and his humility, humanity and dynamism did not fit in with the prevalent derogatory attitudes towards the Saracens and Turks. Equally, the expansion of Islam and its intellectual heritage were envied and, out of jealousy, the Prophet's marriages and the Quran become the foci of a rather abrasive criticism. The Crusaders' accounts of Arab Muslims, and the accounts of Marco Polo during his journeys to the East, added to such images of the non-Arab world of Islam all along the Silk Route.[12]

As well as the religious domain, British encounters with Muslims during this early phase also included those in the political, economic and literary domains. While, on the one hand, there was a fear of North African pirates from the Barbary coast and of the Ottomans, there was also a desire to build up a common alliance with them against European rivals. Queen Elizabeth I sought an alliance-based relationship with the Ottoman caliphate against Spain and other common enemies. Curiously, while the British monarchy admired and sought Muslim military prowess, it equally berated the Moors because of their brown or darker complexions. The combination of this fear with denigration accruing from specific cultural and racist denominators has for long continued to dictate British exclusivist attitudes towards non-Europeans. The subsequent Muslim political decline in southern and eastern Europe has further reinforced the negative images of Muslims rooted in the tripolar forces of culture, colour and class. The growth of the slave trade, in the wake of the consolidation of slavery amidst explorations and colonisation involving almost every European community, was the result largely of these exclusionary attitudes and of an increased need for cheap labour in the colonies. The mushrooming of the missionary enterprise overseas following the Inquisition, the Protestant revolution, the Counter-Reformation and colonialism generally provided a moral justification for slavery.[13] Contemporary West European hegemony was erected on the forces of cultural derision, colour-based racism, colonialist exploitation and capitalist and class-based prerogatives. Thus, the Europeanisation of the world, especially of Africa, Asia, the Western hemisphere and Australasia, justified in the name of culture, religion, politics and economy, created a perpetual unevenness in the North–South relationship which, despite recent rhetoric of a more globalised world, remains ascendant. To a great extent, the Muslim world – in both the Muslim heartland and the diaspora – has been on the receiving end of this unequal relationship for quite some time.[14] Its socioeconomic problems, psychological dislocations, various forms of intra-Muslim conflicts especially of the interstate kind, and continued economic underdevelopment aggravated by political suffocation are the manifestations of imbalances incurred during the colonial–national encounters.

THE SOCIO-INTELLECTUAL LEGACY

Muslims, Moors, Mohammedans, Mahometans or *Turks* were the usual terms used in medieval England for the Muslims of the Mediterranean region, at a time when knowledge about Arabia and more distant South Asia was still confined to a few exotic images. Islam in Spain had created both awe and jealousy among European Christians. It was from Spain that the early images of Muslims as warriors and rivals emerged. However, the educated sections, rather than feeling threatened by Muslims, tried to ascertain their religious and secular scholarship. The over-700-year-long Muslim rule provided an enduring backdrop to this Muslim–Christian dialogue. Thus, Muslims were perceived both as barbarians and as cultured people who were fond of books, the arts, beautiful buildings, fountains, gardens and, most of all, were generally free of bigotry. These enemies were envied for their scholarship, worldly power and religious devotion.[15] Bede, the eighth-century monk, criticised the 'swarms of Saracens' for killing the Gauls, until the former paid the penalty at the Battle of Poitiers in 732.[16] By the time the Tudors removed papal authority over England, English had begun to assert itself as the *national* language. However, its vocabulary, textual themes and information about non-Christian peoples came largely from Latin sources.

While Muslim Spain had vanished from the pages of history, the Turks established themselves as the new Mediterranean power and the Christian world 'faced' a new threat from Islam. For the next six centuries, the Turks symbolised whatever was feared about Islam. Terms such as *Moors*, *Mohammedens* and *Turks* became synonymous and early English writers including Christopher Marlowe and William Shakespeare pioneered these images in their plays. In his preface to Marlowe's *Tamburlaine*, Richard Jones observed:

> I have purposely omitted and left out some fond and frivolous gestures, digressing, and, in my poor opinion, far unmeet for the matter, which I thought might seem more tedious unto the wise than any way else to be regarded, though haply they have been of some vain-conceited fondlings greatly gaped at, what time they were shewed upon the stage in their graced deformities.

Divided into two parts – the first performed in 1587 and printed in 1590 with the second – Marlowe's popular drama depicted the bloody and violent conquests by a former shepherd from Central Asia, Tamerlaine (1336–1405), who symbolised exoticism, violence and treachery, all attributed to Islam during the Elizabethan era. Muslims were shown gloating over the defeats of the Christian kings:

> Now will the Christian miscreants be glad
> Ringing with joy their superstitious bells
> And making bonfires for my overthrow.
> (Bajazeth, defeated emperor of the Turks, *Tamburlaine*,
> Part 1, 3, 3, 236–8)

> Traitors, villains, damned Christians!
> Have I not here the articles of peace
> And solemn covenants we have both confirmed,
> He by his Christ and I by Mahomet?
> (Orcanes, King of Natiolia, *ibid.*, Part II, 2, 2, 29–32)

Tamerlaine was shown blaspheming the Prophet and the Quran, a point not lost on English Christians being ruled by Queen Elizabeth I, though such a depiction denied any respect for Islamic symbols:

... where's the Turkish Alcoran
And all the heaps of superstitious books
Found in the temples of Mahomet
Whom I thought a god? They shall be burnt ...
In vain, I see, men worship Mahomet:
My sword hath sent millions of Turks to hell,
Slew all his priests, his kinsmen, and his friends,
And yet I live untouched by Mahomet ...
Now Mahomet, if thou have any power,
Come down thyself and work a miracle,
Thou are not worthy to be worshipped
That suffers flames of fire to burn the writ
Wherein the sum of thy religion rests.
(Tamburlaine in *ibid.*, Part II, 5, 1, 171–4, 177–80, 180–5)[17]

William Shakespeare, the pre-eminent writer of his era, both
repeated and transformed the peculiar image of the Turk, giving him
characteristics ranging from violence to ignorance and falsehood.
Plays such as *Othello* and *Hamlet* reflect such misconceptions:

... in Aleppo once,
Where a malignant and a turban'd Turk
Beat a Venetian and traduced the state,
I took by th' throat the circumcised dog
And smote him.
(*Othello* (1602), 5, 2, 351–4)

Nay, it is true, or else I am a Turk
(*Ibid.*, 2, 1, 114)

Are we turned Turks? and to ourselves do that
Which heaven hath forbid the Ottomites?
For Christian shame, put by this barbarous brawl.
(*Ibid.*, 2, 3, 166–8)

or:

... if the rest of my fortunes turn Turk with me ...
(*Hamlet* (1602) 3, 2, 269–70)

And Ben Johnson, in *The Alchemist* (1610), wrote the following
dialogue about a *chiause* (messenger):

Dapper. ...What do you think of me,
That I am a *Chiause*?
Face. What's that? *Dapper.* The Turk was here –
As one would say, Do you think I am a Turk? ...
Face. This is the Gentleman, and he is no *Chiause*.
(*The Alchemist*, 1, 2, 25–7)

Other contemporary plays portrayed Muslims in similar ways. Thomas Dekker's *Lusts Dominion* (1590) dwelt on a Muslim–Christian marriage, while Thomas Heywood's *The Fair Maid of the West* (1604), in its first part, concentrated on the Moroccan civil war. *The Turks* by John Mason (1607) and William Rowley's *A Tragedy Called All's Lost by Lust* (1619) both dwelt on mixed marriages whereas *The Coffee House: A Comedy* (1664) (anonymous) dealt with a Muslim coffee house owner residing in London with his English wife. Travel accounts by British visitors portrayed mixed images of Muslims from North Africa and the Ottoman empire. Such visitors were themselves equally exotic attractions, especially to North African Muslims, who would flock to see the 'Flaxen-Hair' and 'ruddy Complexion'.[18] Generally, such images were based on curiosity and on denigration, accruing largely from the legacy of the Crusades and the Inquisition. The Ottoman conquests, denigrated by both Orthodoxy and the Catholic Church, also underpinned such prevalent anti-Muslim caricatures. British contacts with the Muslim world were not frequent, largely because Arabia, Persia and India were distant from the British Isles and the Turks now mainly controlled the routes to the East, including the Silk Route to China. However, some contemporary accounts of these societies, from emissaries – in the tradition of Marco Polo – like Sir Thomas Roe, Sir Henry Middleton, Francis Rogers, Sir Anthony Shirley and William Biddulph, were available to British literary and other inquisitive circles. Despite the expulsions from Sicily, Portugal and Spain, Muslims, confident of their religio-cultural heritage, carried a deep sense of superiority over Europeans.[19] The loss of the Iberian Peninsula was, to a great extent, seen by Muslims as being compensated for by the Ottoman conquests in eastern Europe. On the other hand, Western Europeans, especially after vanquishing the Native Americans, did not consider Islam to be a major threat to their emerging mainstream interests. Several writers, however, warned fellow British citizens to observe a special code of manners so as not to offend Muslims – now generally known as *Turks*.[20]

Early British views of Muslims were not based only on religion, for they also reflected the uneven nature of contemporary politics in the Mediterranean–East Atlantic region, where Muslims enjoyed primacy. British seafarers were often afraid of Muslim raids on their ships and on English territories, which resulted in numerous individuals being taken captive. By 1626, reportedly there were 3,000 British captives in Algiers and 1,500 in Sali, Morocco, following frequent 'Turkish' attacks on British islands and ships.[21] Muslims from the Barbary regions seem on occasion to have invaded the south of England, especially Devon and Cornwall, and taken British captives. The British government had to raise special funds for the release of these individuals. Muslims were frequently seen in Britain, generating awe in British aristocratic and ecclesiastic circles, and were perceived as posing a significant 'danger to all Christendom, from Greece to England and from "Muscovy" to Ireland'.[22] The constant spectre of a Muslim threat from both North Africa and the Ottoman caliphate intensified efforts to understand Muslims and several treatises were devoted to their religion and political ethos. Richard Knolles's *The General Historie of the Turkes* (1603) aimed at understanding the 'Great terror of the world'. Some courtiers even advocated a war against Mediterranean Muslims to capture Sally and Algiers. Some British captives and adventurers would convert to Islam, much to the ire of the clergy, and were designated 'renegades', a term itself linked with the Spanish Inquisition, used in a strict sense in English to apply to Christians 'turning Turkes'. Worries about the overpowering 'infidels' were reflected not just in papal edicts but also in the writings of figures such as Martin Luther, William Shakespeare, John Locke, John Calvin, Christopher Marlowe, Dryden and Philip Massinger.

Nabil Matar, in his significant work, has distinguished four different categories of such converts to Islam. The first category consisted of children taken from their parents, either by the Ottomans or the Maghrebis. Under the Ottomans, the system called *devshirme* had begun in the early sixteenth century, but was ended in 1638 by Sultan Murad.[23] The second category included those who had converted to Islam to end their slavery.[24] The third group consisted of those persons who had themselves opted to live among Muslims in North Africa and the Ottoman Empire. They enjoyed Muslim socio-cultural values and had voluntarily converted to Islam. Contemporary writers such as Sir William Shirley warned the English against socialising with the Muslims, as this might lead to their conversion. The plural nature of Muslim society, with its high level of tolerance and accommodation towards all kinds of religio-ethnic communities, impressed British visitors, especially as Muslim regimes, including the Ottomans, in general avoided state-led conversion of non-Muslim subjects.[25] The reason for some conversions may have been economic as well as political. The fourth category of converts consisted of those Christians who were largely ignorant of Christian beliefs and rituals and were easily influenced by the Muslim missionaries. Conversion to Islam, in any case, has never required exhaustive rituals or complex efforts.

The earliest English convert to Islam, according to *The Voyage Made to Tripolis* (1583), was John Nelson, a servant at the royal household.[26] During the 1660s, Charles II made special efforts for the repatriation of several 'English Turks' from North Africa by paying a ransom, but some of them refused to return. Reportedly, their reluctance was attributed to their 'love of Turkish women who are generally very beautiful'.[27] In some cases, such converts lived with their Christian English wives. Though there may have been exaggerations in consular or other such accounts of British conversions to Islam, their co-religionists would even use force for dissuasive purposes. That is partly the reason why early attempts to translate the Quran were received with great suspicion. Interestingly, converts came from various strata of British society, including penury-stricken adventurers who were able to flourish through migration. Visiting ambassadors from North African Muslim kingdoms usually created a favourable image of Muslim societies in their homelands, which further added to the curiosity amongst fortune-seekers. Some of these ambassadors themselves had been European Christians in the past and had ended up attaining high status as *agas* or *beys* in their newly adopted countries.[28] Even after their conversion, efforts continued to bring these 'renegades' back to Christianity. Contemporary plays and novels such as Thomas Kyd's *The Tragedy of Solyman and Perseda* (1588), Thomas Heywood's *The Fair Maid of the West* (1604–10), John Mason's *The Turke* (1607) and Philip Massinger's *The Renegado* (1624) all censored British 'apostates' for 'turning Turke'. As confirmed by Samuel Pepys, some of these converts on their return to the British Isles would be reconverted through the efforts of a highly concerned clergy.[29] Resistant 'renegades' continued to be perceived as a constant threat to the state and church.

Curiosity about Islam led to increased scholarly work, including the early Quranic translations. Before George Sale's well-known translation of the Quran in 1734, the earliest English version, by Alexander Ross, had appeared in 1649. Under ecclesiastic pressure, the printer was incarcerated till the copies had been officially impounded. Ross defended his rather awkward translation by suggesting that the book did not pose a threat to Anglican values. He used the Quran to generate more interest in the Protestant religion as well as attacking Cromwellian authority. Despite its shortcomings and specific motives, Ross's translation remained quite crucial among literary circles. The 'Turkish BIBLE' was quoted in 1698 by the New England theologian, Cotton Mather.[30] Another important source on early Islam was the translation of Abu Faraj's biography of the Prophet in 1650 by Edward Pococke, Professor of Arabic at Oxford. This is considered to be the first serious scholarly effort to understand Islam, though the Arabist himself remained a practising Christian.[31] That Pococke composed Arabic poetry and read celebratory poems on special royal occasions puts into question the view that Islam did not engage a wide variety of British groups in these early modern centuries. John Milton, Thomas Hobbes, Robert Burton and other British writers showed varying degrees of knowledge of Islamic subjects, especially of Muslim contributions in the realms of the sciences, philosophy and medicine. Avicenna, Averroes, Geber, Alhazen and Hayy ibn Yaqzan were some of the names which were familiar amongst British intellectuals. The survival of the Coptic, Nestorian, Jacobite, Chaldean Orthodox, Armenian and Catholic denominations within the Ottoman Empire presented an enviable contrast to the intolerant regimentation of the Anglicans and Catholics on the same continent. Matar has rightly observed:

> The fact that there were so many allusions to the Qur'an and to Muslim theology in English religious and political writings in this period is important. For Islam was the religion of a military adversary, and it was also a religion which challenged Christianity. Writers recognized that it was not a minor heresy that would soon fade away, but an empire that stretched from Central Europe to India, and from Aden to Baghdad and Crete. Like Catholicism, it was an imperial religion which people in England and the rest of the British isles were being compelled to confront seriously because it was a religion that was backed by military and evangelistic might: it was a civilization that was flourishing – and in the case of Ottoman Islam, expanding – notwithstanding the prayers of Britons and the wars of Christendom.[32]

Coffee – sometimes referred to as 'Mahometan gruel' – became a major debating point in mid-seventeenth-century England. Individuals like Edward Pococke considered drinking coffee beneficial to health, whereas its opponents considered it ominous as it made one vulnerable to 'Mahometanism'. The first coffee house, built in London in 1652, was followed two years later by a similar house in Oxford. This caused much pamphleteering amongst its protagonists and detractors. It was rumoured to be under a Turkish spell and to be possessed of satanic characteristics that made Christians vulnerable to unwanted Islamic or even Jewish influences. The growing number of 'English Turks' was attributed to an expanding use of the drink in Britain, and contemporary cartoons about coffee houses showed turban-clad Muslims serving coffee to innocuous-looking Britons. Sometimes an African slave would be attending the patrons – men and women – with a watchful 'Turk' keeping an eye on the prospective converts. Some of these portrayals speak volumes about the enduring image of the Muslim, sporting turban, aquiline nose, pointed beard and mischievous smile. By contrast, the English clientele are shown as well-groomed, plain-looking individuals exhibiting courtesy and receptivity. Such portrayals have reverberated in the subsequent images of Muslims or Turks, in which turban, beard and long dress remain part and parcel of Muslim identity – bearing a close affinity with the appearance of the Turkish sultans.

Driven by evangelical zeal and interdenominational rivalry, the churches soon pursued their efforts to convert Muslims. Exaggerated reports of conversions in the Muslim world by the Jesuits – especially the French – encouraged Anglicans to enter the arena. Queen Elizabeth, without openly professing such a desire, nevertheless tried to establish closer relationships with the Muslim rulers in Istanbul, Persia and India. She corresponded with the Safavids in 1561, and then sent special gifts to Sultan Murad and his wife, Sultana Safiyya.[33] After Murad's death in 1595, she corresponded with his son, Mohammad III, who was a close friend of the royal envoy, Sir Richard Burton. The first-ever conversion of a Muslim in England occurred in 1586, greatly celebrated in Anglican ecclesiastic circles. By that time, and especially after the English victory over the Spanish armada in 1588, English seafarers had taken hundreds of Muslim captives from Spanish ships. Many of them ended up in England and became the focus of evangelical activities. Most of these Muslims sought English help to enable them to return to the Ottoman Empire and very few of them, despite several contemporary exaggerated accounts, stayed on after having converted to Anglicanism.[34] As in Spain, several of these Moriscos converted out of convenience and not out of conviction as depicted in Shakespeare's *Othello*. In their missionary zeal, the Quakers even went as far afield as Istanbul and Palestine in their attempts personally to convert the caliph and Muslim nobility. They received a warm welcome but a polite refusal, which displayed a high degree of tolerance by the Muslim elite. George Robinson and Mary Fisher were two such missionaries who enjoyed personal audiences with the Muslim rulers.[35] Despite various evangelical efforts, the contemporary Muslim rulers avoided being drawn into the interdenominational jealousies and volatile feuds between Catholics and Protestants.

However, it is amazing to see the categorisation of Muslims as Arabs, Saracens, Turks or even the subsequent caricatures as infidels. Given Turkish power during the early modern era, Muslims were generally called Turks, though, in literary works, they were also referred to as Moors. The term 'Arabs' was applied to the Muslims of earlier centuries. With the growth of English racism under the Tudors and Stuarts, following the colonisation of the Irish and the Native Americans, Muslims emerged as the 'new' enemies, also being identified as infidels. In the prevalent eschatology, both Jews and Muslim (or Saracens) were greatly hated for their religion (culture) and skin colour. In some quarters, Jews received more sympathy than Muslims on the assumption that they would finally destroy the Islamic 'heresy'. Following the failure of the Crusades, despite the fiery leadership of Richard the Lionheart, the Jews were invested with the hope of destroying the Saracens. The Saracens' ultimate destruction was seen as a divine prophesy, and this ushered in a more positive attitude towards Jews: 'The Ottoman danger played a major role in frightening Englishmen into hoping for the Restoration of the Jews to what was intended to become, after the God-ordained Jewish victory and conversion, a Protestant Palestine.' It was believed by the British restorationists that

> the Jews would be willing to undertake a Christian crusade because they hated the Muslims. By so believing, these writers ignored the extensive evidence which showed that the Jews were not particularly hostile to the Muslims, on the contrary, they favoured them over Christians.[36]

Such Christian optimism stemmed from a large Jewish presence first in Muslim Spain and then across the Ottoman Empire, ignoring the fact that Jews had prospered under Muslim protection and were also the victims of Christian fanatics. However, the sudden love of Luther and other Protestants for the Jews was due to anti-Muslim sentiments. Long before the introduction of Arabic at Oxford and Cambridge, these universities had established chairs of Hebrew. Jewish rabbis and Christian theologians and academics wrote extensively on Judaism and Christianity, producing a huge corpus on a multiplicity of subjects. By contrast, Muslims did not make any regular effort to introduce Islamic theology and it is only in recent years that one notices the modest beginning of such a tradition. Not a single book was ever written by a Muslim addressing a British readership. On the other hand, Orientalists including Simon Ockley, Edward Pococke the Younger and George Sale studied Arabic as the 'dead' language, with Islam as a bygone glory. The lack of proper information about Islam only added to stigmatisation which, especially during the closing centuries of the Ottoman empire, turned into a virile form of Islamophobia.[37] The religious, academic and media coverage of the Greek war of independence, the Bulgarian crises and the entire course of the Eastern Question (Balkan problems) dwelt on Muslim atrocities, while almost totally ignoring the plight of Muslim minorities and their forcible expulsion from these places. Islam helped Britain, and especially England, in defining her own identity through a multidimensional relationship in this early era.

The decline of Muslim power after the Ottoman defeat in Vienna in 1683 coincided with the gradual emergence of English power and the subsequent huge colonial empire, which included vast regions of the Muslim world. Fed with specific images and now enjoying primacy, it became difficult for the English elite to attribute equality to their Muslim counterparts. As discussed by Edward Said, Orientalism became the medium of understanding and representing the Islamic world and of justifying a complete subordination of Muslims to a superior British ideology.[38] Bereft of reciprocity and a proper appreciation of Islamic heritage, Muslims became the victims of British indifference and anger, as seen time and again in missionary enterprises, treatises and the official colonial policies with regard to recurring disputes afflicting Muslim regions such as Kashmir, Palestine, Bosnia, Afghanistan, Iraq and Chechnya.

MODERNITY AND HEGEMONY

Colonialism as spearheaded by nearly all the Western European countries (and by Russia as well) had its roots in various socioeconomic developments, collectively called modernity. Modernity's positive attributes, such as industrialism, rationalism, gradual democratisation, inter-gender equality and the evolution of civil liberties, have for a long time remained largely confined to Western communities across the globe, strengthening their hegemonic military power over the colonised and indigenous communities. By contrast, its negative attributes, such as slavery, racism, disempowerment, even the extinction of traditional communities subsequent to their economic exploitation and socio-intellectual marginalisation – all these have been the share of the colonised societies. In an aura of sheer disempowerment,[39] the latter lost self-confidence, until a generation of modernisers, themselves the beneficiaries of Western institutions, began to address the vital issue of identity formation. These elites sought independence by advocating territory- or culture-based nationalisms, as they felt that without a cumulative political sovereignty, the socioeconomic and intellectual regeneration of colonised societies will remain chimerical.

Despite several decades of political independence, the former colonies, including nearly all the Muslim countries, remain beset with serious socio-political and economic problems. The masses remain disempowered, illiterate and vulnerable to statist and societal manipulation. While the regimes remain lethargic, corrupt and coercive, societal trajectories such as ethno-religious groups progressively debilitate them. Accompanied by such maladies, the global politico-economic and cultural domination by the Western nations further marginalises these communities, adding to their multiple dependence on the West. While colonialism triggered a limited scale of industrialisation and scientific education in the colonies, it equally initiated a discourse of hegemony, inequality and dependence. The trajectories of Orientalism, evangelism, racism, uneven economic development, the politics of patronage, bringing unfair advantages to certain dynasties and families, and a discretionary form of territorial nationalism ensured the continued drift and inefficiency of these regions long after their independence. Border conflicts, ethnic dissension, monopolist groups, overdeveloped bureaucracies, both civil and military, feudalist economies, anti-egalitarianism with a prioritised authoritarianism have all continued to sap the civic forces and scarce resources in these countries. The identity crisis remains transcendant in these countries, especially in view of authoritarianism and continued preferences for colonial legacies and hierarchies. The responses, varying from political Islam (as in the Middle East), socialism, trans-regional nationalism (Pan-Africanism or Pan-Arabism), secularism (which has assumed a dogmatic status in Kemalist Turkey) and weak democracies such as Pakistan, Malaysia and Bangladesh, provide numerous instances in which substantive reformist institution-building is lacking.[40]

The Orientalist discourse created in Britain and elsewhere becomes more relevant here in understanding the underlying forces that have continued to fashion popular, official and intellectual attitudes towards Islam and Muslims. The power-centred and complex paradigm of colonialism was not the mere political subjugation of millions across Asia and Africa, it was equally a new, multidisciplinary project involving various fields including science, religion, literature, gender, sports, environment, anthropology, pedagogy, arts and philosophy. Imperialism as an ideology based on unrestricted unevenness, as the studies by Edward Said, John MacKenzie and others reveal, was not merely geared towards defining and subjugating colonised peoples, but equally defined the British identity itself.[41] The hierarchical reconstruction of the world through specific prisms and its recurrent epistemology, as portrayed in the media, in academic debate and in official policies in the West, have yet disallowed the evolution of a post-Orientalist world. As borne out by various studies by scholars[42] and human rights groups such as the Runnymede Trust, the stubborn nature of Islamophobia and its diverse and extensive contours are too immense to ignore.[43]

However, it would be unfair to underestimate the role of colonialism as a factor in accentuating an academic debate, though academic responses have varied from resistance to cooption to reinterpretation of their own situation.[44] In addition, colonialism has triggered a crucial debate among historians, sociologists, religious circles and political analysts who keep on arguing about its impact on the formerly colonised societies.[45] In the same vein, Muslim intellectuals – though they are still few – have begun a tradition of dilating on Western societies and cultures. While Napoleon, in his invasion of Egypt, took along a large number of scholars and experts to initiate French studies of Islam, a few solitary Muslims from contemporary India undertook visits to Europe and left interesting reportage on the lifestyles, churches, universities and political systems in countries such as France, England and Ireland. Belonging to a Persian-speaking Muslim elite, these South Asian Muslim travellers and writers represented the Muslim world undergoing a significant transition.[46] Political decline had set in across the three contemporary Muslim empires of India, Persia and the Near East as Western societies were re-emerging, imbued with new vibrancy.

The host of writings on Islam by European missionaries, colonial officials, scholars and visitors covered the religious, literary, artistic, philosophical and sociological domains. They showed a Western fascination with the world of Islam, however romanticised, fanciful or totally disdainful they may have been.[47] In addition to such literature, the intellectual and religious preoccupation has continued to the present date,[48] though one sees a growing number of Muslim writings on similar comparative themes emerging in recent years.[49] The objectification of Islam and Muslims gradually appears to be giving way to a more sensitive and egalitarian understanding of mutualities as well as divergences, though, on occasions, tensions have resurfaced, pushing back the gains made through dialogue. For instance, the Salman Rushdie affair in the early 1990s, together with the Gulf crisis, reinvigorated old negative images of Islam. A few gains were again made in the mid 1990s, to be lost amidst the anti-terror campaign, in which the Muslim regions, such as Bosnia, Afghanistan, Kashmir, Iraq, Palestine, as well as the diaspora, bore the brunt of anger. In most cases, this anger was unjustified and Muslims were further marginalised. In Britain, the crisis came at a very inopportune time, since in the summer of 2001 race riots in Oldham, Leeds and Bradford impacted deeply on intercommunity relationships. Muslim youths, victims of segregation and forced marginalisation, took law and order into their own hands following inflammatory moves by the racist British National Party (BNP). The police and the local councils, instead of rectifying the malady through institutional empowerment of these largely ghettoised communities in the former industrial centres, only sought justification by blaming the community leaders.[50] The inquiry reports on the worst ethnic riots in British history looked at social, economic and local causes which had remained unrectified for too long.[51]

THE MUSLIM DIASPORA: SAILORS, SCHOLARS, SUFIS, STATESMEN AND SOJOURNERS

The core–periphery relationship between the dominant Western Europe and its former colonies, and the continued dependence of the latter upon the former, have resulted in the evolution of several immigrant communities. With the early expansion of England one notices the Scots and Irish emigrating into the English counties and eventually providing willing partners to the two most significant British projects of imperialism and migration. The Afro-Asian 'subjects' would visit Britain for specific purposes such as education, business or for participation in the imperial parades. Apart from African slaves, earmarked for shipment to the Americas, or in some cases required specifically for the domestic market, Yemenis and South Asians were the earliest migrants in Britain, who settled in London, Liverpool and other coastal towns in England and Wales.[52] Many had been in the employ of the British East India Company as sailors and came to be called *lascars* in Britain.[53] There were a few Asian women as well, who came as *ayas* with the returning colonial and missionary families.[54] While most of the South Asian alumni, such as Gandhi, Nehru, Gokhale,[55] Iqbal,[56] Johar[57] and Jinnah,[58] would eventually return, some of the elite, such as Dadabhai Nauroji,[59] Syed Ameer Ali,[60] Chaudhary Rahmat Ali[61] and Allama Yusuf Ali,[62] decided to settle in Britain.[63] It is only in the post-Second World War era that one sees a significant influx into Britain of immigrants from its former colonies in order to address the labour shortage. Before the war, there were about 15,000 Muslims in Britain, mostly settled in London, Liverpool, Cardiff, Hull and Sheffield.[64] W. H. Quillam, a Liverpudlian solicitor, was one of the earliest converts, who accepted Islam in 1887 after visiting Morocco. His activism and essays brought several other adherents to Islam. From 1893 to 1908, he published the weekly *Crescent,* and became an international Muslim celebrity by receiving patronage from the Ottoman caliph and the Persian king. The Afghan king gave a special grant to establish an Islamic institute in Liverpool and the caliph designated him as Shaikhul Islam for Britain. The shah of Persia appointed him the consul for Persia in Liverpool. However, with his departure from the country in 1908 his movement seems to have subsided.

The Shahjahan mosque in Woking – an institution of great significance – owes its origins to the efforts of Dr Leitner, a well-known Hungarian scholar at the University of Punjab, and also to the financial support that he received from Nawab Shahjahan Begum of Bhopal. After his retirement from Lahore, Leitner engaged in a campaign to construct a mosque and an Islamic centre in Woking for Muslim adherents and was able to accomplish this in 1889. He died ten years later, but the mosque and a hostel survive today with an active Muslim community residing in the vicinity. During the 1920s and 1930s, the Woking mosque became quite active under the leadership of two Muslims: Lord Headley, who had converted to Islam in India in 1913, and Khawaja Kamal ud-Din. The latter maintained a high profile in British official and ecclesiastic circles until his death in 1932, though his reputation was somewhat compromised because of his involvement with the Ahmadis. Marmaduke Pickthall (d. 1936), the translator of the Quran and a noted scholar, attended Woking mosque for prayers, along with Syed Ameer Ali.[65] In 1924, 1,000 native British Muslims and about 10,000 from overseas resided in the United Kingdom and considered the Woking mosque as the religio-social hub of the community. The number of Muslim students in Britain during these years, especially from India, also registered a major increase, though many of them went back. In 1880 there were 100 Indian students; in 1910 their number rose to 700, while in 1931 there were 3,100 studying at various institutions across Britain.[66]

Despite an apparent openness, racist attitudes embedded in an imperialist ideology would cause occasional consternation amongst certain sections of British society. Such resentment, which sometimes led to racist attacks, was largely directed at Muslim residents in Britain: long gone were the days when Muslims received adulation or harmless curiosity. Now they were the representatives of enslaved, inferior races in a presumably pure, white and powerful Britain. For instance, Queen Victoria's two Indian Muslim employees, Abdul Karim and Mohammed Bux, who arrived at Balmoral in 1887, were routinely stigmatised by her white staff. Abdul Karim eventually became the Munshi and taught Hindustani to the queen, but in several intrigues, involving officials of the royal household and the Indian government back home, every effort was made to downgrade him as a stupid, illiterate person of inferior social status, who might be linked with thugs or anti-state activists. On the orders of the queen, Von Angeli was commissioned in 1890 to paint a portrait of the queen's Indian secretary. In 1894 Abdul Karim rose to the status of Companion of the Order of the Indian Empire (CIE), much to the ire of his antagonists, including Sir Henry Ponsonby, the head of the royal household. The viceroys in India were asked to investigate Karim's origins and to send in press clippings so as to blemish his 'lowly' social origins. The investigation eventually found nothing harmful. On the death of the queen in 1901, Karim's papers were burnt on the orders of King Edward VII. This event took place at Frogmore Cottage, one of the Munshi's lodges. A heartbroken Karim left for India and lived in Agra till his death in 1909, when all his remaining papers were also burnt by official order. His widow was allowed to retain a few personal letters from Queen Victoria merely as a memento.[67]

But the recurrent question remains: How many Muslims are there in Britain? Usually the number is given as between 1.5 and 2 million, though one cannot be sure, because until 2001 in British census reports individuals were not being identified by religion.[68] The other reason underlying the lack of certainty about the exact number of Muslims in the United Kingdom is the hesitation on the part of the first-generation settlers who, in some cases, were reluctant to register themselves for votes or in the census. Their hesitation may stem from a lack of education and proper information on the rules governing such important social surveys. However, the fact remains that Pakistanis and Bangladeshis make up the largest share of British Muslims, whose second generation is well under way and accounts for 65 per cent of the total. In addition, there are many African, Arab, Turkish, Bosnian, Albanian or Kosovar, Afghan, Iranian, West Indian and East Asian Muslims in the United Kingdom. Some of them came in as refugees or exiles. Almost every nationality is represented in Britain, thanks to her imperial legacy. All these settlers are post-Second World War immigrants who initially came to meet the British demands for unskilled and semiskilled labour. Many of them have lived in the inner cities and, over the years, have diversified into various professions.

There are about 1,000 mosques across Britain, including the prayer places provided for Muslims by various factories, colleges and offices. The pre-eminent mosque is the Regent's Park mosque in London, which has a long history behind its construction.[69] There were only 18 mosques across the United Kingdom in the early 1960s, whereas in 1977 the number stood at 136. In 1985 there were 338 mosques across the nation and now the number is over 900. Mosques have played a mostly religious role, though many younger Muslims and women would like them to graduate into fully fledged Islamic centres. There are rough estimates – sometimes exaggerated for various reasons – of the number of converts; interestingly many of these converts are women, who seek stability in Islamic traditions or have Muslim partners. Contrary to the common perception, a major proportion of the community lives in Greater London, followed by the Midlands and North West. The Greater Glasgow area, Cardiff and Edinburgh follow these English regions, with a small presence in Northern Ireland.[70] Since the strengthening of regional-isation within the European Union, many Muslims have been moving to and fro though, as is supported by general observation, most South Asian Muslims prefer to settle in the United Kingdom. The old ties, familiarity with the language, clan (*biradari*) or family-based networks and greater mobility between Britain and South Asia are the main reasons for this.[71]

It is very common to exaggerate the number of Muslims – immigrants and converts – within Europe, which, however innocuous that may be, occasionally results in the conjuring up of a massive Islamic threat. Such exaggerated accounts are not confined to sensational elements in the media: religious and ultra-right groups also make use of them. Muslims are seen by the ideological elites, falling back on formidable religious, nationalist and economic arguments, not merely as a demographic threat with destabilising portents; they are also perceived as violent and irrational polyglots who may turn out to be the 'enemy within'. The lack of proper infor-mation on the multiple reasons for conflict in the postcolonial Muslim world, and the various ramifications of this, lead many Western observers to read too much into it. They assume Muslim groups to constitute a monolithic giant sharpening its teeth to gnaw the achievements of stable Western societies. At the same time, strong reservations against immigrants and political exiles as a liability rather than an asset jell with traditional European racial views and traditions. However, it is forgotten that the immigrants came into Europe largely because Europe needed them in the first place, and following economic recovery Europe then started erecting powerful anti-immigration regimes. As a result, most migrations are now taking place within the developing world itself, while the developed North is interested only in qualified professionals to suit its own needs, no matter how much this exacerbates the brain drain from the South.[72]

The fact remains that except for a few thousand converts, all the other Muslims come from *traditional* Muslim backgrounds. Of course people like Martin Lings, Gai Eaton, Yusaf Islam (formerly Cat Stevens) and Tim Winter are notable cases, but to define Islam as the most popular emerging religion may be an exaggeration.[73] There may be several reasons: firstly, we do not have the exact figures on conversions; secondly, there are no figures on Muslim men and women marrying non-Muslims and thus 'extricating' themselves from their own religious traditions. Despite occasional reportage on forced marriages and general negative images of Islam as a sexist religion, many women find it empowering. Several second-generation British Muslim women – well-placed and highly educated – are rediscovering Islam as a stable and more humane bonding ideology.[74]

The evolution of this Muslim community in Britain is as recent as it is diverse. As has been observed earlier, it is difficult to enumerate it since the census data divided settlers on the basis of their ethno-national origins, as Pakistanis, Bangladeshis, Indians and so on. As of the census of 1981, the total number of Muslims stood at 690,000, while the total in 1991 stood at 1,133,000 (see Table 4.1). Informal estimates put the correct total at well above 1.5 million.

Table 4.1   *Muslims in Britain*

Nationality	1981	1991
Pakistani and Bangladeshi	360,000	636,000
Indian	130,000	134,000
Malaysian	23,000	43,000
Nigerian	15,000	–
Turkish	5,000	26,000
Turkish Cypriot	40,000	45,000
Iranian	20,000	–
African	–	115,000
Total	690,000	1,133,000

Source: Jorgen Nielsen, *Muslims in Europe,* Edinburgh, 1995, p.41. In 1991 Nigerians are included with other Africans; the figure for Iranians remains about the same as in 1981, with some minor increase. The statistics, of course, do not include European or Caribbean Muslims, or African Muslims in 1981.

Economic migration began in the late 1950s but registered an increase in 1960–61, when the introduction of official restrictions was considered to be imminent. Until the Commonwealth Immigration Act of 1962, any Commonwealth citizen could settle in the United Kingdom. Legislation in the 1970s and 1980s under Labour and Conservatives further restricted immigration. These parties were bowing to pressure from certain sections of the society, who feared not only loss of jobs to the 'foreigners' but also of Britishness, which had, so far, hinged on an imperial ideology of colour and culture. Parliamentarians such as Enoch Powell and race riots pushed the two parties towards a consensus in seeking immigration controls and visa restrictions. The backlash by racist groups and yellow journalism underwrote such changes, and elements within the main parties tried to use the race card.[75] The traditional monocultural and colour-based definition of British nationalism hyped up an exclusionary patriotism in which economic refugees were increasingly seen as a cultural and economic threat instead of being viewed as an asset. The lack of any institutionalisation of equal rights and increased racial attacks made settlers vulnerable to various disadvantages as well as to discrimination.

In the 1970s, except for the East African Asians, immigration had already dried up, only allowing limited family reunions governed by rigorous legalistic processes.[76] Settlers increased in number due to family reunions in the 1970s and also because of the British-born children of these parents. Many of these young people are already in the universities and eager to work for various British organisations. While their cultural norms have changed tremendously, British culture itself has undergone major changes. Ethnic minorities, contrary to common perception, have contributed to the British economy in several important ways. For instance, two-thirds of independently owned local shops belong to people from minorities. They contribute about £25 billion to the British economy, out of which the Asian community, for instance, contributes over £5 billion. More than 5,000 businesses in Birmingham alone are owned by individuals from minorities, accounting for 60 per cent of the total economy of Britain's second largest city. On London's Underground 27 per cent of the staff are from minorities; 23 per cent of Britain's doctors and 24 per cent of restaurant employees were born overseas. Curries and Chinese takeaways have become more popular than fish and chips; the curry industry employs more people than the mining, steel and shipbuilding sectors put together. Some 175 million curry meals are served annually in 8,500 British establishments and at least half a million Britons eat curry dishes each day.[77] In the area of education, 12 per cent of students come from minorities, though their share in the national population is 6 per cent. In the newer universities, 30 per cent of the students are from minority ethnic backgrounds. Earlier, the Irish had accounted for the largest ethnic minority in Britain for a number of decades. In the recent immigrant and minority communities, Indians make the largest ethnic group, numbering one million, with 47 per cent of them born in the United Kingdom, 37 per cent in India and 17 per cent in Africa. Pakistanis make up the largest Muslim community in Britain and are mostly settled in the north of England in the former industrial centres of Yorkshire and Lancashire. They are followed by Bangladeshis, most of whom live in London; Bangladeshis are the youngest and the fastest growing of all the main ethnic minority groups.[78]

In some cases, in inner cities like Bradford, Birmingham, Luton, Glasgow and Manchester, the level of socioeconomic achievement is comparatively low, especially among Pakistani and Bangladeshi youths. There are several reasons, ranging from a lack of role models to the institutional vacuum that discourages them from staying on in educational establishments. In several cases, institutional racism simply exacerbates introversion among the more vulnerable elements. Despite a greater Muslim articulation, stereotypical views about their religion and women, and a presumption that segregation is by choice, further discourage many community members from an active trans-communal life. However, the high proportion of these youths in the population and their proactive role through much-needed institutionalisation may help change some of the negative trends. One thing is certain: their life is vastly different from that of the first generation settlers and from that of their cousins in South Asia. Such differences are not necessarily negative but are the natural results of different socio-cultural processes at work, sometimes putting strains especially on arranged marriages. In most cases, parents are becoming more sensitive to such changes, though their nostalgia for traditional mores remains pronounced. Media reportage on arranged marriages, marital breakdown, battered Muslim women seeking outside assistance, and the predictable stigmatisation of wider Muslim issues on television not only depress many British Muslims but also replenish the anti-Muslim idiom. However, despite such disincentives, one cannot ignore the resilience of the pioneer settlers, who, despite handicaps such as the absence of sufficient education, a lack of indigenous reciprocity, and heavy psycho-cultural and economic demands on precarious resources, have been able to establish a modicum of middle-class economic security – more in some cases than their fellow-citizens. According to one study, in 1951 almost every Muslim in Britain was foreign-born. A decade later, 1.2 per cent were British-born; a decade later still the ratio stood at 23.5 per cent and in 1981 it reached 37.5 per cent. In 1991, 47 per cent of the Muslims were native-born. In 2000, according to some reliable estimates, the proportion was nearing 70 per cent.[79]

ATTITUDES AND REALITIES OF RACE IN BRITAIN

It is important to summarise some of the findings of a significant survey conducted by a major British newspaper on race and racism in the country within a comparative perspective. Describing 2001 as a 'momentous year for race relations', the *Observer* recalled the race riots in the north of England amidst growing electoral support for the BNP – 11,000 votes just in Oldham. As mentioned earlier, the riots involved youths and the police. The murder of a Kurdish asylum seeker in Glasgow, increased misunderstanding of asylum seekers and pervasive negative images of the ethnic communities, including exaggerated ideas of their percentage of the total population (three times higher than the reality!), were the other main features of this twelve-page survey, which also included biographical details of various prominent British ethnic citizens. Graphs showed that Indians made up the largest ethnic group, numbering 984,000, 24 per cent of the total ethnic minority population, followed by 675,000 Pakistanis, 17 per cent of the ethnic population. Bangladeshis numbered some 257,000, 7 per cent of the total ethnic community population. Overall, whites accounted for 92.9 per cent of the population and the ethnic minorities for 7.1 per cent. In terms of educational achievement at GCSE level, Indians were ahead of everyone, including the whites (60 per cent and 50 per cent, respectively), with Pakistanis and Bangladeshis trailing behind at 29 per cent. However, ethnic representation in the highest cadres or executive positions was reported to be far behind those of the whites. As far as (white) British attitudes towards ethnic pluralism were concerned, they mostly revealed a positive impression, though 71 per cent felt that immigrants should embrace the British way of life instead of their old lifestyles; 61 per cent of respondents felt that regardless of colour just a feeling of being British was enough, though 30 per cent demanded a solid commitment to the UK rather than their previous homeland. Out of the ten most admired ethnic British, nine came from an Afro-Caribbean background; Prince Nasim Hameed was the only Muslim/Arab nominee. Of white Britons 70 per cent still lived in a racially non-diverse area, though 82 per cent would not object to anyone from their family marrying outside their own racial group; 61 per cent of them felt that the UK had already more than enough asylum seekers, whereas 77 per cent felt that all kinds of religions might be taught in the schools. Almost half of the respondents – 47 per cent – acknowledged that it was more difficult for ethnic candidates to get certain jobs than for whites. Given the anti-Muslim backlash after the terrorist attacks of 11 September, 60 per cent of respondents expected Muslims to make special efforts to state their allegiance to Britain, compared with the 40 per cent who would not demand this. Of such citizens 58 per cent felt that people supporting Osama bin Laden must be deported, whereas the other 42 per cent allowed them the right to differ. On an important question regarding the percentage of the ethnic population within the UK, the median estimate made by respondents was 24 per cent – much higher than the actual percentage of 7.1 per cent. Within the UK population of 57 million, the actual ethnic population is 4 million; the respondents' supposed 24 per cent would require the ethnic population to be 14.3 million.[80] In other words, there are areas where general information on ethnic pluralism is still lacking. Misperceptions of exaggerated percentages persist, as do the common stereotypes of ethnic communities largely being scavengers on welfare. In fact, most immigrants and their families have not only brought in their skills and capital, they also have greater educational achievements and professional excellence.[81]

While there is a greater concern in official and various public circles to eradicate racist policies and attitudes, all kinds of racist attacks, including violent incidents, still happen across Europe. Occasional murders, physical attacks, verbal abuse, denigration of religious places such as mosques and cemeteries, attacks by neo-Nazis on refugee halls, shops and houses – both reported and unreported – persist, along with an institutionalised form of racism at various levels, as was accepted in the report following the police inquiry into the murder of Stephen Lawrence (Macpherson Report, 1999). This latter form of racism is not easy to detect, despite a greater sensitivity in creating equal opportunities. Areas including sports, academia, media and high executive positions are still not fully and equitably accessible to minorities, though government promises are not lacking.[82]

Although Islam is the second largest religion in Europe, Muslims remain divided into various ethno-national and sectarian groups. In addition, their intra-religious differences, and a lack of awareness, especially among unskilled workers from a rural background, of the rules and privileges governing citizenship, hinder a greater social mobility. Despite exaggerated accounts of a monolithic Islam, Muslims are the most divided community in Europe. Such divisions are further criss-crossed by cleavages thrown up by class-based differences. However, there is a possibility that with the new local-born generation, with its greater access to local socio-cultural and economic institutions, coupled with positive discrimination and other political measures, minorities including the Muslims may be able to level many of these differences. On the other hand, they may articulate their efforts for a better understanding effectively, yet fall vulnerable to further divisive forces rooted in doctrinal and other diversities.

The recent vital demographic changes have propelled the diverse demands for more mosques,[83] *madrassas*,[84] grants for Muslim schools and equitable opportunities.[85] However, separate from these issues, as was evident in the riots of the summer of 2001, is the question of wider and confident participation in local and national affairs through available and cooptive institutions.[86] Neither a total apologia nor a defensive introversion will be helpful in meeting the challenges faced at various levels. Muslims live in the heart of Western modernity, which does not totally debar them from pursuing their own cultural values, but instead offers them democratic structures and space to develop a multidimensional dialogue. A greater awareness on all sides of divergence as well as of commonalities should help to achieve a balanced and stable position, where Muslims may play an effective role as mediators between diverse cultural traditions. Avoiding the extremes of segregation and unquestioned assimilation, the plural ethos needs to be cherished in collaboration with other ethno-religious communities. After all, democracy, gender equity, greater mobility, socioeconomic opportunities, educational and artistic pursuits available in the United Kingdom are all positive attributes of modernity with numerous benefits for the Muslim diaspora. The enduring and often ambivalent encounter between Britain and Islam is a *fait accompli* and needs to be cherished and channelled in the wider human interest. It is not just an ideal, but an attainable objective, that Muslim intellectuals, politicians and other activists, assisted by the more concerned and appreciative fellow citizens, should bridge the divergences so as to become the harbingers of a more vibrant form of an overdue Islamic renaissance strongly rooted in the United Kingdom.

5 Muslims in Britain: Multiculturalism and the Emerging Discourse

Avenge America: Kill a Muslim today! (Graffito on a mosque in South Shields)

Islam in Britain is far from being a monolith; it is a matrix of national, ethnic, doctrinal and economic diversities where variables like age, education, class, ethno-regional background and attitudes towards religion and the non-Muslim communities determine an entire plethora of variegated responses. Indisputably, the basic belief system and practices remain the same, yet sectarian and other such diversities characterise the Muslim diaspora in the United Kingdom. This diversity is not to belie a Utopian desire amongst both the religio-intellectual elite and the masses to establish a greater communitarian bond by striving to achieve a common platform as a united *ummah*. The issues before Muslims in Britain are both mundane and spiritual; secular and sacred; the problematic of old and new identities; the relationship with the old and the new home; and the aim to evolve strategies to cope with serious socioeconomic challenges, especially in view of indifferent if not overtly hostile attitudes from a number of quarters. While there are genuine worries among the lower strata regarding job opportunities, educational facilities for the younger generation and secure housing, the elite are concerned about the institutional depiction of Islam and the overall place of the community within a multicultural setting.

These worries greatly increased during 2001–03 after a multi-dimensional and often harsh spotlight was trained on Islam and following the detention or profiling of a number of Muslims on suspicion of terror. Though leaders like George Bush and Tony Blair tried to allay Muslim fears by rejecting the notion that the war on terror was the expression of a clash of civilisations, common Muslim perceptions considered the campaign against terror to be inherently anti-Muslim. Bush's analogy with the Crusades and Blair's moralist stance on Iraq against a pervasive public opinion only heightened such worries. Certainly, the large number of civilian deaths in

Afghanistan, the destruction of its infrastructure and ecology following the most sustained bombing in recent times and the plight of millions of refugees across the country created a grave sense of disempowerment and anger among Muslims. Simultaneously, the green light given to the states of Israel, India and Russia forcefully to combat movements for political rights further dismayed Muslims in the West and elsewhere. It felt as if the West, in its vengeance and arrogance, had plainly refused to apply strategies similar to those used in other serious conflicts in those volatile regions and had single-mindedly focused on Muslim populations. Many Muslims felt that the few gains made through intercommunity dialogue had been lost overnight as Islamic civilisation was maligned by both obscurantists and the Western establishments.

In spite of the widely shared socioeconomic and human concerns, an increasing number of middle-class intellectuals have begun to debate Islam-related themes. Such a post-Orientalist tradition is, of course, a positive development, though it is characterised by its own inherent dissension and cliches. Our present chapter begins with a discussion on this diasporic diversity, followed by a focus on some of the recurrent sociological issues within the context of strains on multiculturalism as exposed in the Runnymede Trust report, *Islamophobia* (1997), a significant document with far-reaching implications. The middle section of the chapter features some of the current intercommunitarian and intra-Muslim discourses focusing on macro- and micro-issues. The final section encompasses the quest for identity through a wider intellectual context, within a multicultural milieu. The diasporic corpus of literary writings and audiovisual presentations reviewed here may have copiously dwelt on issues of immigration, pluralism and minority–majority interaction without categorising them as an intentional discourse on British Islam. Thus, it needs to be noticed in the first instance that Muslim-related writings or artistic presentations – both fictional and otherwise – are quite varied and that authors such as Salman Rushdie, Tariq Ali, Ayyub Khan Din and Hanif Kureishi have not been writing as Muslim authors per se. On the other hand, writers like Ziauddin Sardar, Yasmin Alibhai-Brown, Akbar Ahmed, Rana Kabbani and Abdullah Hussain, and artists such as Nusrat Fateh Ali Khan, Ustad Wilayat Khan, Najma Akhtar and others, have consciously underlined their Muslim identity. To the latter category, being Muslim is a cultural and ethnic statement rather than a mere theocratic specificity.

DISCURSIVE CONTOURS OF A SOCIOLOGICAL DEBATE

The current debate on Muslim identity at academic institutions and professional research institutes is led by a generation of sociologists, historians and ethnologists who themselves, in many cases, come from a plural background. In its recent embodiment, this debate began modestly in the late 1980s, soon after the Honeyford affair, but blossomed in the 1990s, especially following the publication of *The Satanic Verses*, to become almost an industry in the late 1990s. The earlier discourse largely centred on broader themes including immigration policies, the British imperial legacy, party politics and the first-generation settlers. The latter phase dealt with more mundane issues such as schooling, housing and jobs, especially in view of the familial needs of the 'pioneer' settlers. Demands for either the abolition of blasphemy laws or their extension to all religious traditions, and the outlawing of religious discrimination have been raised in recent decades.[1] The third and more contemporary phase seems to concentrate on fighting racism at various levels by establishing and celebrating multiculturalism against the backdrop of the Rushdie saga, when a convergence between certain British liberals and ultra-right groups became so obvious. The long-drawn-out bloodshed in Bosnia (despite the Bosnians' avowal of secularism), involving the brutalisation of an overwhelmingly Muslim country in Europe and the rape of a huge number of helpless women, further awakened many British Muslims to their Muslim identity.[2] The sustained bombing campaign in Afghanistan and the Israeli brutalisation of Palestinians, and similar yet under-reported Russian and Indian campaigns against the Chechens and Kashmiris in more recent years, have alerted concerned Muslims to the scale of the denigration and misunderstanding of Islam across the world. The global peace movement in 2001–03 further encouraged Muslims to explore this issue of identity. According to a pervasive Muslim view, political and economic issues, such as those in Iraq and elsewhere, are being dealt with through the use of brutal force, while simultaneously Muslims are widely characterised as religious fundamentalists.[3] However, it is quite ironic to note that only two extreme positions – confrontation or submission – have been attributed to the Muslim diaspora. The so-called Huntingtonian 'clash of civilisations' thesis compartmentalises Muslims as an inherently confrontational monolith, while the premise of total submission presumes the absence of resistance, disallowing any communitarian initiative.

When the Labour home secretary, David Blunkett, demanded the use of the English language as a litmus test for Britishness, it reminded everyone of Norman Tebbitt's exhortation to Asians to support the English cricket team. Blunkett's statement came at a time when the government was already embarked on rolling back civil liberties as part of the anti-terror campaign and Muslims were in negative focus.[4] It somehow overlooked the fact that the Asian youths involved in the summer 2001 riots were all English-speaking, and, in several cases, well-educated British citizens.[5] At an intellectual level, the recent debate on multiculturalism focused on various ideological positions linking the civil rights of the Muslims with the common perceptions of left–liberal elements.[6] Most commentators and activists have felt that the traditional official approach to multiculturalism has not only failed to stem racism but has also been ineffective in ending intercommunity segregation. The peace rallies and vigils involving millions of British citizens from various walks of life established a greater solidarity with Afghans, Iraqis, Palestinians and British Muslims. However, the current debate seems to be centred around certain local and transregional issues such as schools, mixed marriages, job opportunities and an overall redefinition of British identity. The erstwhile territorial or national identities seem to be giving way to holistic identities, such as British Sikhs, British Hindus and British Muslims, in place of the sole categorisation as Indians, Bangladeshis or Pakistanis.[7]

The focus hitherto in several sociological studies has been largely on statistics which, for all their due significance, somehow fail to pinpoint various other socio-psychological denominators. Firstly, most of the studies on the diaspora still centre on immigration, an approach which is becoming somewhat redundant due to strict and extremely restrictive regimes all across 'fortress Europe'. Secondly, like census reports in the past, the statistics merely identify place of origin, whereas the current demographic realities militate against such enumeration. Not only are a clear majority of 'ethnic Britons' – almost 70 per cent – native-born, but the links with the ancestral homeland are also changing radically.[8] The older generation is still worried about education, jobs, marriage and overall cultural orientation of the Muslim youth, and at the same time trying to retain traditional linkages with the families and *biradries* (kinships) back home. The local ethnic media is daily replete with 'stories from home' and gives wide coverage to visiting dignitaries, including clerical, spiritual and political leaders.[9] While some sociological studies may focus on intergenerational divergences, it is amazing to notice a number of mutualities based on religion, food, music and clothes.[10] While the study of the diaspora is quite crucial in order to highlight theoretical and substantial issues, a focus on conflictive, differing and even occasionally oppositional patterns may not be very productive as such an approach simply mythifies an unbridgeable gulf.

A focus on ethnic differences, however pertinent it is and however much it is based on visible economic denominators, might inadvertently prove problematic. Such a focus might reinforce stereotypes of a particular community and could shatter a well-needed sense of achievement. For instance, it is quite common in seminars and conferences to see Indians, Pakistanis, Bangladeshis and Afro-Caribbeans being compared with the *white* British in sectors such as educational achievements, housing and jobs. This might sometimes be helpful in shedding light on murky areas. But a context-free comparative focus in these specific realms without ascertaining other critical variables might transmit doubts as to whether Bangladeshis and Pakistanis could ever move up the ladder. In the same manner, any analysis which sees Afro-Caribbean lifestyles as 'Irish' or Asian lifestyles as 'Jewish' is also too simplistic.[11] Studies need to be more than mere historical surveys or collections of statistics and must move forward beyond minority–majority paradigms. Apart from the undesirable and impractical extremes of total assimilation or eternal conflict, intercultural interaction is a continuous process of negotiation and may even establish a 'third culture' – an altogether new and immensely functional paradigm.[12] Pluralism, thus, becomes a medley of several interactive third cultures redefining the entire ambit of identities.

Like the African Americans, Muslim communities in Britain and Western Europe are not mere mute spectators on the sidelines but constitute active constellations negotiating several strategies of cooption and resistance. However, it is to be remembered that it has been a long and arduous march for minorities in Europe, who, until recently, have been viewed through narrowly defined nationalist periscopes. Jews, Gypsies, Muslims and other such minorities have remained marginal, though greater democratisation, wider empowerment and an accent on equal opportunities are transforming erstwhile exclusionary attitudes. But in view of the ebb and flow of the Right across Europe though parties such as the BNP, the National Front in France and similar ultranationalist and neo-Nazi organisations in Germany, Austria, Belgium, Denmark, Holland, Switzerland and elsewhere, one cannot be too docile and over-optimistic about these acculturative processes.

Another major problem with the current sociological debate is its unquestioned acceptance of the universality of historical and contemporary processes across the United Kingdom. It is forgotten that the evolution and acculturation of Muslim communities, especially those of South Asian origin, may be different in Scotland from those of such communities in England. Fieldwork and publications by certain 'pioneers' from Scotland, for instance, without ignoring the similarities, underline such differences. South Asian visitors to Scotland are reported as early as 1505 in the court of King James IV, though Gypsies of Indian origin had been in the country for a long time. Quite a few Scots served in India during colonial times, whereas the first known Indian prince to live in Scotland was Duleep Singh, son of Maharajah Ranjeet Singh, who, following the British conquest of the Punjab, was brought to Britain. It was in the late nineteenth century that several Indian students and some lascars started arriving in Edinburgh, Glasgow and Dundee.[13]

The earliest immigrants to Scotland from India were mostly Punjabi Muslims from the district of Jallandhar, who earned their living as vendors in the post-First World War decades. These rural vendors, from villages such as Nakodar/Jagraon, included men such as Nathoo Muhammad, N. M. Tanda, Sundhi Din and Muhammad Ashraf. Through their hard work, and undeterred by racist outbursts, these pioneer pedlars of the 1920s eventually expanded their retail businesses into wholesale textile concerns. After 1947, many of their relatives in India migrated to Pakistan and settled in Lyallpur (now Faisalabad), but some young people continued to emigrate to Scotland to join their cousins. Thus several of these *biradari* linkages resulted in a successful Punjabi Muslim diaspora. Their self-sufficiency and active participation in Scottish political life earned them considerable respect among the Scots. By the 1990s, there were 50,000 Asians in Scotland, a clear majority of them of Pakistani/Punjabi origins.[14]

The experiences of the lascars in north-east England and Yorkshire are different from those of their counterparts in the south-east. These lascars, predominantly Yemenis, suffered from a pervasive racism, but developed their own networks and strategies for protection. Handicaps such as their lack of lingual skills and exploitation by employers did not deter them from offering military service to their adopted country during both world wars. Out of a 3,000-strong Arab community in South Shields, 700 lost their lives during the First World War, a great sacrifice for such a small community. However, soon after the war, local groups started harassing the community demanding their expulsion from the country. During the Second World War, British Arabs from Tyneside again joined the armed forces. In the 1950s they had to confront another wave of racism. However, by the 1960s, they were again able to establish several positive mutualities with their fellow English citizens. Still, it is only in recent times that the services rendered to the country and the region by these 'Black Geordies' have started to receive an overdue acknowledgement.[15]

The geopolitical events underwriting Western policies towards the Muslim world have impacted the Muslim diaspora. It is widely believed that Western governments are not fully sensitive and responsive to a pervasive Muslim anguish. The terrorist attacks on New York and Washington in 2001 have certainly proved to be a turning point for both multiculturalism and the Muslim diaspora. For many, Muslims became the punchbags of racism and class-based denigration, whereas for others, the terrorist events only rekindled an existing racist bias in the mainstream Western establishment. The way in which the United States reacted so angrily and violently against an impoverished and war-torn country like Afghanistan, requiring 50 Muslim states to support the military strikes, rudely awakened the Muslim world to the horrors of a contemporary war. While most Muslims decried terrorist attacks, a majority remained critical of Anglo-American policy of singling out a Muslim country for such massive destruction. There were some elements which had earlier supported Osama bin Laden's irresponsible verbosity, but now, seeing millions of new refugees and the large-scale destruction of a decimated country, they were made mindful of the further marginalisation of the Muslim factor in global affairs. The UN, the Organisation of the Islamic Conference (OIC) and the Arab League, all remained redundant as Muslim rulers hastened to appease the United States, leaving ordinary Afghans to the perils of a sustained bombing over several months. There were three dimensions to this saga: it caused a huge and unnecessary havoc in Afghanistan, besides destabilising the entire region; it accentuated anti-Muslim feeling across the world and especially in the West; and it gave an excuse to regimes to introduce draconian laws on immigration and interrogation, resulting in bans on several Muslim charities and the internment of some Muslims clerics on minor suspicions. The exaggerated media accounts of British Muslims fighting in Afghanistan on the side of the Taleban also seriously affected inter-community relations in the United Kingdom.[16] In Afghanistan, as calculated by Professor Marc Herold of the University of New Hampshire, the bombing had caused 3,767 civilian deaths by mid-December 2001, and the number of others killed in Qala-i-Jangi,[17] Kandahar[18] and Tora Bora[19] may have exceeded 12,000. Even after all this devastation, neither Osama bin Laden nor Mullah Omar could be apprehended, though the Taleban regime dissolved, to be replaced with regional warlords:

> There will be no official two-minute silence for the Afghan dead, no newspaper obituaries or memorial services attended by the prime minister, as there were for the victims of the twin towers. But what has been cruelly demonstrated is that the US and its camp followers are prepared to sacrifice thousands of innocents in a coward's war.[20]

In the wake of the retaliatory campaign, there were individual incidents of violence directed against Muslims and vandalisation of some mosques, while negative media coverage increased Muslim introversion.[21] The introduction of restrictive laws by the Labour government led to the detention of Muslim immigrants, and hyped-up anti-immigration propaganda led to the third consecutive victory of John Howard in Australia. All over the Continent, Muslim activists, dissidents and vocal elements were either directly harassed or were put under surveillance. Even Lord Nazir Ahmed, the Labour politician from Rotherham, was cautioned by his peers in the party and had his phone tapped.[22] It is, however, important to remember that according to the early media reports many Afghans in the diaspora themselves opposed the bombing campaign. In the same vein, Anglo-American resolve on attacking Iraq massively dismayed the Muslim diaspora, though the solidarity with the peace movement was reassuring.

THE RUNNYMEDE TRUST REPORT

Various think-tanks and non-governmental organisations in Britain are committed to investigative and ameliorative reports on discrim-inatory regimes in both the private and public realms. The Runnymede Trust, like the Policy Studies Institute (PSI), enjoys a pre-eminent position in sponsoring non-partisan studies on various socioeconomic issues in Britain. Its most important contribution in recent years was *Islamophobia*, a report about the pervasive negative images of Muslims in Britain. It is based on the extensive research and findings of a high-profile committee headed by Sir Gordon Conway, the former vice-chancellor of the University of Sussex. The committee was established in 1996; a number of technical hurdles and other handicaps had taken almost four years to overcome before a final remit was agreed upon. The well-documented and substantial report establishes the existence of multiple forms of racism in British society, from popular prejudices to negative media portrayals of Muslims, in addition to severe cases of harassment and discrimination at certain levels. By using a wide variety of tabulated material and diverse documentary evidence, it underlined the persistence of a strong anti-Muslim tendency across the board. Muslims were shown to suffer from discrimination due to factors including colour, class, culture and creed. The report is not incriminatory of the entire British society, but highlights some of the major echelons that are biased. The report suggests a more target-oriented role for the official agencies, media and academia in eradicating pervasive biases and discriminatory policies, also known as institutionalised racism. Rather than the fallacious denial of its existence and its negative role in the efficient working of pluralism, institutional racism requires committed and holistic efforts for its extinction.

Soon after its formation, the committee sent hundreds of copies of its consultation paper across Britain, soliciting first-hand opinions and experiences of being a British Muslim. It also carried out extensive surveys of UK residents and examined print media. The early findings were published in 1997 and, given the nature of the issues raised in the report and the committee's own high profile, *Islamophobia* received wide media coverage. The commission did not invent the term 'Islamophobia' but took it on board; it had been in currency for quite some time in Muslim intellectual circles. The earliest use of the term was in February 1991 in an American journal, *Insight,* with reference to Soviet policy towards Afghanistan.[23] In the British context, Islamophobia was perceived as 'describing prejudices and discrimination which they (Muslims) experienced in their everyday lives'. Professor Conway, in his foreword, noted that 'it is evident from the responses which we received that Islamophobia describes a real and growing phenomenon – an ugly word for an ugly reality. Hardly a day now goes by without references to

Islamophobia in the media'.[24] In its eleven chapters (including intro-
ductory and concluding sections) the report concentrates on subjects
such as Islam in Britain, media portrayals, verbal and physical
violence against Muslims, the exclusionary definition of British
nationalism, areas of mutualities, and judicial recourse for redress.
Substantiated by first-hand information gathered through the
working paper, surveys and recent publications by reputable authors
and institutions, this major document contains graphs, bullet points,
extracts from important speeches, interviews and list of publications,
besides autobiographical case studies reproduced in special boxes.
The report shows great professionalism in its organisation of diverse
material and general structuring. Its varied sources and investigative
analysis make it a pertinent document on pluralism without
becoming polemical. Rather than simply narrating the facts, it
emphasises corrective strategies in the form of recommendations
under separate headings and can thus be considered compulsory
reading on multiculturalism.

The report acknowledges recurrent misperceptions on both sides
owing to historical and contemporary factors. That Muslims may
bear a grudge against the West is not because Islam has taught them
to do so: there are millions of devout and upright Muslims who retain
respect for Christianity. The earliest encounter between the West and
Islam was through the Crusades, which, according to the report, left
a lasting imprint. The Ottoman conquest of Constantinople further
added to such biases. Many well-known Europeans, such as Ernest
Renan, reflecting the colonial mentality, displayed prejudice towards
Islam: in Renan's view a Muslim is 'incapable of learning anything
or of opening himself to a new idea'.[25] Muslim immigrants including
lascars, students and semiskilled professionals over the last two
centuries have failed to remove these prejudices and Islam has been
conceived as an enemy rather than a partner. In some cases, the
stereotypes and discrimination have multiplied. Some of these all-
too-familiar stereotypes posit Islam as a monolithic, problematic,
segregationist, inferior, hostile, manipulative, anti-Western and anti-
feminist ideology, of which criticism is justifiable. At the same time,
positive views of Islam acknowledge its diverse, genuine, interactive,
participatory, honest, frugal and considerate aspects, though this
remains confined to specific sections of society. While quoting several
examples, the report apportions responsibility in general to media
pundits for denigrating Islamic culture. For instance, it quotes from

an article by Anthony Burgess in the *Observer* which for the first time in recent years used the term 'fundamentalism' with reference to political Islam. The article referred to 'the phenomenon of the new and rather very old Islam, the dangerous fundamentalism revived by the ayatollahs and their admirers as a device, indistinguishable from a weapon, for running a modern state'. To Burgess, Muslim states like Iran were 'little more than intolerant, bloody, and finally incompetent animations of the Holy Book [the Quran]'.[26]

The report found 194 items containing the word 'fundamentalist' in the online archives of the *Daily Telegraph* from November 1994 to May 1997. Of these 142 items contained the world 'Islamic' and only 20 contained 'Christian'. Peregrine Worsthorne found in Islam a great civilisation of the past which had now 'degenerated into a primitive enemy fit only to be sensitively subjugated'.[27] Following the Huntingtonian thesis, English broadsheets in the 1990s seemed to compete with the tabloids in hyping up fears of a presumed Islamic threat. Bernard Levin – another well-known columnist – when commenting on the Oklahama tragedy of 1995, opined: 'Do you realise that in perhaps half a century, not more and perhaps a good deal less, there will be wars, in which fanatical Muslims will be winning? As for Oklahama, it will be called Khartoum-on-the-Mississippi, and woe betide anyone who calls it anything else.'[28]

According to the report, Muslim views of the West, especially genuine complaints on a number of issues, are rejected out of hand as fanaticism and not worth any attention. Thus Islamophobia, at different levels, emerges as a complex phenomenon where exclusion (from jobs, promotion, politics and managerial positions), violence (physical and verbal), prejudices (media-based or in daily parlance) and the daily occurrences of discrimination (in education, health, services, transport and employment) form its major components. While using the available census data and related studies from Oxford, Warwick, the PSI and the Commission for Racial Equality, the report noted that British Muslims, in most cases from South Asia, preferred to work in smaller businesses as it made it easier for them to perform their religious duties.[29]

However, the growing number of Muslim professionals, especially from the second generation – which itself accounts for about 70 per cent of the total – displays increasing mobility and professional diversification. In addition to building simple mosques, the emphasis is turning towards multipurpose Islamic centres to serve various echelons of the communitiy, which in itself increases the demand for locally trained imams. Such significant changes expose the hollowness of stereotypes and add pressure on the private and public sectors to employ qualified British professionals. In the same vein, Islam – and Hinduism, Sikhism, Buddhism and other religions – can no longer be defined as *foreign*. Muslim organisations are being supplemented by regional and national associations such as the Muslim Council of Britain (MCB), the British Muslim Association (BMA), the Oxford Centre for Islamic Studies, Leicester's Islamic Foundation, the Association of Muslim Social Scientists (AMSS) and the UK Action Committee on Islamic Affairs (UKACIA) – though localist, sectarian and ethnic divisions and interclass differences continue to sap Muslim abilities to take on common and larger issues. The growing quality of newspapers and magazines such as *Q News*, the *Muslim News, Impact, Dialogue*, the *Nation, Al-Hayat* and the *News* International, in addition to various radio stations and television channels, is allowing a greater Muslim articulation and interaction varying 'from home to home'.[30]

While global issues such as Palestine, Kurdistan, Abkhazia, Kashmir, Bosnia, Chechnya, Kosovo, and problems in individual Muslim countries such as Iraq and Afghanistan, may still engage British Muslims in the towns and universities, the focus is shifting mainly to *domestic* issues by articulating more robust institutional representation and strategies to tackle discrimination. But, as the Trust's report brings out quite forcefully, media portrayals usually concentrate on themes like gender inequities and violence, imputing them *universally* to Islam. Through copious reproduction of numerous extracts from the tabloids and broadsheets that essentialise Islam with violence, the report focuses on exclusionary attitudes towards Muslims. For instance, Clifford Longley is quoted to have observed:

> Islam has the greatest difficulty in coming to terms with the values of western secular society, which it is much more inclined to regard as satanic than as the greatest achievement of human civilisation to date ... Behind the Muslim demand that they be given their own schools out of public funds is a hidden agenda of discrimination and intolerance – just as one may suspect there is a hidden agenda, but this time a sound one, behind the Government's refusal.[31]

Refusal to assist Muslim schools on such grounds was untenable especially when several other denominational schools – both Christian and Jewish – were grant-maintained irrespective of any 'hidden agendas'. The report rather candidly observed: 'Currently there are almost 7,000 state schools with an explicit religious affiliation. Not a single one is Muslim. About 4,800 are Church of England, 2,140 Roman Catholic, 28 Methodist and 23 Jewish.'[32] On the question of quality at GCSE, Muslim schools, contrary to common misperceptions, were 'close to, or in some instances vastly exceeded, the national average with regard to the numbers of pupils achieving five or more GCSE passes at grades A–C'.[33] Though objections may be raised in some quarters to assisting 'separate' Muslim schools, out of fear of a self-imposed segregation that may eventually turn out to be harmful, yet the fact remains that such official patronage will instil a greater amount of self-reliance. Polly Toynbee, in a piece in the mid 1990s, felt that official funding for Muslim schools may end up hampering the intellectual progress and sociological integration of about half a million British Muslim children. To her, such 'sectarian schools' may mean that

> the state will educate children to believe women are of inferior status, one step behind in the divine order of things. The state will acquiesce in the repression of young girls, putting their parents' cultural rights above the duty to educate all British girls equally.[34]

Whereas a half-baked pedagogy justified in the name of a narrowly defined religious ordinance may be dangerous, given the shortage of qualified Muslim teachers, such a view equally displays stereotyped views of Islamic attitudes towards women. While Muslim women, like many men, may be largely disadvantaged, still their inequities accrue from a host of socioeconomic and political factors and not essentially from the early Islamic precepts as such. Muslim feminism, in fact, rejects the notion of an Islam-based inequality. The demand for financial assistance for 'separate' Muslim schools was misinterpreted as a 'divisive' effort tending towards 'apartheid'.[35] The report rightly felt 'that anti-Muslim prejudice has played a part in the rejections, since the official reasons given by the Government have seemed generally unconvincing'.[36]

While suggesting ameliorative measures – some of them already happening – the report focused on various individuals and organisations undertaking interfaith discourse or creating bridges between communities. The Prince of Wales's speech at Wilton Park, Sussex, in December 1996, with a message similar to that of an earlier speech at Oxford, urged his audience to seek fresher and greater moral and social support from Islamic values. Various other individuals have addressed the need to engage in dialogue, for instance among Jews and Muslims, or Muslims and Hindus, so as to share common strategies and ideals within the context of multiculturalism. While sections of British society might continue, sporadically, to frown upon the composition and cultural traits of a multicultural society, it was felt that, in the holistic interest, they should not deflate such efforts. The report suggested legislative strategies to remove anomalies, for instance the outlawing of discrimination on the basis of religion. Examples of successful litigation were employed to suggest that such precedents might help the community to move forward. The report's authors felt that it might be difficult to pinpoint religious discrimination as specifically warranting statutory intervention, and that some minority practices 'currently illegal might become defensible on religious grounds'; still, that must not impede any legislative activism to outlaw religious discrimination. Moreover, the report reviewed divergent public views on the blasphemy laws. Muslims and a few other observers have demanded their extension to cover every religious tradition as well as the official church, whereas another group urged their total abolition. The report summed up its own recommendation: 'We recommend that the law on blasphemy in Britain should be reviewed, and that reports on how relevant legislation in other countries works in practice should be explored, and proposals made.'[37] In its last section, the report offered 60 vital recommendations to be adopted by the government, media and other private and public organisations to ensure for minorities fair practice, the working of an egalitarian multiculturalism, and a fully fledged citizenship.

THE CURRENT DEBATE AND ITS SOCIO-INTELLECTUAL CONTOURS

The academic debate involving the Muslim diaspora and a host of opinion groups and institutions has moved on since the Rushdie affair. In more recent years, organisational efforts by Muslim academics and activists have led to institutionalisation of the debate, with a greater emphasis on intra-communitarian linkages. Such a post-objectification phase is quite positive and of immense significance because it involves Muslims from diverse professional, gender and intellectual persuasions. It also shows that, benefiting from the democratic and conducive environment of societies such as Britain,

Muslim intellectuals are gradually negotiating a vital discourse on their own status and identity by negating the stereotypic images of a segregated and sterile stalemate. Participation by the younger generation in the role of activist-scholars and also in the peace movement, especially participation by women, is adding a special dimension to this emerging intellectual tradition with positive ramifications for Islam in the West and elsewhere. The thematic issues are of both a general and a specific nature: for instance, the relationship between Islam and the West; media portrayals; concern over the Muslim predicament in Palestine, Iraq, Kashmir, Chechnya, the Balkans, the Philippines and elsewhere; and the political instability in most of the Muslim countries. There is concern over the issues of poverty, ethno-sectarian conflicts, interstate dissension and lack of transparent governance in almost all the Muslim regions. There are worries about the continued factionalist and fragmentary nature of various national communities, kowtowing to external partisan interests and a perceived disempowerment of the global Muslim communities.

Specific concerns include majority–minority relationships, the reinterpretation of Islam, intergenerational dialogue, the evolution of a Muslim identity over and above factionalism, research on Muslim feminism, the recognition of Islamic ethics and aesthetics, the reformulation of Islamic *ijtihad* to suit the demands and challenges in the diaspora and the future socio-political role for Muslims in their adopted homelands.[38] The Muslim debate is not encouraged by a host of impediments and dispiriting developments in the Muslim world in general, but many scholars feel that a long-term legacy requires sustained effort for a reconstructive dialogue. In addition, some Muslims remain worried that monolinguality, persuasive as well as dissuasive pressures from the non-Muslim communities, and powerful yet culturally alien trajectories may be gradually weaning Muslims from the core cultural ethos. Forced marriages and emphasis on the rote learning of Arabic, which lacks spontaneity and dynamic interpretation, are chasing some youngsters away from traditional religious instruction.[39]

While, in a general sense, there is a move towards establishing Islamic or Muslim centres instead of *mere* mosques, the issue-orientated approach is engaging intellectuals and artistes more vigorously. The debate is no longer centred on rights; it has moved on to responsibilities in the broader context of Islamic altruism. The reclamation of the Muslim contribution to social welfare, with a view to leading Muslims towards 'making history' in a secularised context, is perceived as a new frontier. The interface between Islamic Sharia and Western juridical traditions is another upcoming area of research. Similarly, the discussion on globalisation has engendered various Muslim responses and discourses, varying from Muslim globalism to a multicultural and universal globalism based on both temporal and spiritual components. In the same vein, the issues of colour, culture, class, political mobilisation and feminism are being animatedly discussed, though neither to establish a segregated niche nor to seek unquestioning integration. Studies of philology, imperialism, hegemony and hierarchic globalism are some other exciting themes which Muslim social scientists have gradually started investigating. In other words, the statistical and primary nature of needs-based discourse has moved on to newer parameters, especially among the younger generation, and encompasses a steady multiethnic and multidisciplinary interaction.

However, before one apportions too many positive attributes to this nascent intellectual tradition one must not overlook the indigenous and exogenous impediments. The inner cities, where most Muslims in Britain still live, are usually characterised by 'low achievement', and the subtle problems of institutional racism still prevent Muslim social scientists and professionals from achieving higher positions. The defence establishment, the Foreign Office, Parliament, the universities, colleges, funding councils, the BBC, the British Council, DFID, and other such major public organisations are still subtly reluctant to open up executive positions to ethnic members.[40] The entire regime of equal opportunities is largely confined to paperwork instead of providing proactive help to otherwise qualified professionals. Institutional racism is a very slippery terrain and hard to detect and codify, but any fieldwork based on individual surveys of candidates applying but not getting shortlisted, or not being considered for promotion, can, of course, bring shocking revelations.[41] Conditions may be better in some areas in Europe, including Britain, but in places like Austria, Germany, France or the Iberian Peninsula, such discrepancies are numerous and are experienced by a vast majority of ethnic professionals. Even within the United Kingdom there are regional variations in terms of facilities and opportunities for ethnic minorities, so optimism regarding the impact of such a debate has to be guarded.

WRITERS AND LITERARY ARTICULATIONS

Amongst British writers – sometimes mistakenly called Commonwealth writers – are well-known Muslim names, including Salman Rushdie, Hanif Kureishi, Tariq Ali, Ayub Khan Din, Rana Kabbani, Shabbir Akhtar, Ziauddin Sardar, Martin Lings, Gai Eaton, Zaki Badawi, Tariq Modood, M.A. Sherif, Saadia Sherif, Yasmin Alibhai-Brown and Bobby Saiyid, though the list could be extended.[42] In addition, there are Muslim activists such as Yusaf Islam (formerly Cat Stevens), organisations such as the Al-Khoei Foundation, Islam 21, the Muslim Council of Britain (MCB), the Islamic Relief, Tablighi Jama'at, Kashmir Freedom Movement, the Association of Muslim Social Scientists, the Calamus Foundation for interfaith dialogue, and other bodies for socialisation such as the Ar-Rum, the Hyderabad Muslim Association and various Pakistani, Yemeni, Bangladeshi and other such *anjumans*. Mosque and community-based organisations run into thousands; while literary groups holding *mushairra* or literary evenings, and university-based youth groups, such as Islamic societies or extreme constellations like the al-Muhajiroon, Hizbul Tahrir, and others, have evolved in more recent years. But not all are engaged in a serious debate on Muslim identity; some may be attempting a more theocratic, uniformist vision of Islam falling short of a much-needed synthesis and reinterpretation. In some cases, such efforts are too localised and sectarian. Here we are more concerned with some prominent individuals, who through their writings and literary outpourings, have been part of a wider debate on Muslim identity. Some of them may not even like to be pigeonholed as Muslim, but their works deal with Muslim subjects and, in some cases, have caused considerable controversy and hurt among Muslims. Salman Rushdie, of course, tops the list among controversial Muslim writers.

Long before Rushdie's *The Satanic Verses* came out, he was already an established literary figure. A Bombay-born writer, Rushdie has Muslim relatives in both India and Pakistan, whereas he himself came to England to study at Rugby School and then at Cambridge. His career began as a novelist and *Midnight's Children* (1981) elevated him to a distinguished status. This novel depicted the story of Partition and, despite its satirical features, turned out to be an important historical fiction interspersed with some autobiographical details. His other novels such as *Grimus* and *Shame* again focused on South Asian historical and political themes. *Shame* was resented both in India and Pakistan by the ruling elites, which it satirised. However, it was with *The Satanic Verses* that Rushdie incurred wider condemnation among Muslims. Despite dissuasive remarks by referees such as Khushwant Singh, Penguin went ahead with its publication and soon the novel became the most controversial of its type. Though it is an amalgam of history, politics, immigration, racism, Thatcherism in the UK and Bollywood, yet it mainly focuses on the life of the Prophet, the most venerated personality for Muslims of all sects. Rushdie would certainly have foreseen the uproar that his satire of the Prophet would cause among Muslims, but, out of sheer greed or simple obstinacy, he still went ahead. Faxes based on some of the most insulting portions of the text went from London across the world, and India, South Africa and Pakistan banned the offending work. Demonstrations against Rushdie in the Muslim world turned violent, while in Bradford the book was symbolically burnt.[43] Muslims were mainly aggrieved that Rushdie, an 'insider', had caused hurt by mocking the Prophet to appease his liberal and other anti-Islamic friends. Liberal writers like Tariq Ali defended Rushdie simplistically by interpreting the entire saga as the age-old confrontation within Islam between the purist and the artist. Ali's contemporary play, *Iranian Nights*, was mainly written for Western audiences in an Orientalist style.

To more serious intellectuals, with this novel Rushdie had repudiated himself. Earlier, in his fiction and reviews, he had combined political issues with literary subject matter, but now he had forsaken this political project to write merely for a Western readership. In other words, Rushdie, by leaving accountability and political issues aside, had turned into a latter-day Orientalist.[44] He appeared closer to V. S. Naipaul in his satire of Islam. In the United Kingdom, both liberal and conservative Muslim groups appeared annoyed over his blaspheming of Islam and demanded a ban or expressed their anguish in different ways. It was not merely Rushdie who was the object of this grudge, it was a newer generation of British Muslims who, in fact, were assuming the vanguard role by replacing first-generation immigrants who, to them, always appeared law-abiding and rather introvert and submissive. These new-generation Muslims were articulating their identity with reference to racial discrimination and fewer job opportunities. They demanded an equitable use of the blasphemy laws, which hitherto had applied only to Christianity. In addition, the Brelvi and Deobandi factions (two main South Asian Muslim doctrinal groups) were competing for a greater say in community affairs, with Allama Khomeini assuming the role of an international Muslim leader by issuing a fatwa.[45] Though many liberal Muslims[46] disagreed with the fatwa they denounced Rushdie's unnecessary provocations and the resultant hurt and furore. Rushdie's supporters, such as Fay Weldon, felt that Muslims were denying the author his right to speak,[47] whereas several Muslim intellectuals felt that Rushdie, through his rabble-rousing, was acting merely as an Orientalist and not as a secular intellectual.[48]

Rushdie's other novels and story books, including *Haroun and the Sea of Stories* (1990), *The Moor's Last Sigh* (1995) and *The Ground Beneath Her Feet* (2000) mostly dwell on South Asian themes. Bollywood characters, folktales and Muslim themes are combined together with various effects. Some of these stories, including the episode of the theft of the Prophet's hair in 1965 from the Hazratbal shrine in Srinagar, clearly concern *Muslim* issues in South Asian settings. His prose mixes English with Urdu, Hindi and occasional Arabic and Persian words showing not only his literary versatility but also the problematic nature of his own Muslim identity. Rushdie is not divorced from India,[49] especially its literary personages, its pluralism and its Bollywood. As is clear from his *Vintage Book of Indian Writing 1947–1997*, he has a great regard for the Indian literary heritage, especially in English, but also a special taste for Urdu poetry. His relationship with Islam is equally problematic; on the one hand, he is well versed in Islamic history and the early sources of Islamic religion, but at the same time he enjoys satirising some of the Muslim precepts by assuming the role of a demolition man. In some of his reviews, Rushdie, in fact, has defended Muslim cultures. For instance, reviewing Naipaul's *Among the Believers,* Rushdie pinpointed various problems and superficialities within the travelogue, which consisted of the author's visit to Iran, Pakistan, Indonesia and Malaysia. In the same vein, he has been critical of the South Asian elite, including Indira Gandhi and Benazir Bhutto, for being irreverent towards their own societal imperatives.

In one of his essays, while talking of migration from India to Pakistan and then to Britain, Rushdie empathised with the immigrants, observing: 'I have been in a minority group all my life.'[50] In the early 1990s, while living the life of a fugitive under the constant protection of the British police, Rushdie seems to have broken down. To the dismay of his liberal detractors, he reiterated his commitment to Islam, but stopped short of tendering an unfettered apology to Muslims.[51] After the lifting of the fatwa in 1999, Rushdie's movements became more public though he still avoided coming out in the open. While most Muslims remain hurt over Rushdie's caricature, they are not serious in implementing the fatwa. Privately, they complain of the European bias against Islam and the continued derision for the Muslim creed. To them, the European powers and the establishments therein are snobbish and irreverent towards Muslim sensibilities. In addition, they complain of the double standards employed in Western policies. In 1999, Rushdie was made Commander of the Order of Arts and Letters, France's highest artistic honour, and received similar distinctions from various other countries; this did not help alleviate Muslim anger against an egotistical co-religionist who had been 'playing to the gallery'.

Another well-known British writer of Muslim origin is Hanif Kureishi, whose plays, short stories, film scripts and novels show a unique and equally interesting mixture of East and West. His characters are mostly Pakistanis interacting with their British counterparts in various encounters – sexual and emotional in particular. Kureishi was born to a Pakistani father and a British mother in Kent at a time when his father was posted to Pakistan's High Commission in London. His education took place in Britain and all his stories are located within that country. In 1984, he wrote the script for My Beautiful Launderette, which turned out to be a popular movie. His novel *The Buddha of Suburbia* (1990) won the Whitbread Award and was serialised by the BBC in 1993. These two literary efforts, mostly based on South Asian diasporic stories, made the young Kureishi into a familiar name. *Love in a Blue Time*, another collection of his stories, brought him more fame, especially when 'My Son the Fanatic' was adopted as a film in 1990. It is the story of a Pakistani taxi driver who mostly works during the night in a northern industrial city. This middle-aged man is popular with prostitutes, one of whom in particular he escorts around during the night. He is intimate with her, besides quite often swigging whisky. In the meantime, his son has become a practising Muslim, offering regular prayers and spending most of his time with fellow religious Muslims. He is critical of his father for his libertine lifestyle and this friction, symbolic of an intergenerational tension, turns into a tortuous story of suspense. The despondent father confides in the prostitute, showing a cross-cultural relationship between two members of different ethnicities and gender yet very much part of the same working class sharing each other's agonies. Kureishi's other stories focus on drug culture, stifling urban life, the monotony of a working-class existence, especially for immigrants, sexual liaisons between Asian men and white women, and the interplay of complex emotions and erotica.[52] His fiction deals with the disappointment, boredom and depression of lost generations, including immigrants and others, who existentially try to seek solace in drugs and extramarital sex. For instance, his novel, *The Black Album* (1995), written about London against the backdrop of the fall of the Berlin Wall in 1989, centres on themes like religion, sex and ecstasy, with several characters, including some Muslim students, engaging in such activities. Kureishi, through his characterisation and locales, tries to show the meaninglessness of life in post-industrial society and comes out as a serious chronicler and a ruthless critic.

Tariq Ali, another well-known London-based writer, is of Pakistani origin with an elitist background combining feudal and urban strands, and since his activist days at Oxford in the 1960s has been writing both fiction and political commentaries. Beginning as a Marxist, Ali, like other such ideologues, presumed Pakistan to be an aberration which, under its landed and military hegemonic elements, had no chance of survival. Pakistan's creation was superficial for Ali, thanks to the Muslim League's emphasis on an otherwise untenable religious separatism. Tariq Ali, like his father, Mazhar Ali Khan – an affluent Lahore-based journalist – saw South Asia only through the prism of class and an East–West rivalry, which they imagined the East to be winning. Pakistan and other such countries were kowtowing to capitalist imperialism, adding to their own internal contradictions. Ali never felt happy with Zulfikar Ali Bhutto, the proponent of Islamic socialism in Pakistan in the early 1970s. Curiously, both Bhutto and Ali (and Benazir Bhutto) had similar pampered backgrounds augmented by an Oxford sojourn. Ali's TV programmes, such as Bandung Files for Channel 4, have addressed various vital politico-economic issues in the postcolonial world, in which he refuses to be identified only with Pakistan. He continues to articulate his views as a critic and humanist.

Following the dissolution of the Soviet Union and the end of the Cold War, Ali has, interestingly, immersed himself in historical fiction steeped in the Muslim past. In his novels on the medieval Muslim past he seems to be reliving, in a postmodernist style, his own past as a revolutionary. His *Shadows of the Pomegranate Tree* (1992) is a romantic reconstruction of the dying days of Andalusia and, while highlighting the horrors of the *Reconquista*, also generously dwells on the lifestyle of a Moorish Granada characterised by uninhibited sexual norms. The novel is the story of the al-Hudayls, Spanish Muslims of Arab origins, who live close to Granada and witness the rise and fall of the last small vestige of Muslim presence in an erstwhile multicultural Spain. Despite its humorous and often shocking details, the novel is also an elegy to a liberal, tolerant and artistic Spain. Ali's *The Book of Saladin* (1999) is also focused on Muslim–Christian dissension, this time during the Crusades. The ultimate hero is Salah-ud-Din Ayubi, though he also appears fallible in Ali's postmodernist verdict. Apart from jesting, literary innuendo and a boisterous effort to introduce rather superfluous incidents of extramarital sex or homosexuality, Ali's novels reveal his nostalgia for a glorious Muslim past. His 'political correctness' in catering to the postmodernist irreverence for gender specificities reads like a literary extravaganza, yet his own knowledge of the Muslim past in Spain and the Muslim predicament at the hands of the Crusaders both reveal his new-born interest in Islam, essentially intellectual and cultural, not religious at all. *The Stone Woman*, the third novel in his Islamic Quartet, is a fictional sojourn through the late Ottoman era and features several interpersonal and ethno-cultural tensions.[53] Ali is both fascinated in and irreverent towards this Muslim past, yet makes a special effort to transplant his reader back to an era which may still hold relevance for post-industrial societies. Ali again came to the fore as a political activist during the autumn of 2001 when he addressed anti-war rallies, highlighting the double standards in Western policies.[54]

Ayyub Khan Din, the son of an Azad Kashmiri immigrant and an English mother, made his mark on the literary scene with an auto-biographical play, *East is East*, which was initially staged at London's Royal Court Theatre in the mid 1990s. Subsequently, it was trans-formed into a popular comedy, at a time when several other television sitcoms, such as Goodness Gracious Me, reflected a new phase in British Asian cultural pursuits. Din, in his script, depicts the story of his family, living in a North of England industrial centre, where all his brothers, with two exceptions, are becoming typical working-class British youngsters. One, though, is religious and another is an introvert. The father is adamant that they all eat halal meat, offer regular prayers and follow strict Muslim rules at home and outside. The mother is obedient and the children follow the father's dictates as long as he is around. But, in his absence, they become rowdy and even munch pork sausages. The father tries to arrange their marriages, much to the annoyance of his spouse, whom he even slaps, but then turns back to religion to seek solace away from this bicultural conflict. Din, in several interviews, has insisted on the veracity of the story and has presented it in a humorous way without losing its spontaneity. Din's exposé to a great extent demystifies the primacy and near invincibility of the Asian family system.

Shabbir Akhtar, a resident of Bradford with a doctorate in Christian Theology from Cambridge, articulated his views during the Rushdie crisis and, through his letters, articles and a book, tried to defend the Muslim viewpoint.[55] He intended his articulation to expose the flimsiness of the pro-Rushdie debate and to provide a much needed balance. But he had to pay the price. In a subtle way, British academia has tended to neglect him. Akhtar left the UK in desperation and began a teaching career at the International Islamic University at Kuala Lumpur, Malaysia. However, he soon became dejected by the overwhelming Arabisation and hierarchical nature of the university and came back to pursue his own research in Britain.[56] He has frequently written in the *Times Higher Education Supplement (THES)*, occasionally contributing critical reviews. His intellectual articulation is poignant and represents a critical thinking on Islamic identity that has moved away from the simplistic regimentation or Naipaulesque critique of non-Arab Muslims.[57]

Ziauddin Sardar, a London-based intellectual of Pakistani background, achieved prominence during the contentious debate over *The Satanic Verses*. A writer, broadcaster and media expert, Sardar is the author of more than two dozen well-argued works in the realms of history, communication, cultural theory, science and Orientalism. His columns in the *Independent* and *New Statesman* have focused on intercultural issues. Like Akhtar, Sardar has been an active member of think-tanks in Saudi Arabia, Pakistan, North America, Malaysia and Britain.[58]

Akbar S. Ahmed, a former visiting fellow at Selwyn College, Cambridge, has engaged himself in several activities as a modernist Muslim. In the 1990s, Ahmed frequently appeared on British television, published books on modernity and Islam, and engaged in a biographical film about Jinnah. Akbar Ahmed was generally seen as an articulate media specialist[59] whose television series *Discovering Islam* was a successful effort to show the vitality and versatility of Islam and whose film *Jinnah* turned out to be controversial, with the producer being accused of financial bungling. By now, he had become Pakistan's High Commissioner in London and was seen as an apologist for the military regime back home. His financial escapades caught up with him and within a few months he was unceremoniously dismissed by Islamabad. It may take some more years for Ahmed, a former civil servant and currently based in the United States, to reconstruct his academic profile away from the fallout, though his books on Muslim societies such as Pakistan offer an interesting anthropological perspective.[60]

Among the serious and original Muslim analysts of our times, Rana Kabbani figures prominently. Until the Rushdie affair she was an 'underground Muslim'.[61] Rooted in her own traditional Syrian culture, Kabbani had a cosmopolitan upbringing followed by a doctorate at Cambridge. She was never enamoured of her alma mater; as she observes: 'Cambridge struck me as creaking, conservative and misogynistic' and she was faced with sexist affronts from two dons.[62] Her research reviews works by Orientalists such as Galland, Chardin, Chateubriand and Lady Montagu, and the nineteenth-century romanticists such as Shelley, Keats, Coleridge, Moore, Byron and others. According to her, translations of and commentaries on stories like *The Arabian Nights* have continued to influence the views of successive generations of image builders in the West. To Kabbani, the imperialists looked down upon the colonised, in particular Muslim women, and such attitudes continue to reverberate even today: 'Empire's feelings about Oriental women were always ambivalent ones. They fluctuated between desire, pity, contempt and outrage. Oriental women were painted as erotic victims and as scheming witches.'[63] Richard Burton, Rudyard Kipling, Charles Doughty, T.E. Lawrence and other such writers carried on this imperial discourse in their own ways without rectifying an inherent unevenness, as 'the Coleridgean use of the East as a metaphor for sensuality and seductive sorority changed, later in the nineteenth century, into an explicit sexual message'. While Richard Burton became the epitome of the imperialist–scholar, Wilfred S. Blunt offered an opposite but minority discourse based on greater respect for traditional societies plundered by mercantilists and imperialists; as he observed in the case of India: '... if we go on developing the country at the present rate the inhabitants will have, sooner or later, to resort to cannibalism, for there will be nothing left but each other to eat'.[64] To Kabbani, the imperialist discourse based on Orientalism remains ascendant even today in the works of Wilfred Thesiger, Elias Canetti and V.S. Naipaul, whose travelogues fall seriously short of judicious analysis of Muslim peoples. Kabbani's *Letter to Christendom* (1989) and her lecture at University College, Cork (1992), touched upon a number of crucial themes characterising the current phase in the 'East–West encounter'. Kabbani is an articulate writer and an impressive speaker. Her articles on Bosnia and Palestine in the British media during the 1990s displayed a high calibre of both analysis and conviction. She is equally disdainful of the clericalisation of Islam and Muslim chauvinism directed against women. Her television series, *Letter to America*, in 2002, highlighted the agony of Muslims everywhere owing to Western indifference in general and US military and partisan policies in particular.[65]

Another Muslim woman writer to have diligently and effectively engaged in serious debate on the Muslim diaspora in the West is Yasmin Alibhai-Brown, an Ismaili Asian, who, after spending time in Uganda and Oxford, decided to pursue journalism. She defended Islamic humanism in the 1990s soon after the Rushdie affair and through her weekly columns and television programmes tried to highlight the socioeconomic inequities that spawned anger among the Muslim youth in the inner cities.[66] She finds a hegemonic West incriminating Muslims in the former's search for a new enemy. Her books and articles have focused on the issues of racism and other sociological inequities and, in several cases, have attracted immense criticism from certain sections in British society. Her own early family life, turbulent as it was, in addition to a triumvirate of identity – Asian, African and British – is recorded in an interesting autobiography.[67] Her work with the Runnymede Trust, especially the study of multiculturalism, has caused quite a furore in conservative and ultra-patriotic circles in Britain.[68]

Several British Muslim individuals, including Yusaf Islam, Gai Eaton, Martin Lings, Jamil Sherif and Zaki Badawi, have been articulating their views on Islam through a reconstructive debate. Yusaf Islam's Muslim school, his charity – Islamic Relief – and his video on the Prophet have been well received by Muslim communities in Britain. Eaton's writings reflect a deep analysis of Islamic heritage and its relevance to both Westerners and Muslims. Martin Lings is widely respected for his impressive research on Sufi Islam. In the same vein, Jamil Sherif's biography of Allama Yusuf Ali is a well-researched volume on an Indian Muslim intellectual whose translation of the Quran is widely quoted, though his other achievements have largely remained unknown.[69] Sherif's own mother established a charity school for Bosnian orphans in Sarajevo and his wife is a serious scholar of Islam.[70] Zaki Badawi, an Egyptian scholar, was trained at the well-known al-Azhar University in Cairo and at the University of London. His Muslim College in London trains imams by imparting quality education to Muslim men and women, and his other activities include lecturing and advising Muslim and British governments on Islamic jurisprudence. He believes in *ijtihad*, equality for women and a greater emphasis on education, and is one of the architects of interfaith dialogue.[71] Badawi is widely interviewed on television and radio and visits various European capitals presenting Islamic views on crucial legal matters.

The Al-Khoei Foundation is an Iraqi Shia charity engaged in research and publication. It is based in London and brings out a monthly *Dialogue*, which offers balanced views on international and local issues. The Agha Khan-funded Institute for Ismaili Studies in London has, so far, mainly concentrated on teaching and research on Shia Ismaili Islam, though its remit has been broadened under the auspices of the Aga Khan University. In the same vein, the Islamic Foundation in Leicester, founded by Professor Khurshid Ahmad of Pakistan, has over the last two decades sponsored various publications such as indices and review literature. Closely associated with the Jama'at-i-Islami of Pakistan, the foundation is, like several other Muslim organisations, global in its policies but exclusive in its operation, with its management and staff mainly consisting of Jama'at party members.[72] The foundation is in the process of becoming a fully fledged university offering religious and secular instruction.[73] Since the Anglo-American campaign against Afghanistan, Iraq and Muslim activists in the diaspora, many mosques and community centres have become more introvert, dashing any hopes for a mainstream role for them. The well-endowed Centre for Islamic Studies in Oxford, like the Islamic Foundation, chose not to participate in the public debate. Exhortations to more intercommunity dialogue and integration by David Blunkett are seen as ineffective, owing to a prevalent sense of loss and alienation arising from strict new laws on detention, and the severe punitive military campaign against Afghanistan and other Muslim countries. Tony Blair tried to assuage Muslim fears and objections through various symbolic gestures between 2001 and 2003, including a commitment to the reconstruction of Afghanistan, democracy in Iraq and the promise of a Palestinian state, but the sordid realities remained unchanged. The riots in Leeds, Oldham and Bradford, in the north of England during May–July of 2001 and the arrests of several British Muslims in 2002–03 have greatly dampened efforts for greater inter-community dialogue. Further initiatives to allay intercommunity fears and tensions are overdue.

One may draw various conclusions from the above discussion. Firstly, there have been positive signs of a better understanding of the imperatives of pluralism in Britain, though the different communities, especially the dominant ones, still have a long way to go. Rather than seeking integration, one has to understand the parallel processes and seek out possible meeting grounds. As witnessed in the violent riots of the summer of 2001, it is not a question of unwillingness to learn English; instead, economic and socio-structural exclusion has to give way to more cooptive policies. The single-factor focus on Islam and stereotypes of Muslim inability to change must be made to correspond with positive attitudes and healthy policies. The Runnymede Trust's report is a landmark achievement and needs to be corroborated by other similar studies and appropriate ameliorative steps at various levels, especially in view of post-September 2001 anxieties. The most important feature of the Muslim factor in Britain is the evolution of an intellectual and literary tradition as a pioneering discourse on issues of identity. The tradition is nascent, diverse and far from consensual, yet it is encouraging to note that the Muslim communities, in their quest for identity in the changed sociological and historical context, have gradually begun to move the debate away from the usual objectification. It will be interesting and educative to see the further blossoming of this innovative discourse and the accompanying controversies.

6 Muslims in France, Germany and the European Union: Aliens or Allies?

As the nightingale-voice of Shiraz for Baghdad, and for Delhi Dagh
shed bitter tears,
As ibn Badrun's soul lamented when heaven ended Granada's
opulent years,
So to sorrow with you fate has chosen Iqbal, oh this heart that
knows your heart so well!
Whose annals lie lost in your ruins? – those shores and their
echoless music might tell ...
I go with your gift to the Indies, and I who weep here will make
others weep there.

('Sicily' by Muhammad Iqbal)

The relationship between Islam and France evokes such mixed images
as the Battle of Poitiers, the Crusades, Napoleon's invasion of Egypt,
the colonisation of Muslim lands in Africa and Asia, unnecessary
bloodshed in Algeria, Muslim settlers in urban France, the Paris
Mosque, the impressive Arab Institute in Paris, and prominent French
Muslims including Dr Muhammad Hamidullah and Muhammad
Arkoun, scholars of Islam such as Louis Massignon and Maxime
Rodinson, and the sports star, Zidane. Other recent developments,
such as the headscarf issue of the early 1990s, French sleuths
searching for Muslim militants following France's unilateral intervention in Algeria in the 1990s, and the growing emphasis on an
exclusionary nationalism by extreme parties such as the National
Front, display a complex set of attitudes within a country always
known for an assertive avowal of its own culture and strict adherence
to secularism. Although multiculturalism has not yet attained a
positive connotation within the French national parlance, increased
diversification of the Muslim communities in recent years due to the
arrival of Turks, Bosnians, South Asians and others seems to have
spawned an intra-Muslim debate. The absence, owing to ethno-
national divisions and class-based diversities, of a single Muslim
organisational platform – as elsewhere in the North Atlantic regions

– has hindered France's Muslims from playing a communitarian role proportionate to their numbers.

Though Muslims in France may account for more than 3 million inhabitants, including the largest number of converts in Western Europe, their impact on mainstream socio-political institutions and the official establishment still remains minimal, making them vulnerable to various statist and societal prerogatives. On the other hand, the German relationship with Muslims in the past has been more or less neutral and minimal, largely because of the absence of a colonial or other such acrimonious encounter. The Muslim diaspora in Germany, which has a clear majority of Turkish citizens, is a post-Second World War development which, until recently, was perceived as a transient arrangement to overcome a labour shortage. Like Italy and Scandinavia, Germany has been a land of emigration, and Muslims and other settlers are still anomalously defined as *Gastarbeiter* (guest workers). As in France, the Muslim community in Germany is around 3 million, Turks and Kurds accounting for a clear majority, though smaller Balkan, Asian and North African communities have also begun to develop. As elsewhere in the West, ethno-national and sectarian divides characterise this diaspora. How far Germans can be receptive to the concept of a 'nation of immigration', within the context of a redefinition of German identity away from mono-ethnicity, confronts the country's intellectuals and policy planners with a major dilemma in the new millennium.

In both France and Germany, there are thousands of local converts – more than anywhere else excepting the United States – many of whom follow Sufi Islam. The first section of the present chapter is devoted to examining the evolution and specific features of these increasingly plural societies. The final section seeks an overview of Muslim communities in other EU countries as they enter a crucial phase in multiculturalism, offering new challenges and prospects for religio-ethnic minorities.

ISLAM AND FRANCE: AN UNEVEN HISTORY

France's relationship with Muslims dates from the early eighth century, but it has gone through familiar phases such as conquests, Crusades, conversions, colonialism and postcolonial incongruities, as well as growing convergence. The emergence of a powerful, self-confident Europe in the wake of modernity heralded the Europeanisation of the world, Muslim regions falling like dominoes before the expansive British and French colonial campaigns. Even after colonialism, the unevenness in this relationship, as characterised by Orientalist and often hegemonic attitudes, has not totally disappeared. Economically as well as psychologically, Muslims are still gravely disadvantaged and the hierarchical relationship is further marred by subtle reservations emanating from both arrogance and discretion, still pervasive across certain powerful establishments. The Muslim diaspora in France, like its counterpart in Britain, is still diverse and disorganised, and suffers from various institutional, economic and social handicaps. While there has been a growing concern with equal opportunities for underprivileged minorities, attitudes and policies still largely reflect indifference, if not total dismissal. However, the intellectual debate on multiculturalism in France, unlike that in the United Kingdom, is still embryonic, and the official insistence on age-old legislation is posing serious problems for trajectories including secularism and the modernisation of school curricula. Despite France's closer cultural relationship with its former colonies, a hierarchical relationship occasionally bordering on sheer hostility has, until the recent past, also resulted in compulsory deportation or induced re-emigration. Though there is improvement in intercommunitarian relationships, it is too early to suggest that France, at all levels, shares a deep and holistic sensitivity to Muslim cultural and socioeconomic requirements.[1]

The first French–Muslim encounter began with the advent of Islam in Spain and Portugal within a few decades of the Prophet's death. Greatly enthused by their victories over the Visigoths and other kingdoms in the regions, Muslims reached the Basque country and France. In AD 719 Muslims conquered Narbonne and quickly advanced north after capturing Lyon and Burgundy, reaching the suburbs of Toulouse. Advance parties captured Bordeaux and adjoining south-western territories. By this time they had overstretched themselves, and the departure of inspiring generals such as Musa and Tariq made them vulnerable to a concerted French counterattack led by Charles Martel, which resulted in their defeat at Poitiers in 732. This crucial French victory ended Muslim expansion and proved a turning point in French attitudes towards the Arabs. However, Narbonne, the site of the earliest mosque in France, remained under Muslim control until 759. In 793 Muslims made another effort to recapture French territories, resulting in some gains, but Charlemagne retaliated with great force, attacking Spain itself. Eventually, in 810, the emir of Cordoba and Charlemagne signed a treaty agreeing to end any further Muslim invasions of France. In 850, Muslim sailors established a stronghold in the Camargue and organised raids on Marseille, Antibes and Toulon, and for the next 150 years these pioneering Muslim communities maintained their presence in the east and on some islands. In 972, following the kidnap of the abbot of Cluny, a joint French, Italian and Byzantine force recaptured French territories in the Massif Central and re-established Christian authority by expelling the Muslim communities.[2] In the eleventh century, for the third time, some Muslims from neighbouring Spain and North Africa chose to settle in France: there are sporadic accounts of Muslim settlements in France throughout the Middle Ages. However, Muslims had to confront the Christian fury of the Crusades. In 1095–96, Urban II, the elderly French pope, declared the first Crusade with a view to liberating Palestine from the Muslims. It was formally launched from the Massif Central on 25 November 1095 and ended in the French conquest of Palestine. For a century, Palestine was ruled in turn by Godfrey of Bouillon, Baldwin of Boulogne and Fulk of Anjou. Most French cities had powerful connections with the Crusades, with the result that small Muslim communities became the focus of common ire. In the next phase of the Crusades, in 1190, crucial assistance in men and materials was provided by St Bernard of Clairvaux, as King Philip II of France set off from Vezelay on the third Crusade. In 1270, the French king, Louis IX, also known as St Louis, died in Tunisia on the way to Palestine on his second military campaign.

The largest migration of Muslims into France took place in the decades following the fall of Granada, when, amidst the *Reconquista*, many Spanish Muslim refugees moved northwards, seeking respite from vengeful inquisitors. These Moriscos were the descendants of Spanish Muslims who had been forcibly baptised, but secretly practised Islam. During the early seventeenth century, inquisitors discovered the secret adherence of many to Islam, leading Philip III to give them merely 20 days to leave Spain. Many took refuge in North Africa and 120,000 straggled into the Basque region, Narbonne and Bearn. Meanwhile, in 1637, France, eager to acquire colonies, established a trading post at the mouth of the River Senegal. This settlement was named St Louis, after the crusading king, and proved a staging point for further incursions into Africa and other colonial enterprises, including the shipment of slaves to the Western hemisphere. However, the most important phase in Franco-Muslim relationships began with Napoleon's invasion and the French conquest of Egypt in 1798–1801. This aimed at more than mere occupation. The French campaign included a large number of scholars and experts who accompanied the general to conduct a systematic study of the country's cultural and archaeological heritage. It was an ambitious project that, owing to internal French instability, did not reach fruition. However, France remained interested in Egypt and was to play a leading role in the construction of the Suez Canal.

The French occupation of Algeria began in 1830, though it took several more decades of consolidation, in the face of strong Muslim resistance led by Abdal Kader, before France could claim the country. The French occupation of Tunisia occurred in 1882, followed by her acquisition of vast swathes of land in Africa. On the eve of the First World War, France held most of North Africa, including Morocco, as well as vast regions of Western and Central Africa, with millions of Muslims under her control. In 1916, France and Britain, now allies against Germany and Turkey, signed a secret agreement, the Sykes–Picot Pact, stipulating the division of the Ottoman Middle East following Turkey's defeat in the war. Russia, however, another party to the pact, withdrew from it after the October Revolution in 1917. Following the Paris Peace Treaty in 1919, under the system of mandates, France occupied Lebanon and Syria, which remained her possessions until their independence, in 1941 and 1946 respectively. Tunisia and Morocco achieved independence in 1956, followed by Mali and Senegal in 1960; the Algerians had to fight a bloody war to gain their independence in 1962. France was reluctant to relinquish control of Algeria, because the latter was considered to be a province where many of her citizens had settled, aloof from the local Muslim majority. In addition, before the advent of Islam, Algeria had been a stronghold of Catholicism and the home of St Augustine of Hippo. Coastal Algeria, with its developed agriculture and wine industry, was important to France. However, in the French hierarchical order, only those Algerians qualified for citizenship who would renounce their adherence to Islam. Thus, Algeria was more than a colony for France, and its travails worsened with Charles de Gaulle's reluctance to grant her independence.[3] The French had traditionally discouraged Quranic teaching among the Algerians, prohibited them from undertaking pilgrimage to the Hedjaz in Arabia, and discouraged the study of Arabic. Thus, there was very little love lost between the French and the Algerians. After eight years of warfare and millions of Algerian casualties, when the French finally left the country only a few thousand French colonists decided to stay on. Almost a million French citizens, including second-generation descendants and Algerian collaborators, left for France, where the problems of integration awaited these *pied-noirs* ('black feet'). Even today after several decades quite a few of the French continue to bear a grudge against Muslim immigrants.

Relatively recent Muslim migrations into France began with the arrival of Napoleon's Arab soldiers in the Rhone valley, followed by Algerian salesmen – *turcos* – in 1870. By the end of the nineteenth century there were about 800 Muslims in Paris, many of them students from the colonies. Soon Muslim workers started migrating and by 1914 there were 30,000 North Africans in various industrial centres. The war increased demand for immigrants and 132,000 North Africans – largely Algerians – worked on French farms and in factories, and 175,000 served in the French army. Around 25,000 of the latter died in action, though no memorials were erected in their memories. Along with the North Africans, a number of South Asians – especially Punjabis – also fought in France against the occupying German troops. Many of these soldiers of the British Indian Army also lost lives and limbs in the battlefronts across the Continent.[4] After the war only 120,000 North Africans were left in France, as many of the soldiers returned home soon after the hostilities. During the Second World War, thousands of Africans were again drafted into the French armed forces and the postwar labour shortage again attracted a wave of new immigrants. By 1968 there were 1 million North Africans in France, many of them, like the South Asians and Afro-Caribbeans in Britain, unskilled single men. They, too, worked in the automobile and construction industries and by the 1970s their families began joining them in their new home.

Also, during the 1970s, a number of Turkish and Bosnian immigrants settled in France, though, owing to economic recession and increased racism, the government offered various inducements for 'repatriation'. It offered 10,000 francs for voluntary repatriation, and when that failed it refused to renew the work permits of half a million immigrants, most of them Algerians.[5] However, when the socialists came to power in 1981, many of these regressive policies were reversed. In the elections of 1996, conservative Gaullists led by Chirac came to power. The socialist president, Francois Mitterand, was largely helpless faced with a conservative parliament and a growing emphasis on racism in French society. In the elections, the National Front, a right-wing and overtly racist party, polled a high 9.8

per cent of the votes, gaining 35 seats. Chirac introduced new legislation directed against the pluralist dictate and made renewal of work
permits overtly difficult. Illegal immigrants were rounded up from
time to time for deportation, and even young delinquents brought
up in France were expelled from the country. By this time there were
about half a million French-born children of immigrants, generally
known as *beurs*. The census, of course, did not identify them on the
basis of religious denomination, but the majority are Muslims. The
conservatives used the race card, promising stringent measures
restricting immigration and naturalisation. In the elections of 1993,
the conservatives increased their majority and raised the age of naturalisation, even for French-born youngsters (*beurs*), to 16. Earlier,
such children became citizens automatically, but now conferring
French nationality became a state prerogative and the birthright was
put aside. This legislation was called the Pasqua Law after the contemporary interior minister and is still in force; though, following the
elections of 1997, the socialists under Jospin formed the government,
the country was still led by President Jacques Chirac. In 2002, Jean-
Marie Le Pen's National Front took France by storm by obtaining
almost 20 per cent of the votes in the elections. With socialists out
of the contest, Chirac used the Front's electoral performance to his
advantage and got himself re-elected. Despite the pervasive racism,
mostly directed against Muslim and Afro-Asian communities in
France, individual physical attacks on ethnic minorities are still not
widespread. But the situation remains quite problematic:

> While Muslims in France have not suffered the physical attacks
> that Turks in Germany have endured, they must live in a country
> where the extreme right enjoys more electoral success that in any
> other developed European nation apart from Austria.[6]

Though, as in Britain until 2001, the French census does not
identify people on the basis of their religion, it is estimated that there
are around 3 million Muslims in France, with Algerians making the
largest group, followed by Moroccans, Tunisians and Senegalese.[7]
The rest are Malians, Turks, Albanians, Bosnians and Pakistanis. As
stated earlier, a third of the total are French-born. There are between
30,000 and 40,000 French converts to Islam, who have been
influenced by their study of Islam or have interacted with Muslim
Sufis: 'Of all the countries in Europe, France has probably the highest
number of converts to Islam. It is virtually impossible to arrive at a

reliable and agreed figure.'[8] Compared to Britain and Germany, the proportion of Muslims holding professional jobs is higher in France. The proportion of Muslim children attending school is also greater in France than elsewhere and, compared to South Asian women in Britain, a higher percentage of Turkish women in France are in the job and business markets.[9]

Apart from the ruins of the mosque in Narbonne, the first in France, all other mosques are recent and have been largely constructed on a self-help basis, as, by law, public money cannot be spent on religious buildings. Numbering around 1,500 altogether, in many cases they are houses and halls converted for prayer purposes. For instance, in Marseilles, despite a Muslim population of hundreds of thousands there is not a single purpose-built mosque, and the majority community, just like the government, appears indifferent to Muslim needs. On the other hand, the main Paris mosque is a grand and opulent structure built in 1926.[10] For a long time, this mosque was led by Si Kaddour Ghabril who, after his death in 1954, was succeeded as imam by his nephew. The French government appointed an Algerian, Si Hamza Boubaker, as the director of the Paris mosque in 1975; before he retired in 1982 he handed the mosque over to the Algerian government, despite official French protests. However, sectarian and national rivalries among the North African diaspora have occasionally posed challenges for Muslims. Fully fledged efforts were undertaken during the 1980s to bring the various organisations under one banner. In 1967, another mosque was built at 15 rue Belleville, under the auspices of the Association Culturelle Islamique; this is also called the Stalingrad Mosque or the Dawa centre. Of the numerous organisations[11] formed to look after these hundreds of mosques and community centres across France, the most prominent was led by Dr Muhammad Hamidullah, a South Asian Islamic intellectual based in Paris. Dr Hamidullah, a scholar of classical Islam of world renown, hailed from the princely state of Hyderabad and until his death in France in 1999 engaged in teaching and research on Islam.[12] In 1963 he formed his pioneering Association des Etudiants Islamiques en France (AEIF), mainly aimed at reaching Muslim students in France.

The mosque-based or cultural associations in France, like their counterparts in Britain, reflect the personalist or ethno-national prerogatives of their leaders, and in France are usually controlled by various North African groups. The Muslim presence across France is quite visible through a multitude of cultural centres, restaurants, and Arab food, music and taxi businesses. At a more intellectual level, the recently built Arab World Institute symbolises a sustained partnership between Islam and France. Not very far from Notre Dame, its elegant, modernist building houses a massive library, video facilities and a roof-top cafeteria. The incoming light is controlled by automatic steel shutters fitted on the exterior glass wall, which move according to the amount of light needed inside. The library includes manuscripts, newspapers, books and journals in various languages, though most of them are in French and Arabic. The institute is constantly consulted by a significant number of readers and visitors, and reflects an intellectual facet of the world of Islam.

Contemporary French attitudes towards Muslims are similar to those of the British and, in most cases, reflect the colonial legacy of inequity; prejudices emanating from colour, class and culture permeate across the board, albeit less violently. Nor have the role of *Harkis* during Algerian independence or the Franco-Algerian tensions in the 1990s helped to remove intolerance. From time to time, the French government may criticise Israeli expansionist policies, but the public at large remains pro-Israel and expresses its anti-Arab animus through different forms. All Muslims, irrespective of their ethno-regional origins, are simplistically categorised as Arabs, and experience a pervasive anti-Arab bigotry.[13] The British journalist, Adam LeBor, commenting on the general French attitudes towards Muslims, has noted:

> Islam is an obsession for France, an obsession stoked up by politicians and headline-hungry reporters who feed off each other, creating a climate of intolerance and hysteria – it is no exaggeration to describe it thus – that I found nowhere else in Europe or America.[14]

Despite being the second major religion in the republic, as observed by a French Muslim, Islam is still seen as a 'secondary religion'.[15] The demands for halal meat and the wearing of scarves by Muslim women continue to agitate French society, much of which holds that Muslims must conform ungrudgingly to age-old dictates of French secularism. Ironically, many of these French laws themselves predate the Muslim diaspora in France and require serious revision. At various levels, legislation seems to damage Muslim socio-cultural interests. For instance, under the Napoleonic Code – the Concordat of 1802 – Catholicism was accepted as the country's main religion; Catholic priests, Protestant pastors and rabbis were to be paid by the state. This law, which remains in force even now in some parts of France, does not cover Muslim imams, most of whom remain dependent upon their respective less privileged communities. Also, under legislation enacted in 1901, community associations have to be validated by the official bureaucracy, which, given the intra-Muslim schisms, disallows them from receiving official assistance. Finally, in 1905 another law separated the state from church. On the one hand, under Article 1 of this law the state guarantees freedom of religion and opinion, on the other, under Article 2 , 'the Republic does not grant recognition to, pay the salaries of, or provide subsidies for any religion' thus annulling the Concordat of 1802. But this dualism is still in force in some regions, including Alsace.[16] Under this act, while introducing the lycée system, many religious symbols such as crucifixes were removed from educational institutions.[17] In other words, Muslim children are unable to receive religious instruction, as their communities cannot afford proper institutional arrangements on their own, except for small places of worship. Naturally, the laws have evolved over centuries and may not be in total consonance with the cultural imperatives of newer communities in the country. Such a contradiction came into the open in the wake of the Rushdie affair and the headscarf issue.

In October 1989, three Muslim girls in Creil on the outskirts of Paris turned up at their school wearing headscarves, a practice that became a nationwide phenomenon. The incident occurred on the tenth anniversary of the Iranian revolution, which had been viewed unfavourably in France. Coinciding with the anti-Rushdie resentment, the headscarf issue was perceived as an affront to France's secularism and a threat to her cultural identity, and resulted in a major backlash, public and private. A little later, Algeria underwent a volatile phase when the FIS (Islamic Salvation Front), despite winning a majority in elections, was prevented by the army from assuming power. This was done at the strong exhortation of France, much to the anger of Muslims in both countries. In France the edgy authorities tried to impose their will by force. Jean-Marie Le Pen, leader of the National Front, some socialists and a number of intellectuals and media personalities, such as Bernard-Henri Levy, tried their best to exacerbate the public anger directed against Muslims. Many principals opted to ignore the issue and refused to expel scarved girls from their institutions, but the media and the racist groups published exaggerated and presumptuous stories of an internal threat to the republic. In the autumn of 1993, a Moroccan girl suspended for wearing a headscarf went on a hunger strike, triggering a massive demonstration on 4 February 1994, attended by hundreds of Muslims. Although the French government had defended the wearing of skull caps by Jews as a 'non-ostentatious' sign, it now resented the headscarf. However, better sense prevailed, largely due to the efforts of the Socialist leader, Lionel Jospin, and Danielle Mitterand, and the government held back from taking drastic action. Like the Rushdie affair in Britain, the headscarf issue brought into the open the pervasive French attitude whereby secularism seemed more sacrosanct than civil liberties and individual choice, especially in schools: 'For many French Muslims, the headscarf affair, as it became known, was a defining moment, confirming them as perpetual outsiders in French society and pushing them towards a more radical Islam that is less accommodating with life in the late twentieth century.'[18]

Such issues aside,[19] the Muslim community in France has undergone challenges and processes similar to those experienced by Muslims elsewhere in Western Europe. There are serious problems of racism and discrimination at work and in schools, but the younger generation is in many cases debating its own status in a multicultural milieu.[20] There is a growing accent on professionalism and networking, with simultaneous pressure on official and private institutions to assume a more supportive and positive attitude towards pluralism. While Muslims may remain divided into various ethno-sectarian or even class-based clusters, there is still a small community of intellectuals engaged in a multidimensional debate. Scholars such as Muhammad Arkoun are widely respected for their reconstructive efforts; and scholarly works by Catholic intellectuals, including Louis Massignon and Maxime Rodinson, have generated an increasingly serious and respectful interest in Islam.[21] With their increased economic stability and better education and networking through more efficient communication, and with the positive precedents and contributions of other EU nations, Muslims in France and elsewhere are now able to feature more significantly in domestic and foreign policies.

ISLAM AND GERMANY: A NEW PLURALISM IN THE MAKING

Germany and Islam had no major encounter until quite recently, but the German factor played a crucial and destabilising role in West

European colonialism.[22] Soon after unification in 1871, Germany embarked upon an ambitious campaign to acquire colonies and in the process captured Namibia, Zanzibar and some minor Chinese towns. Germany carried out the construction of the Hedjaz railway project in order to increase its influence in the Muslim heartland after befriending a weakened Ottoman caliphate. The Turks were tired of European and Russian encroachments on their territories and saw in Germany a strong new ally. Eventually, Germany was successful in wooing the Turks to the side of the Central Powers, though the Allies used Sharif Hussain – a Turkish vassal for the Hedjaz – to destabilise the Ottomans. Meanwhile, Austria had since 1878 controlled Bosnia and Croatia, and Muslims there had been given some internal autonomy to pursue their religious code (Sharia law). During the First World War, Germany and Austria both tried to use the Muslim factor against the Allies by coopting dissidents in the Franco-British colonies. Muslims in India, along with certain other Indian activists, tried to establish a trans-regional and supra-communal alliance to free the Subcontinent from the British. Groups, including the Pan-Islamists, Sikh activists in the United States and Hindu nationalists, joined hands with the Turks and a number of Austro-German sympathisers to smuggle arms and propaganda literature into India. Thus emerged the Ghadr revolt, which was initiated from San Francisco in 1913 and subsequently quashed in all three continents. Though the Indian activists were able to establish a short-lived provisional government of Azad (independent) Hindustan in Kabul, the British outsmarted them and eventually, through long trials in San Francisco and Lahore, these elements were apprehended and penalised.[23]

This defeat, and a final squeeze on Ottoman Turkey by the Allies, strained relations between Muslims – especially those in South Asia – and the Western colonial powers, who had expected in Germany a strong threat to the existing order of West European hegemony. In addition, the Franco-British acquisition of the Middle East under the so-called mandatory system, British covert support for the establishment of a Jewish state in Palestine, and the West European soft spot for Greece in preference to Turkey deeply annoyed Muslims, who came to see in Hitler a strong rival to this Western hegemony and invincibility.[24] German propaganda was quite strong, among Afro-Asians and the rising numbers of Jewish settlers in Palestine, and the Allies' all-out campaign to establish Israel by expelling Arabs naturally pushed the Palestinians towards Hitler. That is why Amin al-Hussaini, the mufti of Palestine, decided to support Germany against the Allies. In India, not only Muslims, but also many non-Muslims supported Hitler and subsequently Japan in exchange for assurances for Indian independence. Subhas Chandra Bose and several of his colleagues were active in both Germany and Japan and tried to woo Indian prisoners of war to fight against the Allies.[25] Not many people in the Muslim world knew about the Nazi brutalisation of Jews and Gypsies; they saw the Nazis simply as anti-imperialists and good fighters. During the Second World War, Indian and North African soldiers in the colonial forces gained first-hand experience of the German fighting forces and found in them courageous adversaries.

It was much later, in April 1957 in Kiel, that a dozen Turkish craftsmen arrived to help a severe shortage in the German labour market. The postwar West German economy was developing fast and looked to the Mediterranean regions for human resources. Consequently, during the 1960s, the number of Turkish workers increased tenfold. Once they had acquired some basic skills, these workers offered cheap labour that could be easily absorbed into Europe's fastest-growing economy. By the 1970s, Turkish and Kurdish women started arriving as workers or to join their menfolk. Consequently, the Turkish family system and related socio-cultural institutions emerged in urban areas in Germany. Makeshift mosques, zawiyyas (Sufi meeting places), kebab shops, grocery stores and travel agents established auxiliary services for this immigrant community, who mostly lived in the industrial inner cities. As late as 2001, they were still being called *Gastarbeiter*, since Germany refused to accept them as settled immigrants. Many Middle Eastern Christians had also settled in Germany, though Turks, Kurds and North African Muslims were the predominant ethnic groups.[26] Despite its overwhelming Sunni majority, Alwis also made up a major portion of the Turkish diaspora.[27] Other Muslim ethnic groups included Bosnians, Yugoslav Muslims, Jordanians and Iranians. A large number of the Iranians and Afghans came in as political exiles following the Iranian revolution and the tumultuous changes in Afghanistan in 1979.[28] In the 1980s, several thousand Pakistanis also settled in Germany, Ahmadis, who faced persecution in their native Pakistan, accounting for most of them.[29] In fact, Ahmadis had started moving into Germany during the 1950s and 1960s, though the greatest number of them came during the 1980s. German liberal asylum laws (until after unification) allowed these various ethno-regional communities to settle in the country, though the diaspora still mainly consisted of guest workers.

Other than their ethno-national divisions, the Muslim presence in Germany is criss-crossed too by sectarian and class-based cleavages. The Turkish government has tried to influence the largest section of this diaspora through its ministry, Diyanat, by sending in trained imams and by other initiatives undertaken by the consulates. The Turks and Kurds may cooperate as Muslims at one level, but their ideological affiliations may also occasionally spawn tensions. Many Turks belong to the Suleymanci or Nursu movement of the Sufis, which offers a strong sense of community yet is frowned upon by the Turkish government. While Germany's laws and regulations have remained ambiguous (if not totally indifferent) towards ethnically non-German communities, Istanbul has tried to maintain closer liaison with them. As in Britain, the second native-born generation, by definition, does not consist of guest workers. Since the late 1990s, there have been noticeable pressures for German immigration laws to change, though Bonn and Berlin have usually been resistant, largely because in Germany (as in Austria) citizenship is based on racial background rather than on residence. Chancellor Kohl went on record several times as saying that Germany was not 'a nation of immigration'. However, his definition of German identity by reference to mono-ethnicity appears outdated, and criteria such as having a German grandfather appear out of place.

After German unification in 1990, demands for the naturalisation of the diaspora have increased, as has resentment against 'the foreigners', and racist attacks on immigrants, asylum seekers and ethnic communities. German governments have usually shied away from accepting the imperatives of multiculturalism by restricting naturalisation and by reiterating the long-standing definition of German identity, which is unambiguously racial. Although racist attacks on non-German residents have greatly increased since 1990, unlike in Austria and other European countries, no mainstream political party has yet made this into an electoral issue. In May 1993, following an arson attack on a refugee hostel in Solingen by neo-Nazis, Helmut Kohl's spokesman, responding to calls for the Chancellor to visit the site, remarked dryly: 'The Chancellor does not engage in condolence tourism.'[30] The concentration of the Muslim community in urban ghettos, the restrictive policies on immigration, the official disavowal of multiculturalism, and the near-total ineligibility for citizenship of even the native-born – excepting some 50,000 or so cases – under one excuse or another, highlight the uniqueness of the situation in Germany. However, there is reason to accept that matters are gradually changing; for example, the exclusive emphasis on blood and ancestral links with the German race, and the whole concept of *Gastarbeiter*, are slowly disappearing. Hopefully, the better examples from other EU countries may help move Germany towards a greater recognition of pluralism.[31] The German government encourages educational facilities for the children of immigrants, and its socioeconomic policies, at least in spirit, subscribe to equal opportunities. As in France, the Muslim community itself has tried to meet the socio-religious requirements through mosque-based Islamic instruction. Traditionally, the government and the church have collaborated in Germany to sponsor schools and instruction at various levels, but this is not happening with the Muslim diaspora. Their lack of a central organisation, coupled with the unique nature of their residency status, makes it difficult to establish well-provided Muslim schools. It is worth noting that the Austrian government and the Republic of Ireland offer educational facilities to minority children.

Both France and Germany, despite their obviously divergent policies on and experiences of immigration, naturalisation and multiculturalism, seem to be pursuing a policy of integration. While France expects a total, unquestioning cultural assimilation, German (and Austrian) nationhood remains anchored in blood, colour and common descent, which makes it harder for non-Germans to put their views across. In such a situation, factors such as language and class tend to play a decisive role. Many immigrants and refugees, unlike the second-generation Muslims, lack linguistic facility and are confined to ghettoes, making intercultural dialogue rather difficult. This becomes even harder when the host society in general tends to see these 3 to 4 million fellow residents as an aberration, or at least as non-German. That is why German converts to Islam have become the most active agents of change and communication among the various communities. Many of them follow the Sufi *tariqa* and have published extensively on Islam. Their links with Sufi Islam originated about a century back with the visit of Sufi Wilayat Khan from India, or through subsequent interaction with the North African Sufi *silsilahs*. These German Muslims are the most vocal intermediaries and, unlike their counterparts elsewhere, have played a vanguard role on behalf of Muslims in Germany.

SCANDINAVIA, BENELUX AND ITALY

Unlike Germany and Austria, the Nordic countries pursue secular policies and have been usually more accommodating in their immigration and asylum laws. A large number of Turks, Bosnians and North Africans have settled across Scandinavia, though contacts between this region and Islam are only recent. The earliest Muslims to live in Finland were the Tatars and other Caucasian Muslims who came with the Russian army during the nineteenth century, though a strong relationship between Sweden and the Ottoman caliphs existed in the early modern era. Due to this bipartisan relationship, Sweden had relaxed some of the stringent Lutheran laws in order to accommodate Muslims in the seventeenth century. During these contacts with the Ottoman caliphate, quite a few Swedes converted to Islam and engaged in research and publications. In the 1680s, Johan Hjuljammar, a sergeant of the Life Guards, accepted Islam. Gustaf Noring (1861–1937), an author and diplomat, moved to Constantinople and adopted the name of Ali Nouri. A famous Swedish artist, Ivan Agueli (1869–1917), became a Muslim, adopted the name of Abdul Hadi al-Maghrabi and devoted his life to publications, including a Cairo newspaper.[32] However, economic and political developments in more recent years led to significant migrations from the Muslim regions into Scandinavia. The total number of Muslims in all the Nordic countries is still less than half a million, Sweden accounting for 30–40 per cent of them, followed by Denmark, Finland and Norway.[33] There are sizeable communities of Pakistanis in Denmark and Norway, made up of recent settlers. Problems like religious education, linguistic facility and the overall lack of a strong, umbrella organisation characterise this new Muslim diaspora, which has begun to attract more studies.[34] There are several Sufi groups in Scandinavia, including the Naqshbandiya and Alawiya, though the *tariqah* of Wilayat Khan, Idries Shah and Shaykh Fadhlalla Haeri have also gained followers in recent years. The Sufis have built up transregional links, though their main centre remains in Gothenburg. The Ahmadis, with their strong EU-wide networks, remain the best-organised community in the region, whereas the Muslim diaspora in general is relatively new and apolitical. Due to the long-held pacifist tradition of these countries and the high level of foreign assistance to the developing world, they have earned a high level of esteem. Similarly, involvement in the Palestinian–Israeli peace talks in the early 1990s and assistance to Muslim refugees in Asia and

Africa have bestowed a high diplomatic profile to these states. After the terrorist attacks of 11 September 2001, there was no apparently hyped-up preoccupation with Osama bin Laden and his group in this part of Europe, unlike in Britain and the United States.[35] Reported racist incidents in these countries are few, though during the Danish elections of 2001 immigration and political asylum emerged as key issues. Some newspapers and groups even published the names and ethnic origins of individuals who had been granted Danish citizenship in recent years to drum up support for restrictions on immigration.

The Netherlands and Belgium have seen a gradual evolution of Muslim communities that in many ways share characteristics with their counterparts elsewhere in the EU. By virtue of its colonial empire, the Netherlands has maintained historic contacts with Muslim regions, notably the present-day Indonesia, and thus there has been a steady interest in Islam there. In addition, universities such as that at Leiden have maintained a high-profile interest in Islamic affairs through quality publications and by establishing specialised centres.[36] On the eve of the Dutch elections in 2002, anti-Muslim sentiments, as in other EU nations, rose considerably. Brussels, by virtue of its central position in the EU and NATO, has a diverse but sizeable Muslim community marked by ethno-regional and professional variety. The Belgian capital may thus be an appropriate place to study this new but vital bipartisan cultural encounter in the heart of Europe.

The Muslim communities in Switzerland and Italy consist of professionals and unskilled workers. The stringent and community-based Swiss immigration laws disallow a quick naturalisation, whereas Italy has, more or less, pursued EU policies towards exiles and economic immigrants. Southern Italy was a part of the Muslim empire before its integration into a revitalised Catholic society led by the Papal authority, which had always felt uneasy towards the world of Islam.[37] The unification of Italy simultaneously with that of Germany spawned a quest for colonies in an already imperialised world. However, in the twentieth century, Libya, Ethiopia, Eritrea and Somalia came under Italian tutelage, though Italy has become a focus point for Muslim migration only in the last few decades following her economic growth. Most of the Muslim settlers in Italy are from North Africa, Albania and the former Yugoslavia and are a visible presence in a country which until very recently was itself 'a land of emigration'.[38]

7 Ireland and Islam: Green Twins or Worlds Apart?

In my heart I think I always knew I would convert but I was waiting for the right time, using various excuses ... When I eventually said the words it was as if a weight was lifted off my shoulders and at last I could publicly declare what I had felt in my soul for so long. (Amina, an Irish convert to Islam, <www.islamfortoday.com/amina.htm>)

Ireland, an immensely green territory, is an island tucked away from the rest of the British Isles; it has had a turbulent relationship with the United Kingdom, both as a colony and as an independent nation. Other common images it conjures up are of a rich folk culture and a pervasive veneration for St Patrick. Anglo-Irish literature has produced a long list of intellectuals of world renown, including Jonathan Swift, George Bernard Shaw, Oliver Goldsmith, Edmund Burke, James Joyce, W.B. Yeats, Samuel Beckett, Oscar Wilde, Sean O'Casey, Seamus Heaney and others. Ireland, viewed until recently as a country of emigrants, is slowly becoming a land of immigrants. Throughout the nineteenth century, Irish globetrotters worked as the empire's hardy boys, and as tough cattle herders they mapped the American West.[1]

The Irish of today are a prosperous people whose influence is widely acknowledged across North America and in Europe. They are a far cry from their mid-nineteenth century ancestors, who suffered from one of the worst famines in recent human history. The potato crop failure in the 1840s led to widespread misery and mass migration to the United States. The Kennedys, the late Richard Daley (Chicago's well-known mayor), Richard Nixon, Ronald Reagan, Senator Patrick Moynihan and other notable Irish Americans are certainly a privileged generation compared with their forefathers, who left their native shores in penury and abject poverty, especially during the Great Famine. At least 40 million Americans trace their ancestry to Ireland; and 20 per cent of Canadians, 30 per cent of Australians and 15 per cent of New Zealanders claim Irish origins. Following the Great Famine and subsequent crop failures, at least 5 million Irish emigrated abroad and the country remained largely rural, agrarian and underpopulated until quite recently. In 1841, shortly before the famine, the population stood at 8.1 million, while a century later in 1961, due to a constant outflow, it was a mere 4 million. Currently, the Republic's population is 4.5 million and the disputed Northern Ireland accounts for 1.6 million inhabitants.[2] Interestingly, some descendants of former emigrants are returning to settle in a more prosperous and forward-looking country. However, it is ironic to note that until recently this silent revolution after several centuries of hardship has remained unnoticed in the global media. Ireland's own neighbours, east and west, stigmatised her people as tough, hard-drinking, fun-loving but of no great intellectual ability. They were seen as devout Catholics, gullible to authoritarianism but not amenable to progressive ideas, unlike their Protestant and Anglican colonial masters.[3] Understandably, even academia and the media in the developing world have failed to notice the emergence of a new, vibrant and prosperous Ireland. Recent news from Ireland, especially since it joined the European Union on 1 January 1973, along with Britain and Denmark, has been refreshingly positive, if scanty.

This chapter looks at Ireland in its multiple roles vis-à-vis Muslims, as a country, a colony, a coloniser and now a community reflecting a growing multiculturalism. After a brief introduction, it encompasses a discussion on the views held by Sake Dean Mahomed and Abu Talib Khan, the two main South Asian Muslim observers of the triangular relationship involving England, Ireland and India during the late eighteenth century. The last section focuses on the recent evolution in the six counties, as well as the Republic, of a Muslim community, which has roots in the United Kingdom and the Muslim homeland.

IRELAND IN THE BRITISH EMPIRE

An expansive and ambitious England always looked towards its neighbour across the Irish Sea as a land of opportunity for its ambitious monarchy and aristocratic class. Following the schism with the pope and the establishment of the Anglican church under the Tudor king, Henry VIII, the Protestant elements within the English upper class gradually grew intolerant of a persistently Catholic Ireland. The embryonic English imperial project overseas also owed its inception to the Tudor monarchs, whose expansionism began a new era in the Anglo-Irish and Anglo-Scottish relationships.

The Tudors, in their competition with the Spaniards and other continental European powers such as France and the Netherlands, assumed a pioneering role for the English economic and military presence overseas. It was in 1600 in London's Threadneedle Street that a few affluent English entrepreneurs formed the British East India Company as a private enterprise to conduct trade with the East Indies – that is, the regions all the way from the Cape of Good Hope to China.[4] The defeat of the Spanish Armada in 1588 allowed almost unchallenged primacy to the Royal Navy, and America, Africa, India and China offered multiple prospects to enterprising English traders, fortune seekers, seafarers and colonisers. During the seventeenth century, Muslim North African adventurers and pirates targeted Ireland and her ships in intermittent campaigns. Before the Royal Navy was able to thwart the Barbary attacks, Muslim pirates from the Maghreb would quite often venture into southern England and Ireland seeking slaves and booty. In the process, these encounters introduced to these islands, amongst other things, the Islamic religion, Arabic and coffee. There are stories of various converts who were locally decried as renegades for 'going Turke'.[5] Ibn Khaldun,[6] the famous Muslim historian and sociologist from North Africa, referred to Ireland as *'reslandah'* in his classic, *Muqqaddimah*.[7]

The turbulent Stuart dynasty in the seventeenth century failed to contain the growing Protestant power in England and Scotland, and the Cromwellian interlude after the English Civil War caused havoc for the Irish Catholics. This regimented campaign of brutalisation and colonisation led to a long era of turbulence and schisms, especially with the arrival of Sottish Protestants in the north of Ireland. The overthrow of the Stuarts in 1688 sealed the fate of Catholicism in the British Isles once and for all, ensuring the emergence of an ambitious Anglican England embarking upon a more expansive international career. Thus, the seventeenth century in a significant way heralded the primacy of English power over its immediate neighbours as well as its European rivals. Concurrently, it witnessed a steady growth in English commercial and colonial expansion overseas. Starting with the ill-fated Jamestown in Virginia at the turn of the century and the arrival of the Pilgrims in Salem in 1619, the expansion of the New England colonies coincided with the decline of the Spanish and Portuguese factor in Europe and elsewhere, leaving England and France to jostle for global supremacy.

Ireland was, after Wales, the second region to be incorporated in an expanding English empire, followed by Scotland and North

America; gone were the days of the Barbary attacks now that the Royal Navy patrolled and controlled the Atlantic, the Mediterranean and the Indian Ocean. Slaves, tea, spices, opium and silver became the major commodities of this trade, integrating England as the core region into a complex global system of political economy and imperial enterprise.[8] The weakening of the Ottoman, Mughal, Safwid and Qing dynasties, in the Near East, Iran, India and China respectively, left a power vacuum in the vast African and Eurasian territories which, through shrewd and complex diplomacy, militarism and surrogacy, was replaced by British expansion into these regions as the French, the Hapsburgs and the Czars limited their extraterritorial ambitions. Through trajectories such as 'the Great Game' in Central Asia, timely support for the status quo *à la* Metternich in a turbulent Europe following the French Revolution and the Napoleonic campaigns, and manipulation of the vulnerable Ottoman caliphs, Persian shahs, Mughal Emperors and Qing kings, the British were able to establish a universal balance of power with British supremacy at its centre. Short of manpower for such a massive project, England naturally coopted the Scots, the Welsh and the Irish to play high-profile yet still subordinate roles. Thus, Ireland – like Scotland and Wales – curiously emerged as both an imperialist and an imperialised region under British suzerainty over one-quarter of the world's landmass.

IRELAND, ORIENTALISM AND SOUTH ASIA

It is not simply with reference to ethnic conflict and communal or sectarian strife that the former colonised regions such as South Asia share mutualities with Ireland; they were part of the same British Empire, from which several colonial legacies reverberate in collective identities. Gaelic, the native Irish language, belongs to the Indo-European family, though despite high-level official patronage it remains confined to a few rural communities. At one level, the Irish exhibited anti-imperial sentiments: in the United Kingdom and North America, Irish nationalists and their Indian counterparts collaborated against the Raj.[9] But at another, the Irish also materially benefited, by joining the imperial enterprise in both civil and military cadres.[10] The Lawrences (Henry and John) were the most prominent of these Irish empire builders.[11] Regiments in the British Indian Army, such as the Royal Irish Hussars, were manned by Irish volunteers, though the officers were mostly English and Scottish. By the early nineteenth century more than half of the men serving in the British East India Company were from Ireland.[12] It was several decades later, in the early twentieth century, that the various Irish and Indian nationalist elements seeking home rule joined hands together in London and New York, though Theosophists such as Annie Besant and Colonel Olcott went a step further by immersing themselves in Indian spiritual traditions.

As defined by Edward Said, Orientalism – the imagining of an exotic, emotional, yet culturally rich East that is nevertheless 'inferior' to a superior, organised and rational West[13] – puts India and Ireland into a curious equation. They were both prized colonies, but in the imperial hierarchy they stood radically apart. Ireland, due to her Catholicism, underdeveloped economy and political vulnerability, was the *Occidental* Orient yet its empire builders and missionaries proved to be in the vanguard of the entire Orientalist discourse. To them, the empire was still largely a medley of non-Christian peoples, intellectually barren yet fertile for evangelical enterprise, though the arrival of Catholic missions to India for the most part took place at quite a late stage.[14] The study of commonalities between Ireland and India and their complex relationship with the English was pioneered by two Indian Muslim observers in the closing decades of the eighteenth century, who left their valuable impressions in English and Persian, respectively. They offer a unique opportunity in this Muslim–Christian, India–Ireland, East–West, and colony-to-colony dialogue, and were among the earliest Muslim observers of the West, who in the late eighteenth century mainly came from South Asia and left their impressions of the West, including Ireland.[15] This was at a time when Lord Cornwallis,[16] an English squire based in the English colony of Ireland after serving in America and India, headed the colonial administration in Dublin. He had surrendered to the Americans at the decisive battle of Yorktown in 1781 and was deputed to India by the British East India Company as governor general. There were other old India hands who, after making fortunes in India, had settled in Ireland and established a class of English aristocrats set for a major role in the subsequent Anglo-Irish relationship. There were also Africans in Ireland, who had either been brought from Africa as slaves or were employed as house servants by the English aristocracy. Advertisements, such as 'most beautiful black Negro girl, just brought from Carolina, aged eleven or twelve years ... very fit to wait on a lady ...', would routinely appear in the local papers.[17] There were

Indian 'slaves' as well, who worked for country squires, though there is a paucity of material on them.

As late as 1781, years after slavery had been banned in Scotland (though not yet in England), Ireland began a similar debate on slavery. A notice in the *Belfast News-Letter* offering a reward for a runaway 'Indian black' intensified the debate on the moral and immoral dimensions of 'the peculiar institution'. A pre-eminent black abolitionist and a pioneer slave writer and activist was Oloudah Equiano, who was kidnapped from his native West Africa when he was only twelve. Born in 1745, Equiano was taken to the American South via the West Indies before being sent to England. He fought in the British navy but was again sold as a slave and sent back to the West Indies. Despite suffering severe punishments and the taxing drudgery of servility, he was still able to purchase his freedom and returned to England. He became a hairdresser, a musician and a member of a naval expedition to Greenland, finally to emerge as an active abolitionist. In 1789, Equiano published his autobiography, *The Interesting Narrative of Oloudah Equiano, or Gustavus Vassa, the African, Written by Himself*, which ran into several editions, including the first printing in Dublin in 1791. The volume generated significant support for abolitionism and would accompany anti-slavery petitions to Parliament. Equiano (d. 1797) himself undertook an eight-month tour of Ireland, visiting Dublin, Cork and Belfast to raise consciousness on the plight of slaves, and 'sold more copies of his book in Ireland than anywhere else'.[18] The abolitionists found a link between their cause and the Irish anti-colonial struggle, and newspapers such as the *Northern Star* called for an end to the slave trade. But this is not to deny that colonisation offered significant economic opportunities to the Irish. For instance, Belfast owed its growing prosperity and development as a manufacturing town to its commercial links with the Caribbean, preparing broad-fitting shoes and coarse linen to be worn by slaves. Some cotton firms established by Irish magnates depended upon cotton imported from the West Indies and economic prosperity led to greater demand for political rights and dissension with London.[19]

However, Irish views of Islam remained tainted with an Orientalist discourse imported from both Britain and the Continent. For instance, in 1754, a Dublin production of Voltaire's play, *Mahomet the Imposter*, attracted big crowds and rave reviews. The reviewers, in general, found Islam synonymous with Protestantism and equated the Prophet Muhammad with an imperialist English king. Other examples show contemporary literature being used to reinforce partisan views of Islam and the Prophet. For example, Edward Gibbon's biased *Life of Mahomet* was taken from his *Decline and Fall of the Roman Empire* and reprinted in newspapers in Dublin and Cork when they reported on the contemporary parliamentary proceedings on the impeachment of Warren Hastings, the former governor general of India. In the same period, Thomas Moore's *Lalla Rookh* also censored Muslims for persecuting Parsis. Press reports on India usually depended on English sources and offered caricatures of Indian princes and their exotic lifestyles, harems and tiger-hunting expeditions. Most of the coverage was devoted to Shah Alam, the Mughal emperor in Delhi, and Nawab Shujaudullah of Oudh. It was only Sultan Tipu of Mysore who received a unique and comparatively laudatory coverage due to his wars with the British East India Company. On 19 November 1791 *Tippoo Sultan*, a special pantomime, was advertised in the *Dublin Evening Post* as 'a field of fun and humour, ... an operational, historical, tragic, comic and splendid Pantomime in three parts, called TIPPOO SULTAN; EAST INDIA CAMPAIGN, OR THE SIEGE OF BANGALORE. In which will be introduced a view of Tippoo's Black Troops. Encampment etc.'[20] The Irish version of Orientalism was largely an imperial construct, since by that time Irish people were serving in the British Empire and fighting Muslim resistance groups. Curiously, whereas the Irish othering of Islam served a political purpose by offering an excuse to denigrate colonising Protestants, in contemporary English literature, Islam was identified with Catholicism and the Prophet came to symbolise superstitions attributed to Catholics by the Protestants. This malevolent view of Islam on both sides of the Irish Sea struck Dean Mahomed and Abu Talib as an extension of the Orientalism they had both encountered in their native India, and they now tried to counter it through their personal contacts, lectures and writings. Before we resume our discussion of these two South Asian intellectuals, we need to define Orientalism in the context of Islam.

Orientalism is a Western construct rooted in an imperialist discourse and characterised by a multiplicity of unevenness in perceptions and relationships between the imperialising and imperialised nations. Even after the formal end to the physical form of imperial control, Orientalism has managed to spawn itself through different forms of well-entrenched hegemony, including racism, socioeconomic control mechanisms, moral righteousness, intellectual exaltation and a sustained anti-Oriental ethos. Continued politico-economic disempowerment of the masses in the former colonies, owing partly to their inept ruling elites, and partly to a systemic and holistic control of resources and discretionary policies by nations of the North Atlantic region, has ensured its survival. A discourse couched in linguistics and evangelical uprightness in the early colonial and modern eras has come to symbolise a more pervasive and enduring legacy. However, this is not to deny that it had its contributions from the *orientalised* communities, especially from their elites.

India's *do-bhasha* (bilingual) elite, who interacted with Company officials such as Sir William Jones, William Macaulay and others, equally reflected their own complex views on the lack of a coherent Indian or Muslim identity. These elites – mostly Muslim, but some Hindu, especially from Delhi and Oudh – represented 'the old guard' of a receding Mughal nobility,[21] who now hankered for a stronger political hierarchy. This Persian-speaking core group had flourished in conjunction with a powerful state which now suffered from drift, internal chaos and lawlessness, exposing its vulnerabilities to a swift and resourceful Company Bahadur. Used to cooption and patronage, many of this elite were now siding with the Company out of urgency as well as expediency. With their roots in Indo-Muslim culture, and in the knowledge of a weakened Persia and a decadent Ottoman hierarchy, they felt that by siding with the Company they might influence it from within. Their own self-confidence as influential Persian-speaking landowners was reflected in their dealings with the Company's officials. They all enjoyed intellectual pursuits and many found employment with the Fort William College in Calcutta, where they engaged in translation. Their associations shifted from the Mughal Durbar (court) to regional potentates, but eventually came to rest with the Company, especially after the Indian defeat at Buxar (1764) by the latter.[22]

Four Muslim members of this group – Itisam al-Din, Dean Mahomed, Mir Muhammad Husain and Abu Talib Khan – undertook extensive visits to Europe at different times and, on the way, observed the Ottoman, Persian and Arab territories, which afforded them a comparative perspective. Itisam al-Din was a *munshi* (scribe) by profession and worked as an interpreter for the Company in Bengal. Muhammad Husain and Abu Talib, also from the Persian-speaking elite of Oudh (subsequently renamed Uttar Pradesh), had served various princely kingdoms before offering their services to the Company. Itisam al-Din visited Britain in 1767–69, carrying a letter from the Mughal emperor, Shah Alam, for the British monarch, in which the emperor sought his restoration as the emperor of Hindustan after the humiliating defeat at Buxar. It appears that owing to confusion the letter was never presented to the Crown. Mir Muhammad Husain visited Europe during 1775–76 to study science and Dean Mahomed and Abu Talib Khan followed him a few years later to acquaint themselves with Europe. Other members of the same class, such as Murtaza Husain Bilgrami and Ghulam Husain, stayed in Calcutta, seeking occasional employment with the Company. Two other individuals, Abd al Latif and Ahmad bin Muhammad, were born in Persia but came to India seeking employment in British Bengal. Abd al Latif rose to the diplomatic post of a *wakil* (representative) of the princely state of Hyderabad, whereas Ahmad could not obtain such an exalted position and ended up in Patna earning his livelihood through teaching.

Itisam al-Din spent six months at Oxford, met Professor Thomas Hunt, the Regius Professor of Hebrew, and studied Persian manuscripts at the Bodleian including the well-known *Kalila wa Damna*, a classic collection of tales. On his return, he helped Sir William Jones in his studies of Persian and Sanskrit. Despite his aversion to the English language, he studied British history and culture quite closely and, comparing it with the Mughal decline in India, left perceptive observations in his *Shigarf Nama*. A practising Muslim, he nevertheless appreciated the sense of unity and industry amongst several of his hosts. It was Mir Muhammad Husain's interest in science that led him to Europe in 1775. He spent a year in England, and also visited France, Egypt and Jeddah. He picked up a useful knowledge of English, did not like France because of its less attractive food, and found London better and cleaner than Paris. In Egypt he was treated like royalty and on his return to India he engaged in translation work at Calcutta while holding a position with the Company. The participation by the Hindu elite in intercultural discourse began later, during the nineteenth century, with pioneer Bengali intellectuals and reformers like Raja Ram Mohan Rai undertaking organisational efforts to understand the *Aryas* of the East and West.

Sake Dean Mahomed (1759–1851) arrived in Cork in 1784 and settled there after marrying an Irish woman. He lived in Cork for twenty years and wrote the first ever book in English by a South Asian[23] before emigrating to England where he mostly lived in Brighton. During his long residence in Cork, Mahomed witnessed Ireland's multiple involvement in India and its specific views about

Islam. He may even have met Equiano when the latter visited Cork in 1791. Two years earlier, an anonymous author had published a novel, *Hartely House, Calcutta,* in the form of letters by a woman who accompanies her father to Calcutta and sends her impressions of the Indians to her friend back in Ireland. Her letters offer a sympathetic view of Hindus, while Muslims are negatively portrayed. Another novel, *Translations from the Letters of a Hindoo Rajah* by Eliza Hamilton, praised Hindus, who had been 'overthrown by those followers of the imposter of Mecca and by the resistless fury of Fanatic Zela'.[24] Mahomed took upon himself to remove such prejudices and attempted to offer first-hand information on India to a growing readership interested in that part of the world. *The Travels of Dean Mahomed* were advertised in the Irish newspapers, including the *Cork Gazette* in 1793, as a volume by 'a Native of India' which contained 'curious anecdotes of the Inhabitants'. It also highlighted a first-hand account of warfare in India 'with a list of Europeans killed and wounded in the different engagements'.[25] Mahomed's favourable account of India and Indians situates them on a higher pedestal than Europe and Europeans, including Ireland. He finds India to be immensely diverse and an embodiment of natural beauty characterised by a rich soil, multitudes of fragrant flowers

> and the very bowels of the earth enriched with inestimable mines of gold and diamonds.
>
> Possessed of all that is enviable in life, we are still more happy in the exercise of benevolence and good-will to each other, devoid of every species of fraud or low cunning ... The profligacy of manners too conspicuous in other parts of the world, meets here with public indignation and our women, though not so accomplished as those of Europe, are still very engaging for many virtues that exalt the sex.[26]

The book is partly autobiographical, consisting of 38 letters and mentioning his leaving the family to join a Godfrey Baker in the Company's army. The book not only affirms the author's identity as an Indian 'Mahometan', it also establishes his literary credentials. He knowledgably quotes from Milton and popular contemporary Western writers. He narrates his personal relationship with the Nawab of Murhsidabad and informs his readers on Muslim practices. He describes Muslim rituals such as marriage, circumcision and burial 'and sets out to correct prejudices and misunderstandings about

Muslim attitudes to Muhammad and the significance of Allah'.[27] He takes special satisfaction in describing Muslims as 'a very healthful people', who bear sickness 'with much composure of mind' and face death 'with uncommon resignation and fortitude'.[28] He reveals his familiarity with contemporary Western studies of Islam and, without being subjective, offers a positive view of Islam. He is not denunciatory of Hindus and instead supports Rajah Chayt Singh in his battles with Warren Hastings. Insufficient details are available on Mahomed's 23 years in Cork, though Abu Talib ibn Muhammad Khan mentions meeting him there in 1799.[29]

When in 1807, Dean Mahomed and his wife, Jane, moved to Brighton, he established his medical practice there and opened the first ever South Asian restaurant in Britain. He 'championed therapeutic tourism in Brighton, and over the years his aromatic oils and massages treated the Prince of Wales, Robert Peel and even Napoleon III'.[30] In Brighton, Dean Mahomed published his second book, *Shampooing: Or Benefits Resulting from the Use of the Indian Medicated Vapour Bath, as Introduced into this Country by S. D. Mahomed.* Published in 1822, the volume is a commentary on several diseases and their cure, as affirmed by various case studies. Here he gives 1749 as his year of birth – ten years earlier than the one given in the *Travels* – and claims to have been trained as a surgeon in the British Indian Army. His book, synthesising Indian and European medical science, is again an indirect defence of India's wisdom and historicity, especially as, coming after the well-publicised trial of Warren Hastings and Edmund Burke's tirade against corruption in the Company and amongst the Nabobs during the 1780s, India's fame lay in tatters.

Abu Talib Khan ibn (son of) Muhammad Khan Isfahani was the second South Asian Muslim intellectual to undertake an exhaustive visit to Ireland before entering England. He left copious first-hand information on peoples and places in both countries. His Azerbaijani Turkish family originally came from Isfahan, in the long tradition of the Persian elite migrating to Mughal India for better intellectual and worldly prospects. He was born in 1752 at Lucknow in Oudh, which had largely replaced imperial Delhi as the centre for Indo-Muslim culture and scholarship. After study and working in Oudh, he left for Bengal in 1787 in search of employment with the Company. He met Lord Cornwallis and other senior officials in Calcutta, but was unable to obtain an appropriate job. In the process he busied himself in scholarly pursuits and decided to undertake a journey to England. He left Calcutta aboard a Danish ship in February 1799 and, after visiting the Cape of Good Hope and St Helena, landed at Cork. From Cork he travelled to Dublin, observing country life and the charming Irish landscape. After spending some time in Dublin, he departed for London and undertook visits to Windsor and Oxford. He socialised among the British royalty and the aristocracy, including old India hands who by then were serving in higher positions. The royalty and eminent individuals such as Warren Hastings – the former governor general – called him the 'Persian Prince'. Well versed in several languages, including English, he visited France and Malta and then left for Istanbul and Basra. After a short stay in Bombay he finally returned to Calcutta in August 1803. His travels to all these places were recorded in his travelogues and poems, and later in his magnum opus, *Ma'asir-i-Talibi*, in which he wanted to incorporate drawings on the arts and sciences of the West. His volume 'remains one of the most comprehensive accounts of the West by an Indian Muslim'.[31]

Abu Talib Khan identified Ireland as a separate country with its own capital and culture. In his book and articles, he described the landmarks in Dublin, including Trinity College, Christ Church (Dublinia), markets and cafes. He was deeply impressed by the Irish landscape, the fresh air, the charming buildings and scenic villages. He found some of these buildings more beautiful than their counterparts in Constantinople and Genoa. From Cork to Dublin, he passed through the towns of Fermoy, Clonmel, Kilkenny and Carlow and memorialised them in his lucid poems. Of the houses, he noted that many

> were built of stones and it looked as if no plasters were used in their construction, the stones were well and neatly fitted into each other, but the majority of the houses were built of bricks and mortar, neatly laid together. The bricks were of large size and the mortar appeared as white border on their edges. All the houses in the street were of the same height, and the uniformity of appearance was delightful.[32]

Certainly, these houses belonged to the gentry and were tastefully decorated on the inside. He was deeply impressed by the night-time illumination of Dublin, a unique experience for him. In Dublin, he met several former India-related imperial officials, including Lord Cornwallis. He enjoyed the hospitality of George Shee, who had served as a quartermaster in Lucknow and now worked for the treasury under Cornwallis. He operated as an interpreter for Abu Talib in his meetings with Lord Cornwallis and other senior English officials in Dublin. He met his old acquaintance, Captain Baker, with whom he had fought against the Rohila rebels, now a prosperous resident with twelve poorly paid servants to wait upon him. He was a farmer who enjoyed a carefree life on a farm which he had purchased for 20,000 rupees. According to Abu Talib, such a property would have cost five times as much in India. He met another old friend, John Wombwell, who had served with the Indian Army in Lucknow and who could speak fluent Persian. Wombwell had lost his Indian wife in a shipwreck. Abu Talib also socialised with the contemporary Irish literary elite, including Charles Vallancy (1721–1812), a scholar of Persian and Arabic, with whom he discussed the similarities between Gaelic and Hindustani. Abu Talib visited the Trinity College library and saw various Persian manuscripts there, including *Khamsa-i-Nizami* and *Shahnama*, two poetry classics in Persian, composed several centuries earlier by Nizami Ganjvi and Firdausi Khurasani.

Despite finding general similarities between England and Ireland, Abu Talib was keenly aware of the socio-political differences between the two and mentions the Irish revolt, recently suppressed by Cornwallis. The Irish were the Catholics – *millat-i-Pope* – the papal community, but unlike the English, they seemed to him to be moderate in religious matters and less biased than the Scots. He found the Irish balanced, austere and more courageous than the other two nations. In addition, Abu Talib described them as courteous, warm and hospitable towards visitors. The Irish may have been considered inferior to the English in literary and scientific acumen, yet they were quick learners.

> In Ireland, in spite of his being a newly arrived person, he was warmly received and his landlady could follow his broken English, while in London, where he had spent more than two and a half years, the English people were unable to follow his language.[33]

He found the Irish less prosperous than the English and Scots, largely because they spent their earnings on friends and family and pursued carefree lifestyles. Unlike the Scots, the Irish did not try to amass money nor did they attempt to gain higher knowledge or cherished positions in the government. Abu Talib found that the Scots consumed enormous quantities of whisky. The Irish upper class, in its emulation of the English gentry in fashion, manners and lifestyle, was similar to the latter, but the ordinary masses were quite down to earth. Abu Talib studied contemporary media caricatures of the three communities, in which the ambitious Scots would be shown moving into English towns for better jobs and fortune. Typically, a Scot might end up as a steward in some affluent English house in London and eventually lend his savings to his rich employer. Later on, he would marry a rich English widow and settle down to some prominent political or financial position. By contrast, a 'typical' Irishman would serve as a soldier in the Army and on account of bravery might even rise to the position of a general. He would drink heavily, engage in frequent brawls with fellow officers and would, most often, die on the battlefield. An Englishman was caricatured as an obese John Bull, prone to profuse eating and heavy drinking.

Abu Talib Khan described the prevalent English views of the Irish, including the common stereotype of their being heavy drinkers, which, to him, was utterly baseless. He did not seem to have a favourable view of the Scots and accused them of lack of trust and fidelity. His encounters with the Scots were mostly in England, some of them his friends and acquaintances from Lucknow. He expected some reciprocal hospitality from them, but, with one or two exceptions, this was not forthcoming. This discouraged him from visiting Scotland and may equally explain his negative opinion of the Scots. His travels through Ireland had afforded Abu Talib the opportunity of observing the rural peasantry, something that he was not able to do in England. He had noticed the poverty of hamlets consisting of no more than ten or twelve thatched huts. To him, the Irish peasants appeared poorer than their Indian counterparts. Many of these Irish villagers did not own shoes and went about barefoot in the harsh climate. Some of them could not even afford meat and subsisted on potatoes, a staple food that a rather elitist Abu Talib himself did not particularly like. Potato, to him, was the barometer of Irish poverty, as all through his life in India, where rice and meat were luxuries offered only to guests, he had never eaten an *alu* (potato). The Irish diet consisted mainly of wheat, barley, occasional meat and wine. The poor mostly lived on boiled barley, peas and potatoes and they fed their cattle on dried barley crop and, during the snowy winters, turnips. Abu Talib found the Irish soil quite fertile, providing food as well as fuel to its inhabitants. In the houses of the Irish peasantry, Abu Talib noticed sheep, dogs and other livestock sharing the same dwelling as their owners. On the roads, he saw poor people running along beside the coaches, waiting for bits of bread from the passengers. To this Indian Muslim intellectual, Irish poverty arose, among other factors, from three main sources: firstly, the high price of provisions; secondly, the quantity of clothes and fuel needed to keep warm during the long winter months; and thirdly, the large number of children the Irish tended to have.[34]

The next celebrated Muslim visitor to be resident in Ireland was also an Indian intellectual. During the latter half of the nineteenth century, Mir Aulad Ali, from Oudh in northern India, was appointed as Professor of Persian, Arabic and Sanskrit at Trinity College, Dublin. Needless to say this was a prestigious position for anybody to obtain. Married to an English woman, Professor Ali began his tenure in 1861; it ended 37 years later in 1898.[35] Another contemporary visitor from that part of India was Naseeban, a Muslim aya, who frequently visited Europe, Britain and Ireland with colonials returning from India. She was a Pathan governess who had picked up a number of languages, though not much is known about her. Sir Syed Ahmed Khan, the well-known Muslim educationist from India, met her during his voyage to Britain and wrote briefly about her in his travelogue.[36]

IRELAND AND THE MUSLIM WORLD

It is ironic that in recent decades it is usually only with reference to immigration and conflict in Northern Ireland that this region has made the headlines in the global media, while its cultural vitality, its economic vibrancy against the odds and, above all, Irish support for global anti-colonial campaigns have all remained under-reported. It is only in the past few years that the Republic has received some attention, and that mainly because of its growing economic prosperity and reverse migration to the country, which has had its share of adversity and global indifference. Despite being an active member of the European Union, Ireland has always stood for just, humanitarian causes over and above partisan interests. It has traditionally supported the full implementation of UN resolutions on Palestine, and Irish soldiers have lost their lives in some UN operations.[37] It is interesting to note that over the last few decades the small Jewish community in Ireland has migrated to Israel, which may partly explain a pro-Palestinian inclination.

Ireland and the vast Muslim regions have a number of features in common, in addition to their preference for the colour green: for example, their imperial legacy, the English language, an intricate but important relationship with the former colonial power, a vocal diaspora, long-standing economic disparities, a predominantly agrarian economy, religiosity, vicious sectarianism, a rich folk culture, tensions with bigger and more powerful neighbours (such as India, Russia, Serbia and Israel) over a number of issues including territory, and being the object of a global indifference – for Muslims, sometimes amounting to sheer hostility. Ireland's archaeological past, as seen in museums and as exhibited in Dublinia,[38] shows an uncanny resemblance to the ancient civilisations of the Indus Valley and Mesopotamia. Like ancient Egypt, Pakistan, Afghanistan, Turkey, Bosnia and Palestine, Ireland's Celtic populace received waves of invaders including the Vikings, the Normans and the English. For most of their history, except for a small number who make a living from fishing and maritime trade, most of the Irish have remained dependent on subsistence agriculture. Economic adversities and intermittent crop failures pushed millions of them abroad, just as millions of Muslims in recent decades have been trying to eke out an existence elsewhere, with their homelands coming to depend upon their remittances.

It is only in the last four decades that small Muslim communities have evolved from amongst the students at the universities in Dublin and Belfast. Until 1959, they offered prayers in rented buildings or small lecture rooms, though with the aim of building a central mosque in Dublin. In 1983, a former Protestant church on Circular Road was purchased by the Islamic Foundation of Ireland (IFI) to be converted into a multipurpose Muslim complex.[39] With donations from the Gulf sheiks, a bigger and more beautiful Islamic complex was built during the mid-1990s in the suburbs of Dublin, not far from the Dublin College campus.[40] The Dublin Muslim School is adjacent to this Islamic Centre, where a predominantly Irish staff teaches both secular and Islamic subjects to more than 220 Muslim children in a religious environment. Despite being quite religious, Catholic Ireland is the first Western country fully to finance a Muslim school. By contrast, Britain, France and even some Muslim states have often unnecessarily haggled over minor issues, including the donning of headscarves by Muslim girl students.[41] In recent years, Iranians have helped the local Shia Muslim community to construct a similar Islamic Centre with a library and residential facilities.[42] Dublin also holds one of the world's rarest portions of the Islamic heritage, in the form of the Chester Beatty Collection, which consists of 260 rare Quranic scripts, including some of the earliest, in addition to numerous precious miniatures and other pieces of Islamic art. Chester Beatty, an American mining magnate, collected these rarities over the decades from Egypt, India, Iran, China and elsewhere, and before his death, bequeathed this priceless asset to Dublin.[43] The Quranic collection alone is six times larger than its counterpart in the British Museum in London.[44] It is too early yet to be certain about the total number of Muslims in Ireland, but one can see a gradual increase in recent years.[45] On the one hand, British Muslims of South Asian origins have been setting up businesses in the urban centres, while simultaneously Ireland has accepted political exiles from the Middle East and Africa. In recent months, there have been reports of individual racist attacks, generating a debate within the Republic on migration, asylum and pluralism.

Ireland became independent in 1922, 25 years before Pakistan, following a partition – a pattern in decolonisation which was to be repeated in South Asia, Palestine, Cyprus and, more recently, in Bosnia.[46] In both Ireland and many Muslim countries (excluding Turkey, Central Asia, West Africa, Albania and Bosnia) the clergy have remained powerful and hierarchical and it is through folk culture that the masses have tried to break loose. The sacred and the secular often compete to take centre stage. Like the numerous modernist buildings in various Muslim cities, Irish architecture has a strong colonial imprint, especially in the Georgian style, and the economy has largely remained dependent upon Britain's prerogatives. The formation of the elite in Ireland, in a way quite similar to the Muslim world, bears hallmarks of the colonial legacy.[47] However, the politico-economic infrastructure in the entire Muslim world still requires genuine regenerative efforts, whereas in the Republic this has been an ongoing process. Palestine, Kashmir, Afghanistan and Chechnya, as already mentioned, are the bleeding wounds in the Muslim world and many serious Muslims would wish to empower their civil societies through socio-political reform and egalitarian economies. Both the clerical hegemonies and the feudalist oligarchies have retarded Muslim progress and spawned violence and chaos. Fresh paradigms which move away from militarism, fundamentalism, violence, sexism and mono-ethnicity may hold the key to a better future. Both affluent Muslims and the Irish elite relish Oxbridge and Ivy League connections, yet the middle class in the latter case is national, accommodative and progressive, while in the former it is small, ethnicised and sectarianised, lacking national outlook and a progressive agenda. Not only is the Muslim middle class still largely state-dependent, it has become callously opportunistic.[48]

The American influence in both regions is certainly visible but to a varying degree. Washington does not treat Ireland – a small country otherwise – like a third world liability, but deeply respects it, thanks to the Irish vote back in the US, the country's formidable economy and its growing political clout.[49] Ireland, unlike many other states, does not always toe the American official line. Towards the Muslim world, the United States is either patronising or totally indifferent, even hostile on occasions, and lacking the stability, sensitivity and mutuality that it displays towards its east Atlantic neighbour (and towards Israel). The Britons – the big brothers across the Irish Sea – may joke about the Irish, but there is a growing recognition of their cultural identity and economic vitality, whereas in South Asia the Indians, and in the Caucasus the Russians, look down upon their neighbouring Muslim societies and lack reciprocity and warmth towards them. In some cases, they may even collaborate to rain missiles and bombs on Muslim territories.[50] During the American bombing of Afghanistan, which resulted in thousands of Afghan deaths, Mary Robinson, the former president of Ireland and at the time the UN Commissioner for Human Rights, criticised the Anglo-American bombing of a poor country, which displaced another 4 million Afghans. In March 2002, she visited South Asia and conferred with regional leaders and civic groups on issues such as human rights violations in Kashmir, bride burning, honour killings and other vital matters. Her erudite interviews and bold stance on human rights won her rare applause not only in Afghanistan but also in India and Pakistan. During the military strikes on Palestinian settlements in 2001–03 under Ariel Sharon's regime, Robinson, unlike other Western leaders, unequivocally condemned violence. Ireland has acquired great vigour through regional assistance and cooperation, especially from the EU, but Pakistan and India, Iran and Iraq, Egypt and Sudan, Mauritania and Morocco, Turkey and her neighbours, Libya and Chad, invariably all remain at each other's throats without pausing to seek mutualities, with the resultant benefits for their impoverished millions. Both Ireland and Britain seek artistic, economic and cultural commonalities, even sharing nostalgia, whereas the expansionists and xenophobes in the postcolonial world are denying their shared history and equally decry plurality within their own populace.

The greatest difference is in socioeconomic areas, with Ireland representing the wealth, self-confidence and stability of the first world, while the Muslim communities agonise on the farthest margins of the third world. Ireland is a powerhouse of regional cooperation, whereas the Muslim regions either remain peripheralised or suffer from multiple fragmentary processes. Both peoples are equally industrious, but the Muslim world in general lacks capable leadership, sufficient resources and viable strategies to fight its chaos, while Ireland's economic growth, similar to that of postwar Japan, only needs more skilled personnel and markets. To their own detriment, many Muslim nations continue to ignore the Republic, instead concentrating on only a select few Western metropolitan centres.[51] Ireland, given her developed infrastructure, can help Muslim countries in various areas through technology transfer, training of skilled personnel and even by absorbing surplus Muslim labour. Ireland has to be explored and respected as more than a green pasture for the horses of the Aga Khan or Sheikh Hamadan Khalifa.

8   Islam and the United States:
New Friends or Old Enemies?

... the Muslim world's customs no longer seem strange to me. My
hands readily plucked up food from a common dish shared with
brother Muslims; I was drinking without hesitation from the same
glass as others; I was washing from the same little pitcher of water;
and sleeping with eight or ten others on a mat in the open. I
remember one night ... I lay awake among sleeping Muslim
brothers and I learned that pilgrims from every land – every colour,
and class, and rank; officials and beggars alike – all snored in the
same language. (Malcolm X, *Autobiography*)

I don't know a single Arab or Muslim American who does not now
feel that he or she belongs to the enemy camp, and that being in
the United States at this moment provides us with a specially
unpleasant experience of alienation and widespread, quite specifically targeted hostility. (Edward Said, March 2002)

Two developments in late 2001 forcefully symbolised and shaped
the US–Muslim relationship. The terrorist attacks on the World Trade
Center and the Pentagon on 11 September, attributed to al-Qaeda, the
organisation led by the Saudi dissident, Osama bin Laden, deeply
shook the United States. The reaction and consequences were
manifold and immensely painful from the Muslim viewpoint. In its
fury and revenge, America targeted Afghanistan,[1] causing more than
15 thousand deaths, grave decimation of its ecology,[2] and many more
refugees.[3] The campaign indirectly increased racist attacks against
Muslims in the United States and other Western countries. Incidents
of violence, desecration of Muslim properties and mosques, and
further segregation of Muslim communities were the accompanying
realities of this campaign, though both President Bush and Prime
Minister Tony Blair tried to assuage Muslim worries by symbolic
gestures.[4] Many Muslims felt that, coming after the Salman Rushdie
affair, the first Gulf War and the Bosnian tragedy of the 1990s, the
anti-terrorist campaign had dangerously marginalised the Muslim
diaspora.[5] The spotlight on Islam and Muslim communities
undermined intercommunity relations and cheered hatemongers,

racists and other xenophobes who subscribed to the clash of cultures. To many analysts, years of work in interfaith and intercultural harmony had been rubbed out by terror and the counter-terror reaction. It appeared that the terrorists had succeeded in targeting American economic and military might and aggravating Muslim marginalisation in international affairs.

The other major development affecting US–Muslim relations in late 2001 was the first ever UN-convened international conference on racism, held in September in Durban, South Africa. When the United States and Israel withdrew their delegates, following criticism from African and Middle Eastern nations about slavery and Zionism, it was widely felt that not only did the two countries share a common interest on a number of issues, but that they could well afford to antagonise Afro-Asian and Muslim world opinion. The issues in question – the condemnation of violence (including the slave trade), slavery, reparations to African countries, and the brutalisation of Palestinians by Israeli forces – were anathema to the two allies.[6] The United States, being the only superpower, could well afford to be indifferent to wider opinion.[7] This dismissive attitude reflected the continued peripheralisation of the non-white world at a time when globalisation was being hyped up. Moreover, it further affirmed the premise that even a steadily growing Muslim community within the United States was still unable to influence American public opinion and official policies on vital global issues.

The United States had already withdrawn from the Kyoto Agreement on the environment, thus demonstrating insufficient sensitivity to its moral and political obligations on the issue of global warming. In the same vein, the Bush Administration, apparently quite casually, decided to withdraw from protocols on disarmament signed in the early 1970s, causing unease among her West European allies and the Russians. The American about-turn on nuclear proliferation not only weakened the argument against nuclearisation but also exposed American expediency on the subject. But the terrorist attacks simply overshadowed these other events, as the media and politicians concentrated on the fight against terrorism. To many observers, these developments cried out for a review of US foreign policy towards the Middle East and elsewhere, but the Bush administration and the Labour government decided to roll back civil liberties. These events at the beginning of the new millennium are symptomatic of the ambiguous and difficult nature of race relations in the postcolonial, post-civil rights era and also display its extreme

socioeconomic imbalances. Once again, it appears that parts of the
world – such as North America and Western Europe – are heading
towards a more protective regionalism and discretionary globalisation, whereas the former colonised world,[8] including the Muslim
regions, is confronted by the harrowing processes of marginalisation
and fragmentation. Within the same perspective one can delineate
the roots of an enduring uneven relationship between Islam and the
West. The emergence of a strong 'new anti-Semitism' directed against
Muslims seems to have engulfed not only the former colonial powers
in Western Europe; even the 'younger republics', such as the United
States and Australia, themselves founded on immigration, appear to
be pursuing identical attitudes and policies.[9]

Anti-migration legislation, the idea of a fortress West and exaggerated threats to stop asylum seekers and immigrants from coming in
'to sponge' on social benefits, have been used time and again in the
Western democracies and Australia. The electoral success of Le Pen
in France and Pim Fortuyn's List in the Netherlands, and the increase
in support for the British National Party (BNP), are some recent developments in which a racist and exclusive nationalism played a key
role. As was witnessed during the EU summit on immigration and
asylum policies at Seville in June 2002, governments were attempting
to appease the racist sections and parties by introducing stringent
laws. Intermittent arson attacks on refugee centres, physical violence,
verbal abuse and the sheer force of the official agencies have mostly
been concentrated on the non-white communities. The removal of
certain passengers from planes and buses, the impounding of ships
and cargoes from developing countries, selective legislation in the
name of patriotism, and the Anglo-American military build-up across
the Indian Ocean and the Gulf neither operated in favour of globalisation nor did they help the fledgling economies. This is not to deny
that there is an increased acceptance, if not a celebration, of pluralism
and multiculturalism in the present-day West; but it is too soon to
suggest that the scars of the slave trade and its multiple effects on
African societies, the rootlessness of generations of African
Americans, and institutionalised racism have disappeared once and
for all.

Undoubtedly, even amongst the African slaves there was a sizeable
proportion of Muslims, who, after the arduous Atlantic passage,
ended up in the Western hemisphere and within a generation or
two had lost their identities.[10] Notwithstanding the great and
multiple commonalities among Muslims, one cannot ignore the

mutual tensions, the hegemonic nature of globalisation and the strong reservations within the US establishment in dealing with Muslim states and communities, in comparison with its policies towards other communities and countries. Despite the apparent rejection of the Huntingtonian thesis of a clash of civilisations, by a large majority of American scholars, it is still too early to suggest that Islam and the United States have reached a comfortable degree of understanding. US involvement in the Muslim world has been steadily increasing, causing controversy and tension, from its contentious politics in the Middle East to its strictures against states like Iran, Iraq, Libya, Somalia, Sudan, Syria, Pakistan, Indonesia, Yemen and Afghanistan.

Anti-Americanism in the Muslim world has remained significant largely because of Washington's unquestioning support for Israel and its unequivocal stance on sustaining the status quo in the region, mainly to ensure a secure supply of cheap oil. Anti-American sentiment increased following the military operation against the Afghans, with the resultant aggravation of human misery in that country. The Anglo-American insistence on attacks on Iraq in 2002–03, in opposition to a vast global opinion, equally highlighted the serious contradictions in their foreign policies. At the same time, the pervading image of Muslims in the North Atlantic region further worsened, affecting their human rights through subtle forms of institutional racism. However, in both the United States and Western Europe, despite several hesitant sections of society, there is a new curiosity to understand Islam. Courses on Islam and the Middle East are increasingly popular in American universities and the media, despite a certain reservation and bias, show a pronounced interest in Muslim affairs. The complexities and the ambiguities of this relationship are instructive, though one would like to see less emphasis on polarity, and more on the enjoyment of an egalitarian interdependence. Still, this seems to be a distant ideal as long as the relationship continues in its present transitional and disputatious phase.

Our present chapter, within its limited space, attempts to encapsulate a wider subject, which is of growing significance and is being researched using a number of disciplinary tools. The study of Islam in the Americas is a multidisciplinary realm which embraces history, religious studies, sociology, cultural and gender studies, political science, international relations and economics. Concurrently, the study of the United States in the context of the Muslim world involves disciplines like history, political science, strategic studies, economics, diplomacy, popular culture, area studies and communications. Naturally, one cannot cover the historicity and politics of the relationships between 54 Muslim states and the United States, in the same way as one cannot, without being accused of a shallow reductionism, assimilate the study of the scores of various ethnic, doctrinal and sectarian Muslim communities across the USA.[11] However, our effort in this chapter is to locate the historical origins of the Muslim community in the US, then to examine the evolution of more recent intra-Muslim pluralism and an increasing American factor in the larger Muslim world itself.

ISLAM, AFRICA AND THE UNITED STATES

In recent decades, there has been a growing community of Muslims in the United States – among African Americans and the immigrant communities from the 'old world', in addition to a sprinkling of Muslim converts amongst European Americans. Altogether, there are 6 to 7 million Muslims in the United States, making them the second largest religious group after Christians – though in terms of their influence on US policies vis-à-vis the Muslim world their importance is comparatively minimal. Some other communities, long settled in the United States and wielding better institutional networks and more politico-economic weight, proportionately enjoy a greater and more decisive influence. The American Muslim community may, in a sense, be old as well as new, but its visibility is quite recent and, though it includes a large number of professionals, it is still not able to set its imprint to any significant extent on the US government. As seen in the cases of Kashmir, Bosnia, Palestine, Chechnya, or the aerial attacks on Afghanistan and Iraq, the community has largely remained fragmented and localised. By contrast, the pro-Israeli and pro-Indian segments are strong and can easily neutralise any effort that the Muslims may try to mount. The post-11 September US campaign against Muslim countries, communities and even charity organisations has further debilitated Muslim political articulation. The imams, charity groups, students and professionals have been largely depoliticised and the events of the 1990s and 2001–03 have clearly created a great sense of loss, helplessness and alienation amongst Muslims in the West. While there may have been some individuals or smaller groups with contacts with or sympathies for al-Qaeda, to characterise all Muslim socio-political groups as terror-connected was rash and unimaginative.

Historically and ethnically speaking, there are three main categories of Muslim communities across the United States: descendants of slaves, consisting of mainstream Muslims and the Nation of Islam; white Muslim converts; and Muslim immigrants and their families. Each of these categories can be further subdivided on the basis of class, gender, sect, ethnicity, nationality, profession and age. In terms of historicity, the earliest Muslims were Spaniards who reached Mesoamerica and New Spain with the early *conquistadors*. Of course, it is difficult to delineate their numbers or identities, as immediately after the fall of Granada in 1492 most of them had been forcibly converted to Christianity and thus ostensibly represented a new, vibrant and evangelistic Spain in the 'New World'.[12] However, the oldest Muslim community in America consisted of Africans who were brought as slaves several centuries ago, though there is no clear consensus on their exact numbers. Like estimates of the total numbers of Africans uprooted, which range from 10 million to 18 million, estimates of the proportion of Muslims amongst them vary from 20 per cent to 30 per cent. As with their compatriots, a constant dislocation and socio-cultural disempowerment led to the severing of their links with their heritage. It is only in recent years that several historians, through their investigation of transatlantic oral and regional histories and documentary evidence, have started to unearth and reconstruct the experiences of this 'reluctant migration'.

Before the great expansion of the slave trade from Africa, Islam was a major socio-political factor in Central and Western Africa and had established well-known empires in these regions. But their dissolution and fragmentation coincided with the emergence of a new vibrant Europe in the mid-fifteenth century. The dissolution of the Muslim community and state in Spain was the last straw, as now the tables were turned on Muslims and other Africans. Africa was to be conquered and through its human resources the New World was to be harnessed. The fall of Granada was not only the end of the Muslim factor in Western Europe, it was the beginning of the enslavement and colonisation of non-white peoples. The story of Andalusia was to be repeated across the Americas, Africa, Asia and Australia, where, imbued with the forces of modernity, a powerful West ushered in the Europeanisation of the world. The Portuguese and Spaniards, starved of human labour, upon reaching African coastal settlements found it easier to replenish their homes and colonies with the conveniently accessible African labour. The domestication and large-scale proselytisation of the Native Americans had already been a failure, whereas within the ancient European empires, Africa was again seen as a quick solution for labour shortage. Negative images of Africa, based on age-old prejudices and now justified in the name of religion, colour and culture, spawned such an enterprise.[13] Better maps and other navigational aids, swifter ships, the evolution of coastal forts and factories, the patronage of local networks, the development of the middle passage, and the evolution of transatlantic shipping converted slavery – that peculiar institution – into a complex system.[14] The American expansion, the use of vast tracts of land for agricultural purposes and the introduction of crops such as tobacco, cotton and rice fed into the emerging plantation economy, which, in the antebellum (pre-Civil War) American South became immensely dependent upon slave labour.[15]

Slavery within the American context has attracted a massive historiographical debate.[16] While the early literature focused on the moral issues, the antebellum discourse focused on abolitionism, constitutional rights and economic factors. Frederick Douglass (1817–1895)[17] and Booker T. Washington (1858–1915)[18] were the two towering personalities of the nineteenth century in this arena. After the Civil War, the issues of racism and economic and political disempowerment of the former slaves – now scattered in displaced clusters – became the main focus of concern. Socio-legal segregation, regimented through Jim Crow laws and augmented by the Ku Klux Klan and similar other racist groups, was challenged by Douglass and Washington. Washington believed that through economic improvement the blacks would be ultimately able to obtain their political rights, whereas Douglass would not wait for that and called for agitation. However, it was the generation of W.E.B. Du Bois (1868–1963) which offered intellectual and sociological alternatives on the issues of class and colour.[19] Marcus Garvey[20] tried to enthuse his Harlem followers with a greater pride in their African origins, but it was Elijah Muhammad who through his Nation of Islam tried to combine Islam, Africa and America together within his own specific representation of Islam. By the first quarter of the twentieth century, the plantation culture had been replaced by ghetto culture as the Great Migration, soon after the First World War, brought millions of African Americans into cities in the North-east and Midwest. Harlem in New York became the largest African city outside Africa, and the Harlem Renaissance, led by intellectuals and authors such as Langston Hughes, James Weldon Johnson, Claude McKay, Alain Locke, Anne Petry and James Baldwin, dilated on the ideological issues of black identity within American pluralism. Harlem was again the centre for Malcolm X (1925–1965) who, after his pilgrimage to Makkah, entered mainstream Islam and started challenging the Nation's personality- and colour-centred representation of Islam. Parallel to the Nation of Islam, and quite different from the ideology of Malcolm X, Martin Luther King Jr (1929–1968) idealised a synthesised and equal American citizenship, devoid of discrimination.[21] His middle-class Christian views were well received by a large section of African Americans and white activists.[22] However the murders of Malcolm X[23] and of Martin Luther King ended an era of activism, though the civil rights movement had put racial issues at centre stage. Following the death of Elijah Muhammad in 1975, his son Warith D. Muhammad merged the Nation into the larger Muslim community, though Louis Farrakhan tried to carry on a separatist legacy. During the 1980s and 1990s, Jesse Jackson (b. 1941) spoke from the Christian pulpit, while Farrakhan led the Nation, both taking on a number of national and global issues. It is not easy to pinpoint the exact number of the Nation of Islam at the turn of the twenty-first century, out of a total of 31 million African Americans, who make up 13.2 per cent of the total US population.

Other well-known African-American personalities such as Muhammad Ali, Denzel Washington, Amiri Baraka, Toni Morrison, Maya Angelou, Alice Walker, Spike Lee, and leaders like Andrew Young and Al Gregory have all attempted to enhance the interracial gains obtained earlier but now being challenged by the state-led rollback of positive discrimination. Though it is gratifying to note that individuals such as Bill Cosby, Richard Pryor, Sammy Davis Jr, Eddie Murphy, Michael Jackson, Diana Ross, Condoleeza Rice and Colin Powell have obtained pre-eminence in the highest echelons of American life, yet for many African Americans, especially in the urban slums, life is still riddled with challenges and difficulties. The forces of poverty, racism, drug trafficking, violence and break-up of the family system take a larger toll from them than from any other section of US society. The issues of class, colour and gender remain problematic within American pluralism and a sizeable proportion of Black Americans seek succour and identity in religion.

MUSLIM SLAVES IN THE AMERICAS

It is almost impossible to calculate the total number of slaves and the proportion of Muslims amongst them. Since most of the slaves came from West, Central and South-east Africa, one can assume that a fair number were Muslim, since these regions already included large Muslim populations. Of the estimated 10–18 million Africans uprooted between the 1450s and the 1860s and shipped across the Atlantic, the number of casualties accruing from the slave trade on the four continents – Africa, Europe, North and South America – was in all likelihood also significant. Indeed, concern for greater profit eventually ensured that some precautions were taken for the safety of the human cargo. The development of African-American studies and the involvement of scientific tools such as computers in collating information from shipping records, plantation registers, local papers, church registers and other archives are helpful in the reconstructive discourse. The simultaneous development of cliometrics has further enriched the discipline and along with the general increase in black consciousness since the 1960s has led to valuable studies, resulting in books like *Roots* and movies such as *Amistad, Glory,* and *Malcolm X*[24] that enhance the general awareness of black history. Undoubtedly, we are a long way from *The Birth of Nation* (1915), an anti-black, racist movie that increased nostalgia for the pre-Civil War South and helped to revive the Ku Klux Klan.[25] Following pioneering studies by historians such as Curtin, Fogel and Ingerman, slavery is now seen as a complex socioeconomic order and constitutes a field of study in which statistics, monetary calculations and labour-related matters merit greater scholarly attention.[26] It has been recently suggested that from 1662 to 1867 almost 10 million slaves were imported into the Western hemisphere and that if one adds the number sent to Europe the figure could rise by another half million. Modern computerised statistical techniques also provide the places of origin of the slaves, as well as their destinations.

Soon after the American Revolution, with the introduction of the spinning machine, the American South emerged as a cotton kingdom with an insatiable capacity for more slaves.[27] The British outlawed the slave trade in 1808, but European and American ships kept up with the lucrative trade. However, most studies on slavery and race relations in the US still concentrate on the numbers involved and the socioeconomic debate, and in the context of moral and religious issues consider only Christianity and the evolution of the black Christian churches. Even studies of black music tend to link it with nostalgia and Southern Christian themes. Discussion of Islam as the religion of a huge section of the slave population, of their efforts to continue with this heritage in order to preserve their identity, and of the eventual loss of a whole tradition has remained largely absent from such studies until recently.

The arrival of Muslims in the Americas was due to Iberian expansionism and the arrival of African slaves. The Portuguese and Spaniards imported these African slaves from Muslim regions and then started to take them across the Atlantic directly to their colonial possessions, where there was a steady demand for cheap and permanent labourers, peasants and soldiers. Christian fervour, as mentioned earlier, further regimented this socioeconomic factor. The first group of African slaves was brought into Portugal in 1441 and the two Iberian nations monopolised the slave trade for some time. It was in the mid-fifteenth century that Africans were first brought in any numbers into England, where they were seen as exotic beings; earlier English contacts with the Africans – other than during the distant Roman past – were confined to emissaries or pirates from North Africa. It was in 1619 that for the first time Africans reached the English colony of Virginia, where the 20 new arrivals were received rather kindly, although colonial needs and prejudices soon overcame early curiosity and hospitable feelings. In fact, they were offloaded from a Dutch ship in exchange for food for the starving crew. By the 1660s persecution was common, especially for runaway slaves, and most of the colonies had established stringent laws on segregation. For instance, Virginia made slave ownership hereditary through legislation in 1662. In 1672, the Royal African Company came into being to sponsor and regularise shipment of Africans to the colonies, and in 1699 Britain officially opened the slave trade to all her merchants and business conglomerates. It was from the mid-eighteenth century onwards that the slave trade and slavery became a thriving business under the aegis of nationwide institutions. While the Northern United States accounted for 5 to 10 per cent of the total black population of free persons, their treatment smacked of hierarchical if not racial discrimination. An exception to this general attitude was provided by the Quakers, who abhorred slavery and racism and also pioneered abolitionism. The concentration of more than 4 million slaves in the South, especially in the Deep South, resulted in a strong interdependence between masters and African Americans, though it was the office of overseer that remained most feared. At first, church attendance was discouraged, to disallow any possibility of revolt, but separate all-black churches began to emerge gradually and somewhat secretively. Names, religious rituals, languages and cultural values all changed to match the patterns of the masters. Though most Southern planters did not own many slaves, they tolerated slavery on the big plantations as a necessary component of their political economy, racial pride and benevolent paternalism.

Lack of family structure and proper peer institutions soon resulted in a mishmash of identities among the slaves and their descendants, who mostly mimicked their masters in their own religious subculture. Islam and other African religions were soon marginalised or simply vanished, given that the slaves were kept profoundly illiterate, dependent and segregated even from one another. African music, undocumented narratives and occasional references to Africa as a land of origins, all disappeared in the maelstrom of American-ness, with its own unique features. Thus, distinct Muslim identities melted into a hodgepodge of newer identities and, like African languages, Arabic, the Quran, Muslim history and rituals, all gradually disappeared in both practice and memory. The arrival of new slaves in the nineteenth century led to a rekindling of some interest in Islam, but the issues of political and economic disempowerment and the total elimination of contacts with Africa and the Muslim world precluded any continuation of tradition. It is only in the late twentieth century that one notices any revitalisation of this Muslim factor from the American past. The celebrated American pluralism as regards religious and ethno-national identities encompasses every such category, while simply ignoring Islam as a denominator. Even the few occasional autobiographies or rare articles on disparate Muslim communities, such as that at Dearborn in the 1940s, remain unknown. This was the earliest and largest Arab community outside Arabia that evolved in Detroit, when Henry Ford opened his doors to the Middle Eastern labour in the early twentieth century. Quite apart from knowledge of the Muslim diaspora, in the United States even knowledge of the colonised world remained distant and hazy from an average American viewpoint. In recent years, it is almost axiomatic that people all over the world, even in the former communist countries, have known more about America than America has known about them. The localised nature of the American media and the mass production of American education through mainstream courses have not allowed great understanding of the intricacies of global cultures and diverse communities. Despite being a nation of many nations, the United States needs to reorient itself to this dilemma since most Americans, other than those from certain specific sections of society, reveal a lack of interest, if not total indifference and ignorance, towards much of the rest of the world.

The absence of information in the United States on the early Muslims of African and Iberian descent is largely due to the paucity of general studies on Islam and Muslims in Africa until well into the 1950s. The emergence of nation states, and related ideological issues, caused a growing historiography on Africa even though books on slavery continued altogether to ignore Islam and the Muslim factor. It is amazing to see how, until the 1980s, any book on African Americans talked of Africa, Christianity and other aspects of acculturation, but did not have a single sentence on Islam. The Nation of Islam, and the arrival of students and professionals to form a growing Muslim diaspora, led to more interest in Islam, at a time of growing US involvement in the Muslim world and unflinching support for Israel. However, the Muslim factor within studies of the black diaspora would have been totally nonexistent but for the growth of African-American studies and the efforts by specialists such as Allan D. Austin. His comprehensive study entitled *African Muslims in Antebellum America: A Sourcebook* (1984) was the first collection of diverse materials and documents on the subject. In this work he concentrated on a group of Muslim slaves from West Africa, who, in most cases, were elite, well-educated and well-travelled. Some of them left treatises, Arabic texts and autobiographies in English, which are helpful in ascertaining their strategies for survival as well as their religious heritage. This pioneering effort was confined to a small sample of 75 individuals, but established an ambitious tradition in scholarship that is still waiting to be expanded.

Austin, in another volume, focused on nine Muslim Americans of African background who, despite their personal sufferings and separation, retained their identities and left behind a host of diverse source material. Their life histories and works reveal a rich, versatile and vital profile of Africans – far from the Sambo caricature, or the passive victim. Austin's first story is of Job Ben Solomon, who left a 54-page memoir (1734). This 'oldest text in African-American literature' is about a runaway in Maryland. Job talks of his family, ancestry and religion with a great measure of pride and also compares the English nobility with that of his native Senegal. The biography was penned by Thomas Bluett, an English friend, and has been referred to in many studies on slavery.[28] Bluett was a junior contemporary of Yarrow Mamout, whose portrait was made in 1819 by Charles Peale when his subject was 133 years old. Known for his prayers in the street, Mamout wrote Quranic verses in Arabic and kept in touch with his religion while a slave of a Mrs Bell. Known as Mahometan by contemporaries, he was well versed in Arabic, his native Wolof and in English. He was freed on the recommendation of James Oglethorpe, the founder of the colony of Georgia. Ibrahim Abd ar-Rahman, a native of Timbuktu, born in 1762, was captured by slavers and ended up in Mississippi. He became famous after running into John Cox, who had been his guest some 30 years earlier in his native town and had now decided to live in Natchez. Cox tried to get him free, but to no avail. Cox's sudden encounter with the practising Muslim three decades after he had left his native Africa became a cause célèbre in the Deep South. In his old age he was freed and undertook to travel around the United States. Through his demeanour, African Moorish costume and mild manners, he became the best-known African American in the United States in the 1820s. After collecting money for the release of his children and relatives, he returned to Liberia with his wife; but his memoirs continued to be referred to in many accounts.

Another African Muslim, Bilali, originally came from Guinea and was taken to the North American mainland via the Bahamas; he eventually became a plantation manager. Based on Sapelo Island off south-east Georgia, Bilali was an imam who wrote a 13-page manual in Arabic for other Muslim slaves – the *Ummah* in Georgia. In the 1930s his descendants discovered more of his writings, though some of them have yet to be translated. On neighbouring St Simon's island, Salih Bilali, Bilali's friend, who had a similar attitude, wrote a long letter to William Brown Hodgson, dilating on African intellect and Islam. Another African Muslim, caught as a slave and brought to North Carolina, was Umar ibn Said, who also enjoyed literary pursuits. His 16-page memoir – *Life* – was composed in Arabic in 1831 and combines Christian prayers with Islamic recitations. Opposed to contemporary missionary beliefs, he never forsook Islam nor did he believe in Jesus as the last prophet. Umar corresponded with Lamine Kebe, another Muslim slave, who was introduced to him through a common friend. Kebe, a Guinean Muslim, went back to Liberia in 1836, a year after writing down his comments on teaching, though not much is known of his early life. Austin has also researched the papers of Mohammah G. Baquaqua, a native of Benin, who was shipped to Brazil and later corresponded with an American academic. His 65-page autobiography was published in 1854 in Michigan.

Mohammed Ali ben Said or Nicholas Said (b. 1833) was a slave from present-day Chad who had been marched across the Sahara Desert and made his way to the Arabian Peninsula. He visited the Caucasus, eastern Europe, Russia, western Europe and Britain before reaching the United States. This traveller across five continents became a teacher in Detroit around 1860 and fought with the Union Army, concerning which he wrote a biographical piece, published in the *Atlantic Monthly* in 1868. But Said's work remained unknown until it was researched in the 1980s. It is strange that such a well-travelled and highly versatile person was never approached for an autobiography; one has to depend on fragments of biographical information. Very little is known about his life after he retired from the 55th Regiment of the Massachusetts Colored Volunteers and, eventually, returned to Africa.[29] Like many other well-travelled American Muslims, he remains a little-known subject in American historical accounts. The growing research on Muslim slaves and the Islamic past in the United States will not only offer a fuller historical discourse but may equally establish the early Islamic tradition in America, which could further help African Americans in determining their own tri-polar identities as Muslims, Africans and Americans.

THE NATION OF ISLAM AND MALCOLM X

In any discussion of Islam in the United States, one cannot underestimate the importance of the 1960s. The civil rights and anti-Vietnam war movements, the Beat generation, feminism and increased acceptance of pluralism all brought about a significant socio-political change. Being part of the third world became a shared reality rather than a psychological complex, while minorities such as blacks and Native Americans demanded long overdue empowerment and equality. Even the word 'Muslim' or 'Moslem' began to symbolise radical changes towards community assertion.[30] The black Muslim movement or the Nation of Islam obtained a high profile thanks to three African Americans: Malcolm X, Muhammad Ali and Louis Farrakhan. Ali and Malcolm awoke America and the rest of the world to the revival of Islam in the United States, which coincided with the arrival of thousands of Muslim students and future professionals from the Afro-Asian world. This resurgence of interest in Islam converged with ideological changes within the African-American quest for identity. By the 1920s, Booker T. Washington's economic nationalism had been largely rejected by Du Bois and Marcus Garvey who advocated a fully fledged black nationalism. In place of accommodation, the emphasis now turned to assertion, though during the Great Depression it was the African Americans who suffered most. Whereas, in the 1950s, Dr King's exhortations for accommodation and integration were seen by many African Americans as the way forward, several others found this pacifism inadequate. Instead, Malcolm X and the Black Panthers not only spoke of an empowered black nationalism, they equally advocated a more vigorous separatism.[31] This divergence in strategies and ideologies was reflected in the decades that followed by individuals such as the Reverend Jesse Jackson (b. 1941) and Louis Farrakhan (b. 1933), though they lacked the charisma and appeal of Martin Luther King and Malcolm X.[32] During crises such as race riots, many African Americans turned to Malcolm X for inspiration. More recently Louis Farrakhan has tried to revive the Nation of Islam. By contrast, Warith Din Muhammad, the son of Elijah Muhammad, has assumed more of a mainstream role, avoiding interpersonality friction and emphasising the Islamicisation of the Nation.[33]

The Nation of Islam had its origins in Southern black oral traditions, Garveyism and the encounter between Black Americans and North African Muslim immigrants in Detroit. Disenchantment with white supremacy and Christian denominationalism, mingled with a greater nostalgia for Africa, had already led to the evolution of two religious movements in the eastern United States, especially in and around Harlem. The Great Migration and the Harlem Renaissance had transformed Harlem – 'the capital of Black America'[34] – into a vibrant and cathartic centre where sacred and secular, moral and profane existed side by side.[35] In 1913, Noble Drew Ali opened his Moorish–American Science Temple, which by the 1930s was attracting many former Garveyites by identifying blacks as Moors and Asians. In 1919, Father Divine (George Baker) established his Peace Mission Movement on Long Island advocating a collectivist economy and withdrawal from other fraternal organisations and paying taxes. He opened restaurants and laundries serving only African Americans, combining Garveyism with Washington's economic nationalism. However, Father Divine had no interest in the civil rights movement or raising political consciousness among his followers, though during the Great Depression he provided employment and shelter to many blacks. He led a few demonstrations against departmental stores in New York for discriminating against blacks, but his strategy of self-contentment and containment in a way highlighted self-imposed segregation and an apolitical career. In 1965, he died as a prince in his mansion on a 75-acre estate outside Philadelphia. His mixture of religion, economics, personal glorification and a bit of Garveyite African-ness bound his followers together, but his precedence was eclipsed by Elijah Muhammad, the leader of one of most powerful movements of his age.

The Nation of Islam was founded by Fard D. Muhammad in 1930 in Detroit. Not much is known about his life. Master Fard is reported to have said: 'I am W. D. Fard ... and I came from the Holy City of Mecca. More about myself I will not tell you yet, for the time has not yet come. I am your brother. You have not seen me in my royal robes.'[36] He mysteriously disappeared in 1933 and remains an obscure figure. To his follower and successor, Elijah Muhammad, he was like a god who came to launch the movement and to augur Muhammad's own prophethood, whereas, to others, he was a North African vendor who sold his goods amongst Detroit's Arab and African Americans.[37] To some, he was a man with a criminal record who cashed in on the susceptibilities of black immigrants from the Deep South, only to disappear again in the labyrinths of urban America.[38] His disappearance offered Elijah Poole from Georgia the chance to launch his own leadership under the name of Elijah Muhammad. Muhammad combined Fard Muhammad's teachings, Garveyism and his own personal ambitions in a hodgepodge of beliefs in which he posited himself as the promised Mahdi and Messiah. He identified himself as Muhammad, the Messenger of God, though at that stage it is not certain whether he possessed a substantial knowledge of Islam. His kind of Islam was like the Christianity of the slaves, in which all sorts of beliefs and superstitions were stitched together to create a religious discourse offering psychological solace, spiritual bonding and a parallel realm separate from the slave masters. This Islam was quite racial as it identified blacks as superior to the whites, who were devils and had been separated from the rest by a black scientist – Yakub – in the distant past. In other words, his Islam was personalist as well as segregationist.

Elijah Muhammad continued Fard Muhammad's teachings on the superiority of Africans and their distinctness from everyone else. He also expanded his educational institutions, broadened the middle-class norms based on self-help and advised his followers to buy only from outlets owned by the Nation. His followers were given new names, since the slave owners had deprived them of their real identity, and each city had ministers to tend to the community.

Members – both men and women – shunned tobacco, pork and alcohol and determined to live tidy and disciplined lives. Soon Muhammad shifted to Chicago, which emerged as the headquarters for the Nation, besides housing its future university. His project of Black Nationalism, based on colour and a separatist creed, was acceptable to an emerging youthful black bourgeoisie, though the Nation's expansion remained modest all through the Great Depression and the War years.[39] In 1942 Muhammad and 62 members of the Nation were jailed for three years on a charge of evasion of the military draft. It was in jail that Muhammad encountered a large number of black inmates and found them ready to accept his message, with its new political undertones. But the Nation had to wait for another decade until the advent of Malcolm X to assume a more mass-based embodiment.

Malcolm X, the son of a Garveyite pastor, was born as Malcolm Little in Nebraska in 1925. Soon after his birth the family moved to Lansing, Michigan, where racist elements allegedly killed his father, leaving his body on the railway tracks to suggest that the pastor had committed suicide. His mother lost her mental balance and was confined to an asylum in Kalamazoo and the family fell apart. Malcolm, a bright student in the local school at Holt, was discouraged by a teacher from pursuing his interest in law, and was soon sent to live with his older half-sister in Roxbury, Massachusetts. Here he became involved in criminal activities, stealing and pimping, until he was jailed in Charleston. During his incarceration, Malcolm, prompted by another inmate, developed a scholarly interest in English, history and Latin. He became an avid reader and, under the influence of his sister and a brother – both Muslims – started reading the religious literature of the Nation. In 1952, Malcolm left prison and went to see Elijah Muhammad and soon became one of his closest disciples. Malcolm's general knowledge of history, his experience of race relations and his personal commitment to Black Nationalism as articulated by the Nation turned him into a successful orator. His wit and oratorical skills won him national and international acclaim. Soon Malcolm was heading the community in Harlem – the most crucial centre of the Nation, after its headquarters in Chicago. By 1959 the Nation was itself a major economic concern with an annual income of $3 million.[40]

In a cosmopolitan New York, Malcolm came across a wide variety of Muslim opinion and began entertaining scepticism towards Muhammad's claims of prophethood. In addition, he discovered some scandalous facts about the personal life of the Nation's leader, which eventually led to a break. The final straw came with Malcolm's pilgrimage to Arabia in 1963, where he was deeply moved by the Islamic fraternity, independently of racial and ethnic biases. Malcolm adopted a new name, El-Hajj Malik El-Shahbazz, and on his return organised his own mosque. In addition, following visits to Africa, he involved himself in raising consciousness and support for African sovereignty. Despite his religiosity, Malcolm was extremely political in his exhortations about racism, war, the assassination of Kennedy and on the identity of African Americans, on which he openly differed with Martin Luther King. Malcolm was able to dictate his biography to Alex Hailey before he was murdered while delivering a speech in Harlem on 21 February 1965. His sad and sudden end prevented him from reaching the broader horizons of his new-found global role as an activist and as a leader of the deprived people of America. His autobiography reads like the moving narrative of an angry African American whose eventful life reflects the sordid realities of a young black in the United States. It combines the bitterness, passion, moralism and hopes of a young man who is in a hurry to accomplish several things at once. His journey from the slums to a position as an international thinker is remarkable – in contrast to the middle-class upbringing of Dr King. For many African Americans, it is Malcolm whose experience is closer to their own. Both leaders, in their own separate ways, were reformers, but Malcolm had no patience for Gandhian pacifism, though neither did he subscribe to violence. But he seems closer to Douglass, Du Bois, Garvey and Fanon, whereas Martin Luther King sought redress in integration and accommodation within a Christian context.[41] The assassination of Malcolm X, followed by that of Dr King in 1968, left a great void for African Americans who would not acquiesce to second-class citizenry and were imbued with an activist youthfulness. The US government, despite its growing sensitivity towards civil rights, still displayed a lack of interest, if not outright hostility, towards black activists. Not only had protests confirmed the FBI and its director, J. Edgar Hoover, and other important agencies, as proponents of the status quo, but they also intensified their rancour. The riots of 1968 in Watts, California, and in other big cities such as Detroit, alerted America to the grave state of race relations. However, for many African Americans there was no going back.

With Malcolm X gone, Elijah Muhammad continued with his preaching and economic pursuits. By virtue of his advanced age and public profile he had become more accommodative. He groomed Louis Farrakhan as the successor to Malcolm X in New York. The new minister, a musician, turned out to be a gifted orator and rabble-rouser. Soon after the demise of Muhammad in 1975, the Nation confronted a dilemma: either to persist with its segregationist and Muhammad-centred espousal of Islam or to join the global, mainstream Muslim world. Muhammad's eldest son, Warith, opted for the second choice, but many of the Nation's leaders and followers, including Louis Farrakhan, continued to subscribe to Muhammad's preaching. Warith decided to change the name from black Muslims to Bilallians in order eventually to integrate the Nation into mainstream Islam. His education at Al-Azhar University in Cairo, his own religious views, and interaction with Muslim professionals in America helped him dissolve the separatist character of the Nation; but Farrakhan did not budge. Farrakhan revived the Nation in the mid-1990s by floating the idea of a 'million man march' in Washington, DC.[42] The Jewish lobby did not feel comfortable with his views on race and Zionism, and also criticised his close relationship with some Arab leaders. Farrakhan, in a private interview with a black journalist from the *Washington Post,* used derogatory words for Jews which did not endear him with the latter. His references to Hitler and critique of Zionism resulted in an intense reaction from Jewish groups.[43] With the eclipse of Jesse Jackson's leadership, Farrakhan remained the most important leader of the African-American diaspora.[44]

THE MUSLIM DIASPORA

The post-Second World War evolution of a Muslim diaspora in North America, steadily increasing in size, reflects the realities of the developing world. The diaspora has its old and new components, though the number of professionals has increased in recent years, largely because of the arrival of skilled Muslim immigrants. The middle-class contours of both the Nation and the other African Muslims are also quite recent, but both old and new communities have a long way to go to establish bridges. The long-held forces of racism, even after the abolition of slavery, and the divisive realities of African-American communities, have prevented the socioeconomic uplift of this 13 per cent of the US population. This is not to deny that there is a growing middle class amongst them; yet African Americans also make up the bulk of underachievers. The Muslim immigrants are mostly well qualified and mobile, but they are divided into several national and sectarian groups, having brought in with them their nationalist, ethnic and doctrinal schisms. Unlike the African Americans, it is only in recent years that the Muslim immigrants and their first generation children have started receiving scholarly attention.

The earliest Muslim immigrants to the United States, from Syria and Yemen, came to industrial cities such as Detroit, New York, Chicago and Boston. The largest concentration of Muslim Arabs has been at Dearborn, where most of them worked in the automobile industry. However, most Arab immigrants were Christian, though there was a fair representation of Muslims as well. Albanians and Yugoslav Muslims immigrated to the same regions in the inter-war period and established their mosques and *tekkes* (Sufi circles).[45] South Asian migration was mostly limited to the West Coast and consisted of Punjabi peasants, except for a few professionals in New York. These Punjabis were overwhelmingly Sikh, but a few Muslims also emigrated from British India.[46] Some individual immigrants even celebrated material progress in the United States, while feeling sad for their colonised and underdeveloped communities back home. For writers such as Khalil Gibran, who came from a predominantly Christian Lebanese background, East–West tensions and nostalgia engendered mixed images of the United States.[47] The interaction between Muslim immigrants and the American communities has led to many conversions to Islam, though many Muslims have also gradually lost touch with the Islamic ethos. Most of the converts to Islam, especially from amongst the whites, seek a greater sense of spirituality and bonding in the Islamic experience. To them, Sufi versions of Islam – Muslim mysticism – are generally more attractive; influences have come from personal encounters with Sufis during visits to Muslim regions or through the study of books such as Maulana Rumi's *Mathnawi*.[48]

Studies by El-Kholy, Aswad and Haddad have offered readers greater insight into the 'newer' Muslim communities in the United States, focusing on diverse sociological variables such as ethnicity, religion, sectarian identities, professions and nationalism.[49] Three recent themes encountered in more contemporary studies on the Muslim diaspora are: acculturation; contacts with the Muslim world; and the attitudes prevalent amongst the new generation. Such studies are becoming more critical in locating class-, gender- and sect-based attitudes along with the political affiliations of certain diasporic clusters. For instance, Iranian immigrants have mostly come from the educated urban elite, who tended to support the Shah. However, a number of immigrant Iranian students were critical of the Shah's autocracy and demanded democracy or an Islamic alternative. The Iranian diaspora during the 1970s was quite vocal on the campuses, though after the Islamic Revolution in 1979 support for an Islamic system gradually dwindled. A majority of Iranian Americans – like their counterparts in Europe – have been critical of religio-political policies in Iran and emphasise the centrality of culture over religion. They usually stay away from the religion-based activities of other Muslim groups. The deterioration in US–Iran relations since 1979, the Iran–Iraq War and the imposition of religious punishments have deeply disenchanted many Iranians in the diaspora, especially those who had been beneficiaries of the Shah's policies. Like their compatriots in Europe, most of these Iranians are secular in outlook, though affinity with some Shia practices may also symbolise cultural identity away from the larger Sunni groups. The Turks, on the contrary, in several cases, are not so dismissive of their religious identity, and since the Bosnian crisis many Balkan Muslims have also started rediscovering their Muslim origins. In the same manner, a number of Muslim organisations are actively involved within mainstream academia in influencing US policies towards Palestine. The Afghan diaspora – a recently arrived group – has also attempted to build up anti-Taleban momentum through internet and personal contacts. Pakistanis and Kashmiris have always worked together to neutralise Indian efforts to influence American foreign policy, while the Bosnians and Muslim groups cooperated to influence the Clinton administration during the 1990s.

The Clinton administration caused considerable unease among Muslims by ordering the bombing of the Sudan and Afghanistan in 1998, partly seeking a scapegoat to distract attention from the embarrassing Monica Lewinsky affair and partly to assert US primacy in the post-Soviet years. The terrorist attacks on the US embassies in Kenya and Tanzania, attributed to Osama bin Laden – an erstwhile US ally – were offered as a justification to attack these two poor Muslim states. Clinton is also known to have imposed a record number of sanctions against third-world countries during his two presidential terms. Several of these countries happened to be Muslim, such as Pakistan, which suffered economically and politically due to sanctions imposed following its nuclearisation in May 1998. In fact, both India and Pakistan had sanctions imposed on them, but

Pakistan was singled out rather more harshly.[50] Muslim anger reached
its peak following the recent American vengeful aerial campaign
against Afghanistan and the Israeli and Indian crackdowns on Palestinians and Kashmiris respectively, which were seen to happen with
the connivance of the United States. In the meantime, Russia also
intensified its military campaign in Chechnya. In all three cases the
struggle for self-determination was quickly categorised as terrorist,
by contrast with the military response, though this too, in reality,
was a form of state-led terrorism.

Anti-Muslim measures, which singled out Muslim organisations
for supposed terrorist sympathies, deeply aggrieved American
Muslims, since they saw their human rights being violated in those
very countries that trumpeted the ideals of human rights to the
world at large.[51] The scenes of hooded, chained and drugged
members of al-Qaeda being airlifted from Kandahar to Guantanamo
Bay in Cuba deeply distressed many Muslims and other advocates of
human rights. The US reluctance to define them as POWs, their
inhuman treatment during a long journey and the possibility of their
being executed through hasty military trials caused much concern
at the International Committee of the Red Cross (ICRC), but to no
avail. Many Muslims were aggrieved that once again the United
States was totally indifferent to the Muslim predicament and its own
role in aggravating it. Even Arab Americans of Christian denominations, who resented being cast as Arab *Muslims* for belonging to the
Middle East, remained critical of US policy towards Western Asia.[52]
Having 'double standards' is a common complaint made against the
United States, with people citing the special relationships with Israel
and India, which persist even though the Palestinians and the
Pakistanis have been dependable allies to the United States. In the
wake of the hawkish and unilateral attitude towards Iraq, a vast
majority of Muslims in 2003 felt that the United States had taken
upon itself a neo-colonial role which was inimical to its own interests
as well as to global peace. However, they differentiated between
ordinary Americans and the government and powerful pressure
groups of the establishment.[53]

Political and sectarian fissures, along with pressures from outside,
have prevented American Muslims from evolving a common and
consensual platform. To many observers, that may never be a possibility, given the size and diversity of the community. However, the
new generation of Muslims, in most cases, is well educated and

ideally placed for intercommunity dialogue. Mosque-centred activities are being gradually supplemented by a fresher socio-political activism based on professional camaraderie.[54] The earliest Muslim organisational activities were launched on campuses, where Muslim students mainly organised Friday and Eid prayers. Special lectures and other festivities organised by the growing number of Muslims led to the establishment of regular mosques, which by the late 1990s had emerged all over North America. A few African, South Asian and Middle Eastern postgraduate students during the 1960s undertook the campaign to establish a countrywide organisation to create a common ethos. This came to be known as the Muslim Students' Association (MSA); it would hold annual conferences on Islamic issues and diasporic themes and would also try to speak for an emerging Muslim voice in the West. Local chapters of the MSA would often coopt the local ethnic and national organisations, such as the Arab or Pakistani student associations, who would join in all the religious and political activities. Within the larger Muslim student community, all through the 1970s, one still saw an ideological divide between conservative and liberal elements.

The MSA strove to develop into a trans-regional organisation and, over the following decade, it became the Islamic Society of North America (ISNA) as many of the former graduates became fully fledged professionals. During the 1980s, the ISNA established its own head-quarters in Indiana and branched out into various professions. The ISNA, at the present time, is a broad-based umbrella organisation which incorporates a number of associations of physicians, academics, engineers, scientists and social scientists.[55] Activities such as study circles, Sunday schools, nationality clubs, research publications and periodic conferences are increasing, with a greater focus on younger Muslims and families permanently residing in North America. Mosques, private schools, internet groups, television channels, radio programmes and print media offer alternative channels for communication and articulation. The first Gulf War, the Intifadah, the Bosnian and Kosovar crises, the aerial bombing of Afghanistan, Israeli attacks on the Palestinians, human rights violations in the Kashmir valley by Indian troops and the war against Iraq have been widely shared and commented on in recent years through these networks. Such parallel networks not only facilitate a larger sense of identity, but also compensate for the lack of balanced programmes on Islam in the mainstream print and visual media. The bomb blasts at the World Trade Center in 1993, the Oklahoma bombing in 1995 and then the terrorist attacks on the World Trade Center and the Pentagon in 2001 deeply increased the worries and concerns among Muslims in the West, especially in the United States. Many people felt that the constructive work of creating better images of Islam and Muslims had been lost due to the terrorist activities on 11 September and that the United States was reacting with far greater power and vengeance than was called for. Many American Muslims felt helpless in the face of US policies towards Afghanistan and Iraq. Some even felt that the United States was either indifferent to Muslim sensibilities or was merely playing the role of a neo-colonial power, unrestrained by any moral or human prerogatives. However, the younger voices felt a greater need for better organisation and a refocusing of strategies to avoid any intra-community dissension.

Despite its early encounters with Islam, the United States has largely remained indifferent if not totally hostile to Muslim realities. Such an attitude is due partly to the lack of proper information on Islam, partly to a pervasive misinformation about Muslim politics and societies. The Arab–Israeli conflict, disputes such as that in Kashmir, the rise of certain fringe fundamentalist groups including al-Qaeda and the Taleban, and authoritarian leaders such as Saddam Hussain have been both unknowingly and, in some cases, intentionally universalised and taken to represent the entire 1.4 billion-strong Muslim community across the world. Ultranationalist regimes have used such anti-Muslim inclinations to suppress movements for self-determination in Palestine, Kashmir and Chechnya by portraying them as no more than terrorist trajectories. During the sustained bombing campaigns led by the United States, Islam in general also became the casualty of propaganda, vengeance and misinformation. This is not to deny that there are fundamentalist groups in the Muslim world, but not all Muslims are intolerant and even the trouble spots mentioned earlier, including Afghanistan, Iraq, Palestine and Kashmir, arise from political disputes largely created by outside intervention, including that of the United States. In some cases, Muslim groups have tried to portray politico-economic issues as religious movements by defining them as Jihad, which has not led to a better understanding of the issues. The contraction of Islam from a humane and tolerant civilisation to a mere ritualistic theology is both a Muslim and a non-Muslim problem. Within the United States, information on Islam and the early Muslim arrival in the Western hemisphere has remained comparatively unresearched, and multidisciplinary efforts are needed to reconstruct this discourse. A growing religion like Islam faces both opportunities and challenges in America, and in the context of America's longtime racial legacy it may have a chance to offer itself as a humane, egalitarian, peaceful, non-racial and non-hegemonic discourse of universal relevance. Muslim intellectuals – both secular and practising – in a democratic West can also debate the issues of Muslim feminism, Islam and democracy, and a new world order based on tolerance and cooperation rather than exploitation and unbridled power. Time alone will tell.

Epilogue
Andalusia or Renaissance?

It can be tempting to suggest that Islam and the West are perennial enemies, representing not only differing cultures and communities but also antagonistic forces. Such an assumption is, especially in the light of the post-11 September war on terror, both ahistorical and dangerous. There is great interdependence between the two. Neither the West nor Islam is an unchanging monolith, always thinking and acting in the same way. But it would be superficial to gloss over the differences and tensions that have, over the centuries, characterised the symbiotic relationship between Islam and the West. Augmented by stereotypes, ignorance and geopolitical interests, there is a politics of suspicion and even resentment on both sides, which sometimes leads to mutual denigration and sporadic violence.

One way of thinking of the Islam–West relationship is in terms of 'Islam in the West' and 'the West in Islam'. The Muslim factor in the West and the role of the Judaic–Christian West in the Muslim world has a long history – from the early Prophetic era, through the caliphates, the Crusades, the colonial and then the post-independence phases. Each has discovered the other in numerous ways, each concurrently liking and distrusting the other. Today, the Muslim diaspora is the most prominent interlocutor between the two sides, at a time when one needs a better and more judicious understanding of differing perspectives. The diaspora can offer a fresh view of the Islamic heritage and a better understanding of the Muslim predicament. It is vulnerable to several challenges, such as institution-alised racism and discretionary policies, but it can still avoid the Andalusia syndrome by empowering itself within the Western democratic and intellectual milieu.

The winding down of the Ottoman caliphate (like the fall of Granada), through persistent external assaults as well as internal laxity, reminds Muslims that while Europe prides itself on a triumphal modernity in the forms of democracy, secularism and feminism, still it has failed again and again to protect non-Christian minorities including Jews and Muslims. Within modern Europe these minorities have suffered an intermittent marginalisation, if not a total elimination. Outside Europe, Africans, Native Americans and Aborigines received even worse treatment following the Europeanisation of the world.

In the last decade or so, the pervasive indifference over the Salman Rushdie affair, the official Western nonchalance towards Bosnian Muslims, the sudden indifference towards a war-torn Afghanistan and the Anglo-American invasion of Iraq added to the Muslim anguish felt over European and North American unwillingness to help the Palestinians or Chechens. The 11 September 2001 attacks and the resultant American wrath rekindled racist and exclusionary policies and attitudes at numerous levels, with Muslims becoming the focus for contempt and derision – 'the new Jews', in the words of Rana Kabbani. As the attacks on Muslim countries and communities – in Afghanistan, Kashmir, Palestine, the Philippines, Iraq and Chechnya – became increasingly blatant, the Muslim diaspora faced the most challenging predicament of its history. The ultra-right evangelism of the nations of the North Atlantic region and their camaraderie with their Israeli, Russian and Indian counterparts only exacerbated an anti-Muslim animus. The already marginalised Muslim communities suffered racial attacks, verbal abuse, media denigration and a denial of job and promotion opportunities. Islam-bashing became the order of the day, with academics, politicians, racist groups, religious leaders and opinion makers joining the chorus of hatred. Memories of the Crusades, the Inquisition and ethnic cleansing reverberated, and not without substance when one saw leaders such as George Bush and Tony Blair in the company of Ariel Sharon, L. K. Advani and the like, to whom Islam simply implied terrorism and every Muslim was a potential Osama bin Laden. The proponents of the theory of a clash of civilisations have never been so popular.

The majority of Muslim youth in the West, most of whom were born here, have reacted very aggressively or have withdrawn into apologetic suffering. However, on the margins one notices the emergence of smaller sections cogently and forcefully articulating fresher perspectives, away from the extremes of rejection or introversion. These diasporic clusters of artists, writers, activists and intellectuals – men and women of many different doctrinal and secular persuasions – have modestly begun expounding *Muslim* issues. These diverse individuals, who include Ziauddin Sardar, Rana Kabbani, Najma Akhtar, Yasmin Alibhai-Brown and Bashir Maan, among many others, have been totally misunderstood in their North

Atlantic homes, while at the same time they feel cheated by the few fundamentalists who seem to have hijacked Islamic civilisation by claiming to be its de facto representatives. These critical elements feel deeply let down over the continued corruption and impotence of the ruling elite in nearly all Muslim states. Yet, benefiting from the democratic and civic institutions in the West, these elements have begun a nascent tradition of self-questioning, which may augur well for a Muslim renaissance, though it is still too early to predict its future course.

To these intellectuals and activists, Islam is not a repressive dogma but a dynamic, egalitarian and tolerant human civilisation which has thrived on synthesis and plural human values. This is the civilisation of the Pious Caliphate, Muslim Spain, the Delhi Sultans, Saladin's Syria, Fatimid Egypt, Mughal India and the Ottoman Sultanate, a cherished civilisation which was dynamic and receptive enough to reinvent (modernise!) itself until the forces of obscurantism and repression took over. These Muslim critics embrace Islam's dehegemonising and decolonising role, and refuse to support Western policies in the Muslim regions. At the same time, they are deeply perturbed over its monopolisation by reductionist and intolerant elements. To such critical groups, Islam is not simply Osama, Saddam and the Taleban, nor the West just a revengeful Bush–Blair duo, surrounded by hawks and 'new' Crusaders. These Muslim reconstructionists are seeking a new role for the Prophet as a *human* being, the viability of Islam as a synthesised heritage, the adoptability of its corpus through constant reinterpretations of Sharia in the light of contemporary issues, and the deciphering of a new Islamic vision based on inclusive democracy, egalitarian feminism and discrimination-free socioeconomic systems.

Undoubtedly, Muslims cannot build these edifices on their own, nor by simply rejecting other traditions or even modernity per se. The post-11 September tensions and pressures are demoralising, especially in view of anxieties over Iraq and Palestine, but must be confronted as a new challenge. A significant redeeming reality is the rise and expansion of the peace movement across the Atlantic regions which shows that not only are there vast numbers refusing to pursue and endorse the militarist and partisan policies of their respective regimes, there are also great numbers willing to understand the Muslim predicament.

This book's journey through Muslim Spain is not simple nostalgia for a romanticised past; it shows how Muslim Spain can be seen – in part – as an attainable ideal of a civilised and creative coexistence of Muslims, Christians and Jews. Muslim Spain also illustrates how Islam is not new or alien to the West. Likewise, the Barbary Muslims, Turcos, African slaves, lascars, ayas and the recent generations of Muslim students and immigrants have operated as trans-cultural links between the Islamic world and the West, while Western modernity is represented by territorial, administrative, political, cultural, economic and educational structures in the former colonies.

Certainly, many Muslim states have been unfortunate in largely failing to attain politico-economic stability; these states comprise a large portion of the developing world, but even they are eager practitioners of the various aspects of modernity. In some cases, modernity, in the form of uneven development, has aggravated problems which the postcolonial elite has been unable to resolve. All Muslim states – whether authoritarian or democratic regimes or clerical hierarchies – have tried to use modernity in their own ways. In general, the Muslim world wants to move forward and develop holistically in every area, yet is understandably reluctant to imitate Westernism. But that does not mean that Muslims are against the West per se. Their anxieties concern Western dominance, already experienced through colonialism, which in turn engenders worries about a distinctively Muslim identity being lost.

The ferocious trajectories of modernity, in the extreme forms of abrasive assimilation or total marginalisation, should deeply concern everyone; but the future lies in mutualities and through a due preservation of pluralism. While Western political, economic and societal establishments need to be reminded of the pitfalls of modernity, including injudicious and extreme methods of dealing with pluralism, Muslims themselves need to be reminded of their own pluralism and its imperatives. That is the only possible way to prevent the occurrence of new Andalusias, or of any of the other forms of collective violence that the world has been witnessing since the fifteenth century.

Notes and References

PREFACE

1. Valuable studies on the Muslim diaspora in the West include, among others, works by Philip Lewis, Muhammad Anwar, Humayun Ansari, Jorgen Nielsen, Yvonne Haddad, Pnina Werbner, John Esposito and Gilles Kepel. The edited volume by David Westerlund et al. offers a useful survey of Muslim communities and countries outside the Arab world. Studies on Islam and the West by scholars such as Bernard Lewis, John Esposito, Fred Halliday, Karen Armstrong, Albert Hourani, Maxime Rodinson, Martin Lings, Edward Said and Montgomery Watt are widely read and discussed among academics. On Muslim Spain, there is a growing amount of literature in Spanish, though the works by Montgomery Watt and Anwar Chejne have been the landmark pioneering efforts so far. In recent years, one finds Muslim scholars such as Rana Kabbani, Ziauddin Sardar, Yasmin Alibhai-Brown, Akbar S. Ahmed, Mohammed Arkoun and Shabir Akhtar engaging in debate through the media and publications. While Bernard Lewis, Daniel Pipes and Oriana Fallaci may be widely read due to their rabble-rousing views on Islam, scholars such as Said, Kabbani, Sardar and Bobby Sayyid find themselves arrayed against this 'neo-Orientalist' genre. Their works can be read in conjunction with writings by Noam Chomsky, Arundhati Roy, George Monbiot, John Pilger, Robert Fisk, Madeleine Bunting and Michael Moore. Several of these works have been duly utilised and reviewed, and are included in the bibliography.

    The September attacks, the Taleban, Osama bin Laden and the war on Iraq have themselves led to a flurry of books on political Islam, Jihad and terror amidst an unprecedented media coverage of these contemporary themes and diaspora linkages. Most of this literature is of an alarmist nature and may have its negative ramifications for pluralism, as has been highlighted by valuable reports undertaken by the Runnymede Trust and other similar civic watchdogs. Muslim internet groups, network linkages, print and visual media have also mushroomed in recent years, with the younger generation becoming increasingly involved in identity-related debates, though the media will often focus on specific groups, taking them as representative of the entire community. This is not to deny the existence of several fundamentalist groups in the diaspora who play an interesting but also a damaging game with similar sections of the media. The organisations of Muslim professionals – another recent development – is an interesting phenomenon given their outreach and sobering impact, though mosques and ethno-national centres remain the main foci of socio-religious activities.

1 MODERNITY AND POLITICAL ISLAM: CONTESTANTS OR COMPANIONS?

1. The Rushdie affair was the tip of the iceberg. On the one hand, it signified the dissatisfaction amongst the Muslim youth while, simultaneously, it provided fundamentalists and other exponents of Political Islam an opportunity to assume centre stage in the Muslim states.

2. One daily encounters numerous instances of socioeconomic contrasts between a globalising and regionalising West, opposed to a restive and fragmenting Muslim world. For instance, an English daily in one of its issues carried a headline about the US strikes on Afghanistan, 'War cost America extra $20bn', next to a picture of a 70-year-old weeping Afghan 'as he is forced by starvation to eat bread made from grass'. *The Times*, 8 January 2002.

3. Rana Kabbani, 'Why Muslims fear the future', *Guardian*, 21 August 1992. Some of these fears were upheld in the study conducted by the reputable British Runnymede Trust which, in 1997, published its powerful study – *Islamophobia* – highlighting the Muslim predicament.

4. Jonathan Steele, 'Fighting a wrong war', *Guardian*, 11 December 2001; also Bianca Jagger, 'Selective justice', *ibid.*, 8 December 2001. A commentary observed: 'There will be no official two-minute silence for the Afghan dead, no newspaper obituaries or memorial services attended by the prime minister, as there were for the victims of the twin towers. But what has been cruelly demonstrated is that the US and its camp followers are prepared to sacrifice thousands of innocents in a coward's war.' Seumas Milne, 'The innocent dead in a coward's war', *ibid.*, 20 December 2001.

5. Many observers felt that even without using such destructive power the United States could have apprehended them through diplomatic and other means.

6. As Kabbani observed in a special television report, the entire Muslim world looked like a cantonment as the Western soldiers thundered pass the communities to overawe them with their weapons and noise. 'Correspondent', *BBC 24*, 6 and 13 January 2002.

7. Some commentators have felt that an increased focus on Islam – however negative and pernicious it may be – has led to more curiosity about this religion. Some reports even suggested a growing trend towards conversion. It was opined that the new white converts were coming from well-established elite backgrounds. Giles Whittell, 'A mecca for the middle class: why young Britons are turning to Islam', *The Times*, 7 January 2002. However, caution is needed while accepting such reports, as one may not have the holistic picture; and a number of Muslims, especially in the West or in places like Turkey, have themselves been alienated from Islam for a variety of personal reasons. But presenting Islam as a unique case within the context of official war mania was also seen as a dangerous ploy. Mark Mazower, 'Religion's role in world affairs', *Financial Times*, 23 December 2002.

8. It is unfair to see every political moment in the Muslim world being quickly designated as terrorism or sheer fundamentalist confrontation.

For pertinent studies on the subject, see Fred Halliday, *Islam and the Myth of Confrontation*, London, 1996; and John Esposito, *Islamic Threat: Myth or Reality?* London, 1993.

9. Some case studies have shown the varying models of political Islam to be wanting in several areas. See Khalid bin Sayeed, *Western Dominance and Political Islam: Challenge and Response*, Albany, 1995. To some analysts, Islam remains the main dehegemoniser. See Bobby Sayyid, *A Fundamental Fear: Eurocentrism and the Emergence of Islamism*, London, 1997.

10. Aziz al-Azmeh, *Islams and Modernities*, London, 1994.

11. Sociologists and historians are becoming more cautious in applying terms like modernity and tradition. Erstwhile dialectical use is instead being replaced with a focus on seeking an interface between them. Anthony Giddens and Ernest Gellner have written extensively on modernity; several scholars, however, have redefined tradition with reference to social stability and an essential process for continuity. See Edward A. Shils, *Tradition*, London, 1981.

12. Theorists have used various categories to define such Third World states (and some from the former Second World as well). See Fouad Ajami, *The Arab Predicament: Arab Political Thought and Practice Since 1967*, Cambridge, 1992. Some of these problem-ridden states have been defined as 'disrupted' states. See Amin Saikal, 'Dimensions of state disruptions and international responses', *Third World Quarterly*, XXI, 1, 39–49.

13. No wonder that the twentieth century, despite being the epitome of development and enlightenment, turned out to be the most violent period in human history. More than 180 million people lost their lives in wars and other areas of collective violence since science and politics combined to launch some of the most horrible weapons of total destruction.

14. Neil MacMaster, *Racism in Europe*, Basingstoke, 2001, p.1.

15. A survey conducted by the *Reader's Digest* in November 2000 revealed that eight out of ten British adults believed that refugees came to Britain since they regarded it as 'a soft touch'. Two-thirds thought there were too many immigrants, at immense cost, whereas 40 per cent felt that immigrants should not be allowed to retain the cultures and lifestyles of their previous homelands. The Mori survey of 2,118 adults throughout the United Kingdom revealed that most of these opinions were based on a sketchy knowledge. *Reader's Digest*, November 2000.

16. In fact, most contemporary migrations have taken place within the developing world. The number of refugees lost on the seas, in containers or in cross-border shootouts will never be known.

17. Ali Rattansi and Sallie Westwood (eds), *Racism, Modernity and Identity: On the Western Front*, Cambridge, 1994.

18. For more on this, see Robert Miles, *Racism*, London, 1989; Kenan Malik, *The Meaning of Race: Race, History and Culture in Western Society*, Basingstoke, 1996; and Michael Banton, *Ethnic and Racial Consciousness*, London, 1997.

19. Jane Austen, Macaulay, Kipling, Richard Burton and several other writers fed into this Orientalist discourse which, as Foucault and Said have suggested, remains common even today. For details, see Edward Said, *Culture and Imperialism*, London, 1994; Stuart Hall (ed.), *Representation*,

Cultural Representations and Signifying Practices, London, 1997; and Rana Kabbani, Imperial Fictions: Empire's Myths of Orient, London, 1994.

20. Various think-tanks, such as the Policy Studies Institute (PSI) and the Runnymede Trust, have documented the areas in British public and private domains where institutional racism is at work. The European Union and think-tanks elsewhere, including Amnesty International, Minority Rights Group and Human Rights Watch, offer documented evidence on race relations and policies affecting minorities.

21. Even in the West, where once military regimes were heralded as modernising forces, disenchantment with them in recent years has been quite apparent.

22. Western attitudes towards a secular Turkey on the issue of human rights face a persistent dilemma, with Turkey's secularist preferences often being contradicted by democratic and plural imperatives. The Kemalist vision may be progressive and liberal, bringing together Turkey's elite and Western leaders, yet it also causes consternation amongst diverse and plural forces within society, who seek different alternatives. The West finds itself in a quandary, continuing to use a 'carrot-and-stick' approach towards Turkey, while not coming out openly in accepting her membership of the European Union.

On the contrary, the West has, en masse, rejected Khomeinism and the post-Shah mode of Political Islam in Iran. While supporting reformist elements in Teheran, the West equally finds itself at variance with the democratic verdict in that country.

The Taleban, members of Afghanistan's Northern Alliance and certain other Jihadi groups, including the much wanted fundamentalist Osama bin Laden, to a large extent owed their existence and sustenance to Western covert support, especially during the resistance against the former Soviet Union. These Mujahideen of yesterday, from Omar bin Abdar Rahman to Osama, had by the late 1990s changed from the best allies to the worst and most wanted enemies of the Western powers.

In the same vein, France, like other Western powers, has always decreed in favour of democratisation, despite keeping a continued high-profile interest and often meddling in the internal affairs of its former colonies. The most vivid case is that of Algeria, where France compelled other Western allies to reject the election results favourable to Islamic parties. Paris did not allow the formation of the elected government and instead encouraged the military authorities to carry on with their discretionary policies, causing havoc and bloodshed in that country. This is not to deny the responsibility of the local elite for such mishaps, but the West remains deeply involved in all these turbulent spots across the Muslim world. The post-1991 carte blanche to Russia to impose her Monroe Doctrine on her southern neighbours has allowed the West to ignore the militarist–nationalist campaigns all the way from Tajikistan to Abkhazia and Chechnya. In Bosnia, the foot-dragging over a meaningful and pre-emptive intervention and continued global inaction, added to an arms embargo and Bosnia's quarantining from any external support for her self-defence, simply caused her populace to bleed for five long years. The situation in Palestine equally exposes the primacy of Western expediency over human rights imperatives. UN resolutions are routinely defied by Israel, whereas ordinary Palestinians continue to suffer, as do the Iraqis and Kashmiris. Considering as terrorist activities only those of certain groups, while absolving states of any such massive crime, has exacerbated alienation in these regions.

Such a discretionary policy of pick-and-choose is definitely not in good taste and creates strong anti-West feelings.

23. Both of them, in some curious cases, see secularism itself turning into intolerant dogmatism. However, postmodernists will not forsake a humanist secularism for a dogmatic theocracy as it may re-medievalise society, whereas to the Islamicists, going back to a revered past and glorified transition remains the ultimate dream and ideal. Some clusters within these two ideological groups share a common strand of anti-Americanism. See Ziauddin Sardar and Merryl W. Davies, *Why Do People Hate America?* London, 2002.

24. These were the *ulama* associated with the two pre-eminent seminaries in Northern India based at the towns of Deoband and Rai Bareilli. The former adhered to a strict allegiance to purist Islamic teachings and felt that the Muslim renaissance was not possible without going back to pristine values. On the other hand, the Brelvi *ulama* and *mashaikh* accepted the channel of the saints, sufis and *pirs* though they also yearned for an Islamic utopia. Most of the *ulama* and *mashaikh* in South and South-western Asia have been trained by the alumni of these two major seminaries.

25. Azad, a great scholar in his own right, was also a political activist. In the 1940s, he was elected as the president of the Indian National Congress, the largest and the most effective Indian national party. He feared that a partition of India would strictly stipulate the partition of Muslims, and while leading his Jamiat-i-Ulama-i-Hind and the Indian National Congress, differed with Jinnah's and Iqbal's idea of a separate Muslim state. See his autobiography, *India Wins Freedom*, New Delhi, 1991.

26. Mawdudi was born in the Osmanli state of Hyderabad, the last significant Muslim princely state in India, enjoying powerful links with the Ottomans. After a sojourn in journalism, he devoted his life to a purist interpretation of the Quran. He rejected modernism in all its manifestations and moved to Lahore in the late 1930s. In 1941, he established his Jama'at-i-Islami (JI), the most powerful, well-organised vehicle for his version of an Islamic revolution. Mawdudi, like Azad, did not believe in a separate statehood, because he abhorred nationalism as a Western device to divide the *Ummah* and also because he did not trust the Islamic credentials of the Muslim Leaguers espousing the case for Pakistan. Eventually, he settled in Pakistan and spent a lifetime elaborating the Quranic teachings and leading his religio-political party. Even almost two decades after his death, he remains one of the most vocal and influential spokespersons for an Islamic revolution. The JI has its own autonomous parties all over South Asia. For more on him, see Seyed Vali Reza Nasr, *Mawdudi and the Making of an Islamic Revolution*, London, 1994.

27. Nationalism was a liberating as well as liberal ideology in the post-French Revolution era as it unified disparate communities into one nationhood

by achieving sovereignty. As seen during the fascist era, and more recently with the evolution of a xenophobic form of ultra-right nationalism, in several cases, it is changing into a repressive ideology. For a secular view of nationalism, see E. Kedourie, *Nationalism*, London, 1961. For a useful theoretical discussion, see E. Hobsbawm, *Nations and Nationalism since 1780: Programme, Myth and Reality*, Cambridge, 1990.

28. For more on the Khilafat Movement, see Gail Minault, *The Khilafat Movement*, New York, 1982.

29. A sad example is that of Afghanistan, where successive Mujahideen and Taleban governments, despite their avowals to create ideal Islamic polities, have radically disempowered women and minorities. For more on this, see William Malet (ed.) *Fundamentalism Reborn? Afghanistan and the Taliban*, London, 1998; Peter Marsden, *The Taliban*, London, 1997; and Ahmed Rashid, *Taliban: Islam, Oil and the New Great Game in Central Asia*, London, 2001.

30. For a useful commentary, see Khalid bin Sayeed, *Western Dominance and Political Islam*.

31. I am grateful to Jamil Sherif (the author of *In Search of Solace*, the only biography of Allama Yusuf Ali) for arranging a meeting with Abdul Karim Surush in London in early November 1998.

2 THE SAGA OF MUSLIM SPAIN: PLURALISM TO ELIMINATION

1. 'We may also be surprised that the departure took place so gallantly, as if the intermittent conflict between Muslims and Christians throughout the Middle Ages – in the long run a sort of civil war – had been no more than a kind of practice bout. It is somehow symbolic that 898/1492 was both the year of the taking of Granada and the discovery of America.' Emilio Garcia Gomez, 'Moorish Spain', in Bernard Lewis (ed.) *The World of Islam*, London, 1997, p.225.

2. The term was used by Muslims for the entire Iberian Peninsula, though in present-day Spain it is only the southern part of the country which is called Andalusia. Literally, al-Andalus means the Land of Vandals, the early rulers and inhabitants of the Iberian Peninsula. Spain itself was called *Hispania* in all the Muslim languages, and this is the present name of the country – *Espagna*, pronounced just like its Arabic equivalent.

3. Gomez, 'Moorish Spain'.

4. By 1249, Portugal, the erstwhile part of Muslim Iberia, after expelling the Muslims had carved out its own separate identity.

5. Jan Read, *The Moors in Spain and Portugal*, Totowa (NJ), 1975, p.217.

6. Quoted in *ibid.*, p.218.

7. 'Moors' has for quite some time been used as a derogatory term in European literature because of its colour-based connotation. The Moors were viewed as the barbarian, dark-skinned Africans who were to be removed from Christian Europe which, in contemporary understanding, symbolised culture, whiteness and racial supremacy. Such an ideology went very well with the racist stereotypes rooted in vendetta and missionary zeal. The recent continentalisation, accomplished during

the early modern period by Western cartographers to regionalise the world, had accentuated segregationist views on differences and distinctions. The issues of slavery and persistent racism legitimated themselves through this handy and derogatory view of Africans. Such a dangerous form of Orientalist discourse was also internalised by the several colonised peoples including the Arabs to differentiate themselves from Africans. In our present study, Moors would include Muslims of various ethno-regional backgrounds within Spain.

8. *Ibid.*, p.224.

9. 'This had been implanted from the very beginning of Moorish rule in the Iberian Peninsula, and by the twelfth and thirteenth centuries had become all-pervasive.' Jan Carew, 'The end of Moorish enlightenment and the beginning of the Columbian era', *Race and Class*, 33, 3, 1992, p.3.

10.

It was through old and familiar ideas that the New World was made known to Europe. The voyages that commenced in 1492 ended up endorsing and further legitimising a great lie. Instead of an encounter, Columbus's voyage inaugurated a sundering of Europe from Other People, a rupture that has yet to be healed and overcome. (Ziauddin Sardar, Ashis Nandy and Merryl Wyn Davies, *Barbaric Others: A Manifesto on Western Racism*, London, 1993, pp.1–2)

11.

Even the hand that signed the sailing orders of the Admiral of the Ocean Sea was the same hand that signed the ultimatum to the Jews, that of Juan de Coloma. Now, in 1492, Columbus, possessing the essential mind of the West with all its twisted religiosity, its background of classical geography and medieval folklore, and its recent acquisitions of technical skills, was ready to seek out new worlds. During his lifetime the Indies would thus inevitably become the New World analogue of the Crusades. Here, once again, under the cover of righteous Christian outreach, criminal rapaciousness would be sanctioned. (*Ibid.*, pp.40–1)

12. Basil Davidson, 'Columbus: the bones and blood of racism', *Race and Class*, 33, 3, pp.17–18.

13. Chris Searle, 'Unlearning Columbus: a review article', *ibid.*, 33, 3, p.67.

14. John Dyson, *Columbus: For Gold, God and Glory*, quoted in *ibid.*, p.67. The book contains commemorative pictures and text retracing the Columbian expedition. It was in July 1990 that a replica of the *Nino*, crewed by a Spanish professor and his students, re-ennacted the Columbian voyage. It is interesting to note that in July 1998, several Native American groups in South America put Columbus on trial *in absentia* for his 'crimes against humanity'. Based on an ITV report, monitored in Oxford on 21 July 1998.

15.

Even though Columbus was a European, and his first voyage predated the American revolution by nearly 300 years, he is revered by many as the first American hero. The nation's capital is named in his honour, as are several cities, streets, parks and schools including one of the country's oldest and most prestigious universities. [His birthday is an annual holiday across the United States.] (Barbara Ransby, 'Columbus and the making of historical myth', in Dyson, *Columbus*, pp.79–83)

16. For a contemporary account of slavery and the massacres of Native Americans by Spaniards, see Bartolome De Las Casa, *A Short History of the Destruction of the Indies*, translated by Nigel Griffin, London, 1992.
17. Matthew Carr, 'Spain: the day of the race', *Race and Class*, 33, 3, p.89.
18. The Hispano-Roman peoples of Spain were 'in fact more accomplices than conquered' and supported the Muslim factor. The emergence of Spanish as the new language, largely due to the Muslim factor, and the salience of the Iberian Christians in the Arab and Berber armies, allowed quite a bit of interaction among these peoples. See Gomez, 'Moorish Spain', p.226.
19. It reminds one of the evolution of Muslim communities in Western Europe and North America in the post-Second Word War years, when the erstwhile anti-Jewish cynicism has turned against Muslims.
20. It has been suggested that Roderick may have seduced Julian's beautiful daughter, who had been sent to Toledo for higher education.
21. According to some traditions, he landed at Tarifa, which again has a resemblance to his name.
22. Muhammad Iqbal (1875–1938), in his moving poetic style, celebrated the event in one of his Persian poems, in which Tariq is shown as the epitome of Islamic dynamism. To his sceptical companions, Tariq said that they were far away from their homes and there was no going back as from now on Spain was to be their new home.
23. There are all kinds of stories about the treatment meted out to Musa and Tariq in Damascus, where they are reputed to have died in penury. A similar fate is attributed to Muhammad bin Qasim, the Ummayyid conqueror of Sindh, who had been recalled from the Punjab. Such stories reflect the anguish and grief of some contemporary Muslim historians, who felt that by halting the conquests, Caliph Sulayman had done a major disservice to Islam.
24. It is not clear how many people paid poll tax. To Sir Montgomery Watt, Muslims did not force conversion on local people for financial reasons, but if such converts volunteered to join the army they were encouraged. See W. Montgomery Watt, *A History of Muslim Spain*, Edinburgh, 1996 (reprint), p.20.
25. He is known as al-Dakhil: the entrant.
26. He was called Amir-ul Momineen Nasir ud Din-al Allah, meaning Leader of the Faithful and Helper of Allah's Religion.
27. Watt, *History of Muslim Spain*, p.68.
28.

We see in Cordoba under the caliphs not only the glory but also the inherent tragedy of Spanish Islam. Foreign to the Christians of the North, who were half-brothers by blood; foreign also to the peoples of the East, its brothers by race, culture and religion, the great kingdom of the South appears to us as an airy mirage, a blazing sun on a misplaced orbit, which as the poet ibn Hazm once said of himself, had the fault of rising in the West. (Gomez, 'Moorish Spain', p.229)

29. Carew, 'The end of Moorish enlightenment', p.14.
30. On the other hand, even several centuries later, great writers like Cervantes had to suffer in penury as the state and church lacked any interest in literary pursuits: 'With the end of the Moorish power, the Spanish not only went on a book-burning spree, they also tried to erase every vestige of Moorish cultural influence from their consciousness.' *Ibid.*, pp.5–6.
31. Literally, it meant the one who gained victory through God's assistance. As a chamberlain, in 981, Mansur moved the offices of the caliphate from Cordoba's al-Cazar to a new palace at Madinat al-Zahara so as to isolate the young caliph from outside contacts.
32. Literally 'those who come back'. They were inspired by a Sufi, ibn Yasin.
33. For a comprehensive account, see Anwar G. Chejne, *Muslim Spain: its History and Culture*, Minneapolis, 1974.
34. The emirate under the Moravids offered its loyalty to the Abbasid caliph in Baghdad and thus marked the end of a separate Spanish caliphate.
35. 'Furthermore, it is a poignant elegy for Moorish Andalusia, a remarkable work of autobiography, an incisive evocation of Cordoba under the Umayyads, and the Middle Ages' finest collection of erotic stories.' Gomez, 'Moorish Spain', p.230.
36. *Ibid.*, pp.233–4.
37. Carew, 'The end of Moorish enlightenment', p.14.
38. Chejne, *Muslim Spain*, pp.329–33.

3 MUSLIMS IN SPAIN: BEGINNING OF AN END

1. The three South Asian writers were born in British India and debated the issue of Muslim identity during the period of decline and morass. Iqbal's philosophical writings and poetic compositions, Sharrar's novel and plays and several of Hejazi's novels alerted millions of Muslims in India and elsewhere to the Muslim saga in Spain. Hejazi was the youngest of the three and died in Rawalpindi in the 1990s. Kabbani, an eminent Syrian writer and diplomat, had served in Spain and wrote moving and nostalgic poetry.
2. The cathedral took a little more than a century to be completed (1402–1506) and, to date, remains the largest cathedral in the world, covering a total area of 11,520 square metres. Subsequent additions have been made by successive dynasties.
3. The Columbian papers, including the log books, maps and other antiques are housed in Lonja, a separate and magnificent building located across from the cathedral.
4. King Carlos (Charles) V added balconies and royal portraits to commemorate his marriage to Isabel of Portugal but they look totally out of place. Adjoining this magnificent room is a long dining hall and a small apartment built by Philip II.

5. Another massive building not far from the Alcazar, the Fabrica de Tabacos, flourished as a result of trade with the colonies. Riches acquired from the Native Americans and expensive crops like tobacco were stored here by scores of workers before their onward delivery elsewhere. Seville was the earliest centre of the Spanish colonial empire and this building occupied a central position especially in the tobacco trade. Now it is used as the old campus for Seville University and resounds with all kinds of languages and accents.

6. The 135-kilometre route between Seville and Cordoba is scattered with small hilltop villages built around forts and churches. An alternative and more interesting route from Seville, further to the south, passes through Carmona, an old Roman town with a significant Muslim past. At a distance of 30 kilometres from Seville, the picturesque Carmona retains an early imitation of the Giralda, visible from afar.

7. Following its categorisation by UNESCO as an international monument in the early 1970s, several arches facing the courtyard were reopened for the first time since their closure soon after the Reconquest. Latticed wooden windows made of Canadian cedar and special glass have been inserted to provide enough light inside.

8. A walk around the outer wall shows a number of gateways with decorative white and red arches and Kufic calligraphy. Above the Gate of St Stephen – renamed from the original during the Inquisition – one can still see the earliest Quranic inscriptions, dating back to the era of Abdar Rahman II.

9. Charles I of Spain and V of Germany, or Carlos V, the Holy Roman Emperor, had himself been responsible for the destruction of a number of Moorish buildings in Seville and inside the Alhambra. His disgust only shows the extent of the harm done to the original building during the Inquisition. The emperor had earlier given permission to the bishop of Toledo for the construction of the grand chapel within the mosque, but on seeing the demolition work he felt dismayed. He personally saw the sorry state of affairs while on his way to Seville to marry his cousin, Dona Isabel of Portugal.

10. Ferdinand and Isabella built a new Alcazar a little further to the west. Its Arabian style gardens, unlike those of Seville's, are elaborate and refreshing.

11. A unique feature of this part of Cordoba is a historic synagogue at 18 Calle Maimonides, one of the three earliest synagogues in Spain, the other two being in Toledo. It is a small building dating from 1316 and retains excellent stucco work. During the expulsions, the synagogue suffered immensely but has been recently restored, along with its women's gallery. By its entrance there is a turbaned statue of Maimonides, the great philosopher.

12. V. G. Kiernan (translator) *Poems from Iqbal*, Karachi, 1999, pp.96–100.

13. Early morning affords a fragrant coolness emanating from scores of citrus trees in the courtyard. It is said that, amongst several other new crops, oranges were introduced into Spain by Muslims.

14. One encounters several stories of people being taken away for offering prayers after being refused permission to do so. This practice is clearly dis-

criminatory since Christians can pray in the cathedral whereas Muslims are banned from praying in the mosque. The laws of the European Union forbid any kind of discrimination based on race or religion, but it appears that the Spanish authorities are still maintaining the status quo until someone challenges them in the higher courts.

15. It is advisable to wait until a tourist party is allowed inside the enclosure and the lights are turned on. The guides can be quite rude, perhaps due to their protective attitude or because they do not like inquisitive tourists. In any case, the best way is to follow some useful and comprehensive guide rather than one of the chattering guides whose information may not be entirely true besides being exotic and partisan.

16. In the old town there are two newer buildings belonging to the local Muslim community. One of them was locked but the other, a small and beautiful mosque just a few minutes walk to the north of the Cordoba Mosque, was in use. Its imam, a Spanish Muslim, was enthused to see fellow Muslims visiting his well-designed mosque.

17. Note the word 'Ahmar' in his name!

18. The other end of the room has an oratory, next to several niches once used for prayers. The sultan would receive his royal guests in the Mexuar before taking them into the Serallo. The lower margins of the Mexuar's walls are decorated with floral and colourful tiles, something which one finds in almost every building dating from the Muslim and Mudejar era, and which has been revived in recent times due to its unique Spanish roots. The main border is in blue and white tiles with circular, sun-like circles connected with their smaller counterparts, all falling in symmetrical lines and angles. The tiled border does not reach all the way to the floor, leaving a few inches in between to allow the necessary space for carpets. The revival of these tiled margins and motifs in the twentieth century in Spanish private homes, galleries, gift shops and some official buildings is a gradual yet unstated recognition of the indigenousness of Spanish Islamic arts. The Muslim design of rooms with corridors around an open courtyard afforded proper circulation of the air especially during the hot summer. The fountains, flowers and ventilators all added to the cooling effect of these multi-storey houses. In recent years, such a traditional architecture has been shunned all across the Muslim world for more modernist, bungalow-style structures without a central compound.

19. The two most exquisite rooms facing each other across the courtyard are respectively called the Hall of the Abu Cerraj and the Hall of Two Sisters. The former is the larger of the two with an immensely beautiful ceiling of sixteen sides, each supported by stalactite vaulting. Its ornamentation reflects the sunlight beaming through windows in the dome. The dome, like the columnades, is itself a piece of great artistic refinement and lies in a unique symmetry with the two-columned or three-columned arches. The dome is designed like a star, with eight sharp angles each housing two windows to allow sufficient light into this historic room. The ornate work on the ceiling of the dome and its several vaults appears like a honeycomb. Light is also reflected in the fountain and its stained bowl, located in the centre. It is said that the stains on the marble bowl are, in fact, the blood marks of the princes from the

Abu Cerraj tribe, who were murdered by Abul Hasan, the father of Boabdil. Sultan Abul Hasan suspected the chief of the Cerraj of being in love with his favourite princess, Soraiya. This tragic story from the twilight hours of Nasirid rule, mingled with the sad end of the kingdom itself, leaves a very melancholy feeling.

20. After seeing so much art and absorbing Nasirid history, with the numerous tragic stories attached to the rooms in this magnificent palace, one is bound to feel quite heavy at heart. The beauty, symmetry and exquisite originality of these empty buildings, which once resounded with poetry and romance, and the traumatic disappearance of their patrons, leaving the rooms barren and mute, create a deep sense of awe and gloom.

21. Generalife is the Spanish version of *Gennatal Arif*, meaning garden of architects as well as garden of the pious.

22. Bordered by cypresses and myrtle bushes, here lies the Patio de los Cipreses, where Sorayia was rumoured to meet her lover, Hamid, the chief of the Banu Cerraj, who was killed by Boabdil's vengeful father. Ibn Zamrak eternalised the gardens in his poetry by describing their diversity, their beauty and the various joyful sports held here during the different seasons. Roses, bougainvillea, geraniums, carnations, jasmine, vines and citrus trees and several other subtropical plants adorn the Generalife, with its unique bowers and countless rows of flower beds.

23. It appears that the original college was largely demolished to build the cathedral, and a new outer wall, with a rather blatant mix of colours, was added. The caravanserai, the old silk bazaar and the Madrassa must have been the busiest commercial and educational areas of Old Granada – the Moorish Alcaiceria – before the Inquisition superimposed its own cultural and structural choices.

24. Just behind the Royal Palace and adjacent to the palace of Charles V is this monastery which was originally a palace itself. Soon after her death, Isabella's body was kept here until, according to her wishes, the new cathedral was built by Ferdinand at its present site.

25. Within the chapel itself the crown, sceptre and coffer of Isabella and the sword of Ferdinand are on general display. Many pieces of her jewellery and diamonds, originally robbed from the Nasirids, were used to sponsor Columbian campaigns. Basically, this grand Royal Chapel is the mausoleum of the Conquering Couple whose bodies lie in the plain crypt, accessible by stairs. The bodies of Ferdinand, Isabella, their daughter Joanna 'the Mad' and her husband, Felipe 'the Handsome', and of the child prince, Michael, are placed in lead coffins in the crypt. Above them is a grand monument built under the orders of their grandson, Charles V, in the form of sculpted effigies of these four Catholic monarchs, which remains barricaded by iron grills. Isabella, before her death in 1504, had willed for an eternal candle by her coffin, which has now been replaced by an electric bulb. Ferdinand died on 23 January 1516 and his body was taken to lie in the monastery at the Alhambra. On 10 November 1521, the remains of both bodies were brought to the Royal Chapel, which is of Toledan style, buttressed by balustrades and decorative pinnacles. The big windows, steep spires and gargoyles

contribute to the Gothic characteristics of the chapel, whose interior is heavily gilded to suit the great Reconquest. In the portrait gallery of the chapel, amongst a rare collection, a portrait by Botticelli called Oracion del Huerto depicts three saints sleeping on the grass, while Christ is shown receiving the Holy Spirit. Work on the cathedral began in 1521 and went on, with long intermissions, until the eighteenth century.

26. The last Nasirid sultan is not forgotten in Granada. The reproductions of Pradilla's famous painting abound everywhere. In addition, a lane named after him branches off the Reyes Catolicos right across from the city and reaches all the way to Plaza Bib Rambla, once an Arabian structure but now a busy plaza. In addition, there is a bar, as one understands, in Granada named after the defeated sultan.

27. One of the earliest scholars to have duly recognised the literary and intellectual contributions of Muslims in the emergence of the Spanish language, its romantic literature and the richness of Spanish poetry under the Moors, was Julian Ribera. He attributed the evolution of 'Romance Vernacular literature' to the Muslim influence in Andalusia. His researches, followed by those of S.M. Stern and Emilio Garcia Gomez, have resulted

> in disinterring over fifty examples of the verse form known as the *kharja*. These are short passages in Romance, coming at the end of longer Hebrew or Arab poems called *muwashshahs*. As they are the oldest poetic texts in any vernacular language in Europe, their discovery entirely reorientated the investigation of the origins of lyric poetry in the Romance literature. (Emilio Garcia Gomez, 'Moorish Spain', in Bernard Lewis (ed.), *The World of Islam*, London, 1997, p.228)

28. For instance, a prominent university built in recent times, Stanford in California, has borrowed explicit Moorish style in its arcades, corridors and columnades.

29. Samuel Levi, a well-known Jewish financier, was a close advisor of Pedro the Cruel, who subsequently murdered the former to acquire his wealth. Eventually, Jews and Muslims were either banished from Toledo or were forcibly converted to Christianity.

30. Its Renaissance-style gate, impressive lecture halls and corridors, and facade covered by medallions and emblems, make it a unique architectural monument. Thanks to a family of architects in the seventeenth and eighteenth centuries, this beautiful town became known for the Churrigueresque movement in neo-classicism. The name is derived from Jose Churriguera (1665–1723), the doyen of this family of architects, known for flamboyant design.

31. Galicia is not so poor as some other regions of Spain, though in the past, as in Ireland, famines visited the area quite frequently. Economic factors combined with geographic reality created a tradition of seafaring among these people, who have migrated to South America in large numbers: it is said that there are more Gallegos in Buenos Aires than in Galicia itself. A conservative region dominated by the local feudal and religious hierarchies, Galicia has provided Spain with an unending supply of

right-wing leaders, including Francisco Franco and Manuel Frago, the leader of the ultra-right party, Partido Popular.

32. There are all kinds of amusing stories about the pilgrims and the people they came across. The earliest tourist guide about this route was written by a French monk, Aymery Picaud, who recorded all the watering and sheltering places along the route. He gave an account of the bizarre sexual habits of the Navarese Basques 'who exposed themselves when excited, and protected their mules from their neighbours with chastity belts'. Mark Ellingham and John Fisher, *Spain: The Rough Guide*, London, 1997, p.468. Such stories may be true but could also have arisen as ethnocentric satire.

33. In recent times, hikers, bikers and adventurers have joined the pilgrims in traversing the valleys, hilly terrain and plains to reach Santiago.

34. Now, they have become some of Europe's most cherished Mediterranean resorts.

35. Various such towns hold their annual festivals to mark Christian victories over Muslims. For instance, the first Monday of May in Jaca is reserved for commemorating the Battle of Vitoria fought against the Muslims and is characterised by folklorist events and processions.

36. Since 1987, it has housed the provincial parliament.

37. A thankful city has adored its heroes by dedicating its museums to Pablo Picasso, Joan Miro and Antoni Tapies. Its Olympic Village, the famous Ramblas and the Mediterranean white beaches make it a unique place, though its prosperity is not equitably distributed. The natives prefer to identify themselves as Catalonians and do not appreciate being bundled up with the rest of the Spaniards.

4 ISLAM AND BRITAIN: OLD CULTURES, ODD ENCOUNTERS

1. One cannot be dismissive towards a persuasive thesis that the future Muslim intellectual renaissance – long predicted by Muslim reformers such as Jamal ud-Din al-Afghani, Muhammad Abduh, Syed Ahmed Khan, Ameer Ali and Muhammad Iqbal – may come about in the West. The ever-increasing networks among Muslim intellectuals now based in the West are positive indicators of a growing Muslim debate on the issues of identity, still an ideal within the Muslim world itself. Through the intermingling of ethno-national and religious identities within an interdependent Europe, a broader *Muslim* identity seems to be slowly evolving, away from the erstwhile statist and societal strictures. For a similar interesting perspective, see Olivier Roy, 'Muslims in Europe: from ethnic identity to religious recasting', ISIM's *Newsletter*, 5, June 2000, pp.1 and 29.

2. The British media – both broadsheets and tabloid press – carry extensive coverage of these groups, occasionally displaying a little exaggeration. For a serious, first-hand and more balanced view, see Adam LeBor, *A Heart Turned East: Among the Muslims of Europe and America*, London, 1997, pp.98–156. Hussain and Benazir Bhutto, to several analysts, may be outlaws from their own homeland, but there are many other individu-

als who have sought refuge in the United Kingdom from the persecution of their antagonists.

3. Some of them espouse Pan-Islamic agendas and through a rather crude
and exclusivist campaign only cause serious reactions. For instance, in
the early 1990s, Hizbal Tahrir's harassment of Muslim women students
worried several British campuses, which eventually banned the
movement. In the late 1990s, it appeared to be on the wane, though in
2001–02, its splinter group al-Muhajiroon, led by Omar al-Bakri, a Syrian
cleric, gained some publicity. The Jama'at-i-Islami, Tablighi Jama'at and
the Iraqi Shia elements, as well as various Afghan groups and several
other religio-political parties from the Muslim world, maintain their own
offices and networks across Britain. Some of the leading Arabic, Urdu,
Turkish and even English newspapers or weeklies are published from
London, as well as several television channels carrying religious, cultural
and some political programmes. These channels and email facilities have
already evolved into the most effective system of networking.

4. For more on her, see Benazir Bhutto, *Daughter of the East*, London, 1989.
Since her conviction by a superior court in April 1999 on corruption
charges Bhutto has opted to stay on in the safety of Britain. Some of the
charges against her were dropped two years later following the revelations of corrupt practices of the judges involved in the cases.

5. Taking Pakistan as a case study, I have discussed this in greater detail in
my recent book. See Iftikhar H. Malik, *Islam, Nationalism and the West:
Issues of Identity in Pakistan*, Oxford, 1999.

6. Many recent researches show that Islam did not venture to displace Christianity from the Middle East and North Africa. Commonalities in
language, ethnicity and culture, accompanied by the more tolerant
nature of Islamic polities during the caliphates, did not circumscribe the
thriving Christian societies of the Middle East. Christian places of
worship, houses, markets and other such buildings were not demolished
nor were Christians compelled to choose between Islam and Christianity. On the contrary, they received fully fledged religio-cultural freedom
within a stable political environment. Simultaneously, Muslims learnt
about the Greek and Roman heritage, which allowed a greater intellectual interchange leading to the preservation of antiquity, besides various
radical intellectual and philosophical innovations. It is true that some
ecclesiastic enthusiasts tried to hype up a Muslim threat besides attacking
Islam's doctrinal and historical evolution, yet the common populace
remained at ease with the Muslim factor. The eventual popularisation
of Islam in these regions was largely due to several dynamics operating
quite autonomously of the Muslim political establishment. Even
centuries later, the existence of sizeable non-Muslim communities across
the Middle East, the Near East, Iberia and South Asia was due more often
to a continued policy of tolerance and coexistence. For a pertinent perspective, see Norman Daniel, *Islam and the West*, Oxford, 2000.

7. Ziauddin Sardar, *Orientalism*, London, 2000, p.2.

8. This is supposed to be the surviving remnant of 'the most lurid of the
accounts of Urban's speech'. Quoted in Terry Jones and Alan Ereira,
Crusades (based on the BBC Series), London, 1994, pp.10–11.

9. *Ibid.*, p.2.
10. Quoted in *ibid.*, p.52.
11. For more on the Crusades, see Jean Richard, *The Crusades, c.1071–c.1291*, translated by Jean Birrell, Cambridge, 1999; Christoph T. Maier, *Crusade Propaganda and Ideology: Model Sermons for the Preaching of the Cross*, Cambridge, 2000. The first volume is a useful text on the history and the events of the two centuries of warfare whereas the second is based on contemporary sermons used for propaganda purposes.
12. Maxime Rodinson, *Europe and the Mystique of Islam*, London, 1988.
13. Slavery, in recent decades and especially in the United States, has invoked several serious studies in reference to religious, racial, economic, political and intellectual denominators. For a useful overview, see Peter J. Parish, *Slavery*, Keele, 1992 and Winthrop Jordan, *The White Man's Burden: Historical Origins of Racism in the United States*, New York, 1971.
14. Contrary to expectations during the nationalist struggles, the post-colonial realities in several countries are bleak reminders of underdevelopment, elitist monopolies and a growing gap between North and South. The top 20 per cent of humankind now holds 86 per cent of the world's wealth whereas the bottom 20 per cent accounts for only 1.3 per cent. The North–South differential was about 30:1 in 1965, and is now 70:1 and rising. 'The IMF-based liberalism was causing more frustration and even mass suicides.' Based on an Amnesty lecture by Susan George at Oxford, reproduced in Chris Miller, 'The Price of Freedom', *Oxford Today: The University Magazine*, Vol. 11, No. 3, 1999, pp.12–13.
15. R. W. Southern, *The Making of the Middle Ages*, London, 1953, pp.230–1.
16. Bede, *A History of the English Church and People*, Harmondsworth, 1968, p.330.
17. Orcanes, the Turkish king, refers to 'God and his friend Mahomet' and is able to share respect for both Christ and Mohammad after a victory:

> And Christ or Mahomet hath been my friend ...
> ... in my thoughts shall Christ be honoured,
> Not doing Mahomet an injury
> Whose power had share in this our victory.
> (Orcanes in *Tamburlaine*, Part II, 2, 3, 11, 33–5)

18. Joseph Pitts, *A True and Faithful Account of the Religion and Manners of the Mahommetans in which is a particular Relation of their Pilgrimage to Mecca* (London, 1704), as quoted in Nabil Matar, *Islam in Britain, 1558–1685*, Cambridge, 1998, p.1. Pitts' journey has been further studied in Zahra Freeth and H.V.F. Winstone, *Explorers of Arabia: From the Renaissance to the End of the Victorian Era*, London, 1978.
19. Muslims looked at the British as Nazarenes (Christians) who had gone astray from monotheism by worshipping icons. Such icons, to the Muslims, symbolised a salience of paganism over the *Islamic* origins of Christianity.
20. For some of these directives aimed at pleasing Muslims, see William Biddulph in *Purchas His Pilgrimes*, VIII, p.292 and, Sir E. Denison Ross (ed.), *Sir Anthony Shirley and his Persian Adventure*, London, 1933, p.184.
21. Quoted in Matar, *Islam in Britain*, p.7.

22. *Ibid.*, p.9.
23. Many scholars have commented on the merits and demerits of the system. To some, it was a brutal way of separating Balkan Christian children from their parents, while to others it meant being catapulted into the higher rungs of the Ottoman administration, bringing status and prosperity.
24. About 2,000 wives petitioned the king and the Parliament in 1626 for the release of their spouses who, according to them, had been forced to convert. *Ibid.*, p.27.
25. Not to talk of cities like Buda and Belgrade; even Constantinople remained overwhelmingly Christian until the late nineteenth century. It was only following the massive expulsions from Bulgaria and Greece that the demography of the Ottoman capital changed dramatically. For further details, see Philip Mansel, *Constantinople: City of World's Desire*, London, 1995; also on tolerance from a contemporary account, see Sonia P. Anderson, *An English Consul in Turkey: Paul Rycaut at Smyrna, 1667–1678*, Oxford, 1989.
26. Several English converts were also noticed by the British consuls in Constantinople. In addition, there were reports of occasional conversions from amongst the employees of the British East India Company. See Matar, *Islam in Britain*, pp.35–6.
27. Quoted in John B. Wolf, *The Barbary Coast: Algeria Under the Turks: 1500 to 1830*, New York, 1979, p.237, as reproduced in *ibid.*, p.37.
28. One such emissary form Morocco was Alkaid Jaurar bin Abdella, who in his tour of London in September 1637 impressed everyone with his piety and humility. He was a Portuguese convert.
29. *Ibid.*, pp. 66–8.
30. Cotton Mather, *A Pastoral Letter to the English Captives in Africa from New England*, Boston, 1698, as mentioned in *ibid.*, p.81. Earlier, in 1680, George Fox, the Quaker, read Ross's translation and quoted various sections from it.
31. Oliver Cromwell and his Secretary showed their knowledge of the centrality of the Quran in the Islamic faith in their correspondence with the Moroccan kings.
32. Matar, p.110.
33. She herself was a Venetian convert to Islam and corresponded with the queen often applying Christian symbolism.
34. David B. Quinn, *Explorers and Colonies: America, 1500–1625*, London, 1990, pp.197–205, as quoted in Matar, p.127.
35. The Quakers, unlike the Inquisition and some of the other missionary groups, never declared Muslims to be 'infidels', but instead acknowledged the commonalities between Islam and Christianity.
36. Matar, pp.173, 175.
37. Still, there were intellectuals like Dr Johnson during the eighteenth century who viewed Islam ('Mohametanism') and Christianity as the only civilised forces in the world. Quoted in Albert Hourani, *Islam in European Thought*, Cambridge, 1990, p.11.
38. Edward Said, *Orientalism*, London, 2003 (see the latest edition with a new foreword).

39. Analysts and activists like Franz Fanon, Aime Cesaire, al-Afghani, Muhammad Iqbal, Mahatma Gandhi, Leopold Senghor, Nehru, Jinnah, Malcolm X, Martin Luther King Jr and Nelson Mandela struggled in their own ways for a greater empowerment of their communities. Even latter-day activists like Khomeini used Western symbols and strategies to gain political power. Edward Said, Ashis Nandy, Andre Frank and Eqbal Ahmad are some of those most recent scholars for whom colonialism has been much more than a mere political subjugation.

40. A useful comparison with these manifestations of Political Islam is made by Professor Khalid B. Sayeed when he reviews policies in Saudi Arabia, Pakistan and Iran. See his *Western Dominance and Political Islam: Challenge and Response*, Albany, 1995. Khomeinism has been seen as a movement within the rubrics of modernity: see Abdarrahmanian, *Khomeinism*, Albany, 1994. Kemalism and Khomeinism, however, are still two different strands of ideologies aimed at similar goals: Bobby Sayyid, *A Fundamental Fear: Eurocentrism and the Emergence of Islamism*, London, 1997.

41. See Edward Said, *Culture and Imperialism*, London, 1994; John M. MacKenzie, *Orientalism: History, Theory and the Arts*, Manchester, 1996; *Propaganda and Empire: The Manipulation of British Public Opinion, 1880–1960*, Manchester, 1984; and (ed.) *Popular Imperialism and the Military, 1850–1950*, Manchester, 1992.

42. Various Muslim papers and magazines in the United Kingdom, such as the *Muslim News*, the *Jang, Impact, Dialogue, Al-Hayat, Sharqal Ausat* and *Q Magazine*, have frequently published accounts of racist attacks, media-led denigration and desecration of Muslim cemeteries. Such incidents of Muslim-bashing are in addition to the discrimination and global indifference meted out to Muslim *fundamentalists*. As seen in the post-Rushdie era and during the Bosnian tragedy, and especially after the terrorist attacks on the United States in 2001, the very equation of Islam with fundamentalism has become a global cliche. For a useful commentary, see Fred Halliday, *Islam and the Myth of Confrontation*, London, 1996.

43. The Runnymede Trust's Report – a pioneering document – is discussed in a separate section.

44. Such efforts cover almost the entire Muslim world as more and more researches on Muslim modernists continue to be undertaken.

45. The debate is not just confined to the Muslim elite; it has engaged all kinds of communities in the colonised regions. For instance, see Tapan Raychaudhuri, *Europe Reconsidered: Perceptions of the West in Nineteenth Century Bengal*, Delhi, 1988; also, Niall Ferguson, *Empire*, London, 2002.

46. Gulfishan Khan, *Indian Muslim Perceptions of the West during the Eighteenth Century*, Karachi, 1998. (The study is based on a doctoral research completed at Oxford and concentrates on six early Muslim intellectuals.)

47. For a relevant commentary, see Alain Grosrichard, *The Sultan's Court: European Fantasies of the East*, translated by Liz Heron, London, 1998.

48. Some of the leading Christian scholars on Islam include amongst others: Kenneth Craig, Montgomery Watt, Karen Armstrong and Michael Nazir Ali. On this subject, see Kate Zebiri, *Muslims and Christians Face to Face*, Oxford, 1997. The number of serious academic works on Islam, Muslim communities and countries run into hundreds of thousands. Similarly,

there are hundreds of works of fiction – several developed into movies – that offer specific images and stereotypes of Muslims. More recently, there has been a host of writings on Osama bin Laden, al-Qaeda and the Taleban, linking them with Islam and terrorism. These works have been crucial in fashioning Western perceptions and misconceptions about Islam.

49. For instance, Ziauddin Sardar, *Orientalism*, London, 1999; and with Merry W. Davies, *Distorted Imagination: Lessons from the Rushdie Affairs*, London, 1990.

50. The banner headline on the front page ran: 'Riots report blames police, ministers and communities', *Guardian*, 11 December 2001. Earlier, the Ouseley Report on ethnic communities in Bradford in July 2001 had highlighted similar socioeconomic causes. Ironically, the latter report appeared just a few days after the riots between the Asian youths and police, largely ignited by the BNP. For further details on the riots and reports, see <www.guardian.co.uk/race>.

51. The committee led by Ted Cantle, a senior executive from Nottingham, highlighted corrective measures such as common/mixed neighbourhoods, multiethnic schools, a new definition of citizenship and regenerative schemes at local and national levels. For details, see *Guardian*, 12 December 2001.

52. However, many Indians ended up in various British colonies long after the end of the slave trade and engaged as unskilled labourers (coolies) for various imperial projects. For more details, see Hugh Tinker, *A New Kind of Slavery*, London, 1974.

53. Sir Syed Ahmed Khan (1819–1898), the eminent Muslim modernist, founder of the Aligarh College and a prolific writer, visited Britain in the 1870s before embarking on his educational projects.

54. One of them was the Muslim Pathan woman, Naseeban, from the United Provinces (UP), who had made 22 voyages to Europe. She had been to Ireland, Britain, France, Portugal and several other countries and spoke English quite fluently. Sir Syed Ahmed Khan met her during his visit, as is briefly mentioned in his Urdu travelogue, *Musaafiran-i-London*. She was accompanying some Mrs Cooper, and Sir Syed found her life story 'no less a wonder than the Suez Canal'. For details, see Hasan Abidi, 'The Muslim woman voyager', *Dawn Magazine*, 30 December 2001. Also, Rozina Visram, *Asians in Britain: 400 Years of History*, London, 2002.

55. Gandhi and Gokhale came from Western India and belonged to Hindu notable families, whereas Nehru, a Kashmiri Pandit, was from Allahabad, UP. The Nehrus ran a very successful law practice and participated in national politics. Jawaharlal Nehru's father, Motilal, was an active member and president of the Indian National Congress, a party itself established in 1885. Gokhale was a moderate politician who deeply believed in constitutional politics; following his demise in 1915 the Congress came under the control of radicals, until Gandhi turned it into a mass movement. Mahatma Gandhi's charisma and philosophy brought masses into the Congress and transformed the lives of millions, including that of the aristocratic Jawaharlal Nehru.

56. Allama Muhammad Iqbal (1875–1938), the pre-eminent Muslim poet of his time, was born in Sialkot and came to Lahore to study. His higher

education took him to Cambridge, Heidelberg and Munich, where he studied Western and Islamic philosophies. He is credited with advocating an overdue Islamic intellectual renaissance and has effectively influenced generations of Islamic modernists.

57. Muhammad Ali Johar, a Muslim from the UP, studied at Oxford's Lincoln College in the 1890s and established a society of South Asian students, called Majlis. On his return to India, he became a political activist and spearheaded a high-profile campaign during the second decade of the twentieth century. Known as the Khilafat Movement, the campaign tried to protect the Ottoman caliphate from complete annihilation following the Turkish defeat in the war. His brother Ali (Shaukat Ali), their mother (Bi Amma) and hundreds of their supporters were imprisoned for staging a boycott of the Raj, until the movement itself fizzled out due to Kemalism. Ali, along with Iqbal, Jinnah and several other Indian leaders, came to London to participate in parleys with the British officials and on his return in 1931 died in Jerusalem. He was buried there. A fiery orator and writer, Muhammad Ali and his brother Shaukat Ali are known as the Ali Brothers in Indian Muslim history.

58. M.A. Jinnah (1876–1948), also known as the Quaid-i-Azam (the Great Leader), was born in Karachi and studied in London before going back to Bombay to practise law, Eventually he became the leader of the All-India Muslim League (AIML), a moderate Muslim party established in Dhaka in 1906. A constitutionalist to his core, like his mentor Gokhale, Jinnah struggled for an independent state of Pakistan.

59. He was the first Asian to be elected, in 1893, to the House of Commons as the member for Finchley. Jinnah and several other Indian students played critical roles in his election campaign. He came from the Bombay-based Parsi community and through his moderate political activism fired many expatriate Indians to struggle against the Raj.

60. Syed Ameer Ali, a Muslim jurist from Bengal, was deeply disturbed by the misrepresentations of Islam by missionaries and Orientalists. He wrote two pioneering works on Islamic history: *The Spirit of Islam* and *A Short History of the Saracens*. Through his scholarly publications and other such activities he not only counteracted the Orientalist onslaught on Islam, but was equally committed to imparting a greater self-confidence to Muslims in India and elsewhere. He eventually settled in London, where he carried on with his socio-intellectual activities and in 1908 established the London branch of the AIML. He was actively involved in sponsoring various functions of the Muslim Literary Society, which was linked with the Woking Mosque. Ameer Ali died in London in 1928.

61. The author of several books on the future of Muslims in British India, Ali originally came to Cambridge as a student from the British Punjab. In the 1930s and 1940s, he wrote and campaigned for Islamic homelands in India. After the creation of Pakistan, he visited the country, but came back disillusioned and settled in Cambridge where he soon died of diabetes. In one of his works, in 1933, Ali coined the term 'Pakistan' for the Muslim majority areas in India. Every year many Pakistani Muslims visit his grave in Cambridge, duly accrediting this scholar-activist for advocating the case of Muslim political sovereignty.

62. A prominent Muslim ICS (Indian Civil Servant), originally from Surat in western India, Ali decided to live in England after his retirement. In between, on the suggestion of Allama Iqbal, he came to Lahore to head the Islamia College and to complete his English translation of the Quran. Ali lived in London and died in sad circumstances in the early 1950s. Despite the fact that his translation remains the most widely read across the world, there has been, compared with some of his other contemporaries, very little research on Yusuf Ali. For a recent biography, see M.A. Sherif, *Searching for Solace: A Biography of Abdullah Yusuf Ali, Interpreter of the Qur'an*, Kuala Lumpur, 1994.

63. For a historical and multi-channel relationship between the United Kingdom and Muslim South Asia, see Iftikhar H. Malik, *Islam, Nationalism and the West: Issues of Identity in Pakistan*, Oxford, 1999.

64. Fred Halliday, *Arabs in Exile: Yemeni Migrants in Urban Britain*, London, 1992, as quoted in Philip Lewis, *Islamic Britain: Religion, Politics and Identity among British Muslims*, London, 1994, p.11.

65. Lewis, *Islamic Britain*, pp.11–12. Also Peter Clark, *Marmaduke Pickthall, British Muslim*, London, 1986.

66. Lewis, *Islamic Britain*, p.13.

67. For more on this and related themes, see Rozina Visram, *Ayahs, Lascars and Princes: Indians in Britain, 1700–1947*, London, 1986.

68. A safe figure is around 1.8 million. For the demographic features and other important details on British Muslims, see *Guardian*, 17 June 2002.

69. Following the allocation of land for an Anglican cathedral in Cairo, King George VI donated this land for a central mosque in London. He opened the Islamic Centre in November 1944, though the campaign for building the mosque took several years and involved the ambassadors of several Muslim nations. Most of the money came from Saudi Arabia, which has a major say in the management of the Regent's Park Mosque. It was formally inaugurated in 1977 and offers library and other community services.

70. Bradford has the largest Pakistani/Azad Kashmiri population of any British town but Birmingham remains the largest Pakistani city and is only second to London if one includes all the boroughs making Greater London.

71. For a useful statistical, biographical and cultural profile of Muslims, see *Guardian*, 17, 18, 19 and 20 June 2002.

72. Even the many practising Muslims, true to self-justification, subscribe to Islam's growing popularity among Westerners.

73. Some enthusiastic converts themselves tend to exaggerate their numbers. For an interesting report, see Giles Whittell, 'A mecca for the middle class', *The Times*, 7 January 2002.

74. Madeleine Bunting, 'The other side of the veil', and Angelique Chrisafis, 'Under siege', *Guardian Magazine*, 8 December 2001. Channel 4's series on Islam, shown in March 2002 and February 2003, offered detailed and interesting information highlighting the post-September anxieties as well as the issues of political and economic alienation.

75. Such a phenomenon is not confined to the United Kingdom; all across the Continent, inter-party contests have sought to focus on immigration

as a vote-catching strategy. In more recent years, Austria, France, Switzerland and Australia have witnessed demands for restricting immigration. In early 2000, Chancellor Schroeder of Germany inflamed various groups in his country by announcing his interest in sponsoring several thousand Indian IT specialists. In Australia, the Liberal Party won a third term by hyping up anti-refugee sentiments.

76. For a useful background, see John Solomos, *Race and Racism in Britain*, London, 1994.

77. 'Curry's flavour' (editorial), *The Times*, 26 February 2000.

78. E. Cashmore, *The Black Culture Industry*, London, 1997; and, E. Copley, *Not so Green and Pleasant Britain for Minorities*, London, 2001.

79. Jorgen Nielsen, *Muslims in Western Europe*, Edinburgh, 1992, p.42.

80. For details, see 'Race in Britain – 2001', *Observer*, 25 November 2001. The next census results are due in 2002; these may show a slight increase in the ethnic population with a larger ratio of British-born citizens. In addition, one may be able to acquire more exact figures on religious categories.

81. Claire Sanders, 'Minorities are better educated than peers'. *Times Higher Education Supplement*, 23 November 2001. (The report is illustrated with a statistical graph.)

82. For instance, in education, minority students and teachers have often complained of discrimination at various levels. For details, see 'Race myopia in universities', *Times Higher Education Supplement*, 13 July 2001.

83. According to Nielsen, there were 18 mosques in the UK in 1966; 81 in 1974; 314 in 1985 and 452 in 1990. Nielsen, *Muslims in Western Europe*, p.45. However, one sees a steady growth in the number of mosques in recent years to cater to the needs of various linguistic and doctrinal groups, office workers and students all across Britain. One cannot be certain about the exact number. Some British Muslim intellectuals are disturbed with this mushrooming of mosques, especially amongst various sects or linguistic groups, which, to them, may further fragment the community. However, newer mosques are multifunctional, with lecture rooms, computer centres, morgues and some common meeting or residential facilities. Some of the mosques, such as those in Edinburgh, Birmingham and London, reflect a unique architectural synthesis to match the surrounding buildings. The Oxford Centre for Islamic Studies, aimed at conducting research on the Islamic world, in its effort to build a multi-purpose centre, faced severe difficulties largely due to the objections of a small section of the local community who had nefariously exaggerated the presence of minarets amongst the spires. The matter went all the way to the deputy prime minister, John Prescott, who in early 2000 finally gave permission for its construction.

84. Most of these *madrassas* are attached to mosques, as the prayer halls are used for teaching Quranic knowledge to both boys and girls. However, there are fully fledged Muslim schools – one in Brent, opened by Yusuf Islam, and the other in Birmingham, the Hijra School. Unlike many religious schools run by Christian and Jewish organisations, Muslim schools were not allocated any official grants. In the late 1990s, however, these two schools were allocated annual grants.

85. The issue became linked with the performance of locally born Pakistani and Bangladeshi children at state schools. Ray Honeyford, the headmaster of a school in Bradford in the mid 1980s, accused these parents of not properly supporting their children in their homework. He made derogatory remarks with reference to their culture, and especially censored parents for sending their children back home, disrupting their education. Under public protest, he was made to withdraw his remarks, though the polarisation between the antiracist and racist groups turned into a long-drawn struggle. In 1985, after eighteen months of acrimonious exchanges, Honeyford sought early retirement thus bringing the episode to an amicable end. The post-1989 protests against Salman Rushdie equally pushed Muslims to organise themselves nationally over and above their regional and clannish divisions. The episode, however, drew undue attention – mostly negative – to Muslims, leading to further denigration of Islamic values. The events of 2001, the subsequent eavesdropping by the police and MI5, and the detention of a number of people dismayed the community to a major extent.

86. It was authoritatively suggested that the summer 2001 riots were caused by economic and social marginalisation of otherwise sensible British youths, who were immensely let down and even manhandled by the local institutions and police. There was a greater need for fresher and more dynamic policies, away from discrimination and hand-picked peer committees. For a pertinent account by an insider, see Manawar Jan-Khan, 'Bradford must face reality', *Guardian*, 12 July 2001; this viewpoint is corroborated in five letters in the same issue, appearing under the heading 'Why Asians have had enough'.

5 MUSLIMS IN BRITAIN: MULTICULTURALISM AND THE EMERGING DISCOURSE

1. While seeking stringent measures on detention, the Labour government tried to introduce legislation to outlaw incitement to religious hatred, but the initiative was voted down in the House of Lords in December 2001. Many critics felt that instead of merely outlawing such hatred there should be a fully fledged legislation outlawing discrimination of all kinds, including religious discrimination, as was noted by an analyst: 'The incitement to religious hatred offence is at best a sop and at worst an attack on the Muslim community.' Madeleine Bunting, 'The new anti-Semitism', *Guardian*, 3 December 2001.

2. During the 1990s, it was not uncommon to come across various secular and assimilated individuals who no longer felt qualms about their self-definition as Muslims. Some colleagues at British universities surprised the author with their rather sudden avowal of Muslimness.

3. This is not to deny that several extreme groups have used Islam to suit their narrowly defined and often obscurantist activities and have sadly reduced it to mere theology and theocracy. However, it is political marginalisation and economic adversity which, in fact, spawn such responses.

4. Ironically, while mourning the tragic civilian deaths in New York, the Western leaders conveniently forgot the massacre of more than 8,000 innocent Muslims in the UN-declared haven of Srebrenica in Bosnia in 1995. William Dalrymple, 'Scribes of the new racism', *Independent*, 25 September 2001.

5. For an interesting counter-view, see Vikram Dodd, 'Blunkett's blame game', *Guardian*, 11 December 2001.

6. For an interesting though not totally fair critique, see Stephen Chan, 'A left too lazy to look the "other" way', *Times Higher Education Supplement*, 7 December 2001.

7. The new census is to include categories such as religious identity. In earlier censuses, Jews and Sikhs were the only minority categories recorded.

8. At one level, they are becoming looser as the lingual factor is playing a crucial role. British Muslim children are becoming increasingly monolingual and more at ease in Britain than 'back home'. Arranged marriages are faltering as well, though there have been a number of cases (not confined to Muslims only) of forced marriages. However, through email and better travel facilities, the links may also be growing in a holistic way. Simultaneously, there is a fragmentation: for instance, children born to Azad Kashmiri parents define themselves as Kashmiris rather than being identified as Pakistanis whereas their counterparts from amongst the Pakistani, Bangladeshi or African backgrounds are interested in being identified as *Muslims*, British Muslims, or Muslim British.

9. This is not to suggest that the new generation is not interested in their ancestral countries; rather, in some cases, they have vocalised and radicalised their own views on issues such as Palestine, Kashmir and Chechnya. A critical study of newspapers and magazines – especially their English sections – highlights the concerns of the new generations and surprisingly they appear similar to those of the first generation. In some cases the adoption of popular culture through dress styles, music and food further solidifies intergenerational links, contrary to some of the hypotheses underlining the widening gap.

10. The communal socio-religious activities such as Eid Milad (the Prophet's birthday) and Muharram (the anniversary of the martyrdom of the Prophet's grandson) attract quite a few members of the younger generations. In addition, several young British Muslims, irrespective of their national background, are seen in the Tablighi (religious propagation) activities directed from the headquarters in Bury.

11. Such a comparison was made by Professor Ceri Peach, a geographer from the University of Oxford, in the early 1990s and, for a time, attracted some media and academic attention.

12. The term was initially introduced in the 1950s and 1960s by the Useems, professors at Michigan State University, and was subsequently applied in a number of studies. It acknowledges a persistent process of give-and-take through negotiations between two or amongst several cultures. In some cases, the cultures may be asymmetrical owing to their numerical, economic or territorial strength. For instance, immigrants may find the host culture stronger and more established, but may equally devise

strategies to negotiate with it viably. For further discussion on the theoretical aspects of the third culture, see Iftikhar H. Malik, *Pakistanis in
Michigan: A Study in Third Culture and Acculturation*, New York, 1989.

13. By that time Dundee had become the centre of the jute industry. Jute
was brought from Bengal, but the goods were manufactured in eastern
Scotland.

14. I am grateful to several individuals in Glasgow and Edinburgh for this
information. But I owe special gratitude to Mr Bashir Maan, the first-
ever Asian JP and councillor in Scotland, for his generosity. His own book
remains the most comprehensive and original study on this subject. See
Bashir Maan, *The New Scots: The Story of Asians in Scotland*, Edinburgh,
1992.

15. For an interesting study, see Barry Carr, 'Black Geordies', in Robert Colls
and Bill Lancaster (eds) *Geordies: Roots of Regionalism*, Edinburgh, 1992.

16. Despite the early much-repeated stories of scores of Muslim youths in
Afghanistan, only a few had been to that part of the world and five of
them ended up at the US detention centre in Cuba.

17. The massacre took place in a fort used by General Dostum, the local
warlord, when hundreds of Taleban and their foreign supporters were
reportedly torched by the CIA and other special agents. The official
version on CNN, and the Pentagon briefing by Defense Secretary Donald
Rumsfeld, simply attributed it to the usual hazards of warfare. For an
eyewitness account, see Luke Harding, 'Allies direct the death rites of
trapped Taliban fighters', *Guardian*, 27 November 2001; and, for a
critique, see Isabel Hilton, 'We too are responsible for the massacre at
Qala-i-Jhangi', *ibid.*, 29 November 2001. In June 2002, a documentary
introduced in Berlin by a former chair of the Amnesty International
showed first-hand accounts of organised massacres.

18. Some reports suggested that upward of 10,000 inhabitants of Kandahar
were killed through intense bombing by US aircraft. Sky TV report,
monitored in Oxford on 7 December 2001.

19. It was believed that there were quite a few Pushtun and non-Afghan
fighters with their families hiding in the caves in eastern Afghanistan,
who, for days, experienced heavy bombing. Some of them eventually
surrendered, to be further humiliated by the Alliance captors. A few of
them even preferred to be shot rather than being paraded before the
cameras. Most of the POWs were weak, wounded and exhausted and,
despite exaggerated accounts of the strength of their defences, they
presented very sorry figures. Subsequently, when hundreds of them were
flown to the US base in Cuba, the latter refused to classify them as POWs.
Sacks were put over their heads; their feet were chained and their hands
were tied to the seats. Some of them were even drugged on the 20-hour-
long flight. The ICRC and some British organisations raised concerns
over the human rights violations, which the US government routinely
dismissed. The US bombing on the high mountains of Tora Bora and
further south extended over months and caused severe geological
damage, besides starting fires all across the region, which was already
depleted of trees.

20. Seumas Milne, 'The innocent dead in a coward's war', *Guardian*, 20 December 2001.
21. A graffito on a mosque wall in South Shields stated: 'Avenge America: kill a Muslim today'. A young veiled Muslim girl in Swindon, England, was set upon by a group of youths who caused her head injuries; an Afghan taxi driver in London was paralysed after receiving a severe beating.
22. It was a headline in several dailies. See *Guardian*, 18 December 2001.
23. *Insight*, 4 February 1991. According to the Oxford English Dictionary, this was the first-ever printed use of the term. See Runnymede Trust, *Islamophobia: A Challenge for Us All*, (hereafter the *Report*) London, 1997, p.1.
24. Gordon Conway, Foreword, in *ibid.*, p.iii.
25. Quoted by John Esposito, *The Islamic Threat: Myth or Reality*, Oxford, 1992, in *ibid.*, p.5.
26. He compared the Quran to Hitler's *Mein Kampf* and observed that there is 'more blood and stupidity than glamour in the theocracy of the Sons of the prophet'. *Observer*, 27 September 1981. Though the term 'funda-mentalism' was itself coined in the USA in the late nineteenth century within the Protestant context, its first application to the Muslim world was by the *Middle East Journal* in 1957 and then it was Burgess who used it in the above-cited piece. The Iranian revolution, Hizbollah, Hamas, Taleban and various Islamic activists across the Muslim world eventually came to be characterised as fundamentalist or extremist aspects of Islam.
27. *Daily Telegraph*, 1 March 1997.
28. *The Times*, 21 April 1995. When reminded that the Oklahoma bomb blasts were not a Muslim act, he refused to tender an apology. Earlier, Charles Moore, the editor of the *Spectator*, wrote:

> You can be British without speaking English or being Christian or being white, but nevertheless Britain is basically English-speaking, Christian and white, and if one starts to think that it might become basically Urdu-speaking and Muslim and brown, one gets frightened and angry ... Because of our obstinate refusal to have enough babies, Western European civilisation will start to die at the point when it could have been revived with new blood. Then the hooded hordes will win, and the Koran will be taught as Gibbon famously imagined, in the schools of Oxford. ('Time for a more liberal and "racist" immigration policy', *Spectator*, 19 October 1991)

29. One could add several other factors including the demand for such ethnic businesses from within the respective communities besides the limited nature of job opportunities in the open market due to several prejudices. Not only do such small businesses allow social mobility within the community, equally they allow employment for several members of the family, which may not be possible in the outside market.
30. One may attribute this kind of institutionalisation to two parallel factors: firstly, that the community is here to stay and is engaged in redefining its own role in view of the various challenges and prospects; and secondly, that Muslims generally do not find a positive representation in

the available British media and are thus compelled to seek their own forums.

31. *Daily Telegraph*, 3 September 1993.

32. *Report*, p.47.

33. *Ibid.*

34. *Independent*, 14 February 1996.

35. Such views were expressed by James Hutchings in *The Times*, 1 January 1993.

36. *Report*, p.47.

37. *Ibid.*, p.60.

38. Some of these issues recur in the meetings of the Muslim Council of Britain, which came into being in 1998. In addition, the Association of Muslim Social Scientists (AMSS), established in 1999, has been holding periodic, well-attended conferences where such thematic issues have been selected for scholarly deliberation. For more details, see Humayun Ansari, *Muslims in Britian* (an MRG report), London, 2002.

39. In a survey at Oxford University, carried out informally in November 2000, several Muslim observers felt that only 20 per cent of the Muslim students in the higher institutions across the United Kingdom were fully practising Islam in a theocratic sense. However, it was felt that there is a growing number of Muslims becoming aware of their Muslimness over and above their ethno-regional differences. This survey was based on personal questions raised informally after the congregational prayers.

40. This has been admitted time and again by ministers as well as by the heads of such corporations as the BBC. Greg Dyke, the Director of the BBC, in a speech called his organisation 'hideously white'. He gave the example of an annual reception for the Corporation's executives where with one exception all 89 participants were white. *The Times*, 8 January 2001.

41. While selecting the successor to Dr George Carey, the retiring Archbishop of Canterbury, many people feared a racist backlash against the Revd Dr Michael Nazir-Ali, one of the candidates, who is of Pakistani origin. The Bishop of Rochester, Dr Ali was the first non-white to be considered for this highest office of the Anglican Church. But a smear campaign was unleashed against his 'Catholic' past so as to get him disqualified. Dr Nazir-Ali himself, in an interview, feared a racist undertone to this campaign. *Sunday Telegraph*, 14 January 2002.

42. One may mention names such as Aziz al-Azmeh, H. Ansari, Muhammad Anwar, Yunas Samad and a few other academics dilating on sociological and historical themes within the regional or international parameters of Islam.

43. For more on this, see Iftikhar H. Malik, *Islam, Nationalism and the West: Issues of Identity in Pakistan*, London, 1999, pp.13–19.

44. Rana Kabbani, *Letter to Christendom*, London, 1989, pp.65–8.

45. Gilles Kepel, *Allah in the West*, London, 1997, pp.126–44.

46. Ziauddin Sardar and Merryl W. Davies, *The Distorted Imagination*, London, 1991.

47. In her *Sacred Cows* (1989), Weldon found the Quran totally incompatible with Western values. Conor Cruise O'Brien, the Irish editor of the *Observer*, found Islam simply 'repulsive'. *The Times*, 11 May, 1989.

48. Shabbir Akhtar felt that the vocal Western support for Rushdie signalled a serious omen for the Muslim diaspora. In an oft-quoted piece, he observed that 'the next time there are gas chambers in Europe, there is no doubt concerning who'll be inside them'. *Guardian*, 27 February 1989. For an interesting critique of *The Satanic Verses*, see Rana Kabbani, *Women in Muslim Society*, Cork, 1992. Yasmin Alibhai-Brown and several other Muslim intellectuals felt that either the British liberals were being racist towards Muslims or were at least uninterested in respecting their sensitivities.

49. During the riots of 2002 over the Mosque–Temple issue, and its spillover in the Indian state of Gujarat, Rushdie, like several other secular Indians, felt disgusted with the way Indian polity was being pushed towards Hindutva. For his critical comments, see Salman Rushdie, 'Religion, as ever, is the poison in India's blood', *Guardian*, 9 March 2002.

50. Salman Rushdie, *Imaginary Homelands: Essays and Criticism 1981–91*, London, 1992, p.4.

51. Some Muslim notables, such as Dr Zaki Badawi of the Muslim College, London, asked him to apologise openly for the hurt caused to Muslims, to commit himself not to publish the paperback of *The Satanic Verses*, and to give away his royalties from this novel to charity. Rushdie was not forthcoming on the last of these and the efforts for reconciliation broke down.

52. See his *Midnight All Day*, London, 1999; *Love in a Blue Time*, London, 1997; *Intimacy*, London, 1998, and *Sleep With Me*, London, 1999.

53. Tariq Ali, *The Stone Woman*, London, 2000.

54. His recent book is based on the same theme. See Tariq Ali, *The Clash of Fundamentalisms*, London, 2002.

55. See, for instance, Shabbir Akhtar, *Be Careful with Muhammad*, London, 1990.

56. Based on personal interviews with Dr Shabbir Akhtar in Oxford in 1998. In a newspaper article, he lashed out at self-styled Muslim jurists for their obstructionism. See *Times Higher Education Supplement*, 13 February 1997.

57. Shabbir Akhtar, 'God's impatient faithful', *Times Higher Education Supplement*, 15 April 1994; and, 'A grouse for Mr Biswas', *ibid.*, 15 May 1998.

58. Some of his titles include: *The Future of Islamic Civilisation* (1979); *Islamic Futures: The Shape of Ideas to Come* (1985); *Barbaric Others: A Manifesto on Western Racism* (1993); *Introducing Cultural Studies* (1997); *Postmodernism and the Other* (1998), and *Orientalism* (1999); and, with Merryl Wyn Davies, *Why do People Hate America?* (2002). In addition, he edits the journal *Futures*.

59. For an interesting piece comparing Ziauddin Sardar with Akbar Ahmed, see Tomas Gerholm, 'Muslim Intellectuals in the Postmodern West: Akbar Ahmed and Ziauddin Sardar', in Akbar Ahmed and Hastings Donnan (eds) *Islam, Globalization and Postmodernity*, London, 1994, pp.190–212.

60. His various titles include: *Discovering Islam* (1988); *Postmodernism and Islam* (1992); *Living Islam* (1993); and *Jinnah, Pakistan and Islamic Identity: The Search for Saladin* (1997).

61. Rana Kabbani, *Letter to Christendom*, p.ix.

62. Rana Kabbani, *Imperial Fictions: Empire's Myths of Orient*, London, 1994 (reprint), p.vii.

63. *Ibid.*, p.26.

64. Quoted in *ibid.*, p.96. Blunt viewed Islam quite positively in his *The Future of Islam*.

65. A very moving series, which was shown on BBC 24 in January 2002 only after midnight, under the title *Correspondent*.

66. Her various sociological studies include: *The Colour of Love: Mixed Race Relationships* (1992); *Racial Equality in Europe: Problems and Prospects*, with Paul Gordon (1992); and, *True Colours: Attitudes to Multiculturalism and the Role of the Government* (1999). In 2001, she was selected as the BBC Asian writer of the year.

67. Yasmin Alibhai-Brown, *No Place Like Home*, London, 1995.

68. See her *Who Do We Think We Are: Imagining the New Britain*, London, 2000.

69. J.E. Sherif, *Searching for Solace: A Biography of Abdullah Yusuf Ali*, Kuala Lumpur, 1994.

70. The school in Sarajevo was funded by a Muslim charity based in London, which also planned for a similar school in Kosovo.

71. In a lecture at the University of Bath in November 2000, Zaki Badawi highlighted the commonalities between the three Abrahamic traditions and offered a progressive view of Islam. It is no wonder that some of his views are not well received by some Muslim purists. Earlier, at the AMSS conference in London in September 2000, Badawi had urged Muslim women to provide a fresh and dynamic leadership to the community instead of submitting to male prerogatives. See also Jack O'Sullivan, 'Defender of his faith', *Guardian*, 15 January 2003.

72. There are several Muslim artists, poets and professionals whose works dilate on various cross-cultural themes. Among the professionals one can mention Najma Akhtar, Zafar Abbas Malik, Ayyub Malik, Rukhsana Ahmed, Raficq Abdulla and others. There is a whole generation of poets and novelists – both men and women – whose publications make up an entire collection of diasporic literature in languages such as Urdu, Punjabi and Arabic. The credit goes to the late Nusrat Fateh Ali Khan for synthesising Sufi Qawwali music with the Western traditions. Some of these artists and writers have been interviewed in a video about British Muslims, sponsored by the British Foreign and Commonwealth Office. For details, see London Television Service, *Islam in Britain* (two parts), London, 2000.

73. Based on personal interviews with Professor Ahmad at Wilton Park, Sussex, on 26–27 February 2003.

6 MUSLIMS IN FRANCE, GERMANY AND THE EUROPEAN UNION: ALIENS OR ALLIES?

1. It is not unusual to encounter observations in private meetings to the effect that Muslims are 'unable and unwilling to assimilate themselves into the French culture'. Such comments are ironically offered both by

the populist leaders and by some academics specialising in Muslim regions. (A number of interviews were conducted in 1994, 1997 and 2000 at various institutions across France.)

2. The region between Toulon and Frejus is still called Massif des Maures, the Massif of the Moors.

3. The French colonies, like the British Empire, were vast and diverse, yet in several cases, such as Algeria, control was centralised. In addition, the French made conscious efforts to assimilate the colonised peoples culturally, by imposing the French language and culture on them. French cultural and class-based hegemony, even more than colour, caused numerous responses from the colonies. For a useful structural comparison, see David K. Fieldhouse, *Empires*, London, 1993.

4. Several of these injured Indian soldiers were kept in Brighton and other coastal towns in a kind of isolation, away from the local communities. It is ironical to note that despite their frontline role in defence of the colonial masters, the intelligence sleuths kept them under strict surveillance and censored their correspondence with their relatives back home. For an interesting study, see David Omissi, *Indian Voices of the Great War: Soldiers' Letters, 1914–1918*, London, 1999; and, *The Sepoy and the Raj: The Politics of the Indian Army, 1860–1940*, London, 1995.

5. All these statistics are taken from Neal Robinson, 'France', in David Westerlund and Ingvar Svanberg (eds), *Islam Outside the Arab World*, London, 1999, pp.339–40.

6. Adam LeBor, *A Heart Turned East: Among the Muslims of Europe and America*, London, 1997, p.161.

7. According to Robinson, there were 3 million Muslims in France in the mid 1990s, whereas Nielsen and LeBor estimated that there were 4 million. The problem arises due to lack of proper census reports identifying respondents by religion.

8. According to Dr Hamidullah, the pre-eminent Indian scholar based in Paris and the imam of the Dawa Mosque (also known as the Stalingrad Mosque), there were '22,000 conversions of various nationalities for the decade to 1982. More recent studies suggest a total of French converts to Islam in the region of 30,000 to 50,000.' Jorgen Nielsen, *Muslims In Western Europe*, Edinburgh, 1995, pp.10–11.

9. *Ibid.*, p.12.

10. Allama Muhammad Iqbal (1875–1938), the poet-philosopher from Lahore, visited the mosque in 1933 while on his way back from Britain. He had been to London to attend the Round Table Conference convened by the British government to seek Indian political opinion on the future constitutional arrangements in India. Iqbal, during this journey, visited historical Muslim monuments in Andalusia and Sicily. Some of his moving poems are about these buildings, whose architects Iqbal remembers with nostalgia and anger. Iqbal's Urdu poem, *Paris Ki Masjid* (Paris Mosque) reads as follows:

> What should my eyes, but an architect's
> Nimbleness, see in the shrine
> Of the West? It knows nothing of God.

Mosque? the Frankish illusionists
Have smuggled into the carcass
Of a shrine, an idol-hall's soul!

And who built this palace of idols?
The same robbers whose hands have turned
Damascus into a desert.
(Muhammad Iqbal, *Zarb-i-Kaleem* (The Rod of Moses) in *Poems from Iqbal*, translated by Victor Kiernan, Karachi, 1999 (reprint), pp.184–5.)

11. For a long time, French law prohibited the formation of any cultural associations without the prior approval of the Interior Ministry. This law came into force owing to the fascist experience in the 1930s and 1940s. However, it was rescinded in 1981 and since then several local and national associations have come into being.

12. He is considered to be a leading authority on the Muslim concept of Jihad. Author of several volumes and articles, Hamidullah lived a very austere life in the hall above the mosque. For more on his ideas, see Iftikhar H. Malik, 'Islamic discourse on Jihad', *Journal of South Asian and Middle Eastern Studies*, XXI, Summer 1998, pp.47–78.

13. This is similar to 'Paki-bashing' in the United Kingdom.

14. LeBor, *A Heart Turned East*, pp.163–4.

15. Quoted in *ibid.*, p.167.

16. Quoted in Neal Robinson, p.350.

17. This is, of course, a totally different situation from that of the United Kingdom, where the state provides partial funding for Christian and Jewish schools. In the case of Muslims, successive British governments have been reluctant to offer assistance to community schools. It was only in the late 1990s under Tony Blair that for the first time three Muslim schools were designated eligible for official grants.

18. LeBor, pp.168–9.

19. While most Muslims in France are employed to perform menial and unskilled jobs, a class of professionals is steadily growing, despite all the hurdles. However, racism and bigotry, rooted in class, colour, culture and colonialism, still remain overwhelmingly pervasive. Many Muslims visiting France, especially those from Britain, experience unnecessary police controls and checks on passports and immigration documents. The present author, while returning from an international conference at CERI, Paris, in 1998, was stopped by six heavily armed policemen at the Nord train station. Without proper explanation, they demanded my (British) passport and then took their time in verifying it by telephone with their headquarters. In the meantime, in full view of the public, the author was detained by these fierce-looking policemen with their guns at the ready. It was only after about ten minutes that I was allowed to board the Eurostar train, without any explanation or apology. My later protests to the French ambassador in London resulted in a mild explanation suggesting that, given the bomb blasts in Paris, the authorities had to be vigilant. The embassy would not comment on the reasons for my being singled out for this interrogation in public. Obviously, they did not want to mention that my complexion had triggered the entire episode.

20. However, it is ironical to see how different EU member states engage in various sleazy activities of espionage employing members of their own ethnic communities and totally compromising the civil liberties of such individuals. In 1999, a British court was engaged on the case of Shafiq ur Rehman, a Pakistani imam whom MI5 had tried to hire for espionage on British Kashmiris in 1997. 'Muslim cleric was "wooed by MI5"', *Guardian*, 17 August 1999.

   In 2000, the press revealed the underground and underhand activities of the French intelligence agencies on British Muslims. French agents had approached and hired a North African Muslim, not only to spy on Muslim activists, such as Abu Hamza, a Yemeni Afghan war veteran living in London; they had asked him to blow up a mosque as well. For a detailed report, see David Leppard et al., 'French spy reveals dirty tricks in UK', *Sunday Times*, 8 October 2000.

21. There are several French and Muslim scholars writing on Islam as a civilisation and on the various Muslim communities. Writers such as Gilles Kepel, Marco Gaborieau, Olivier Roy, Bruno Etienn, Leila Babes, Jocelyne Cesari and several others are producing well-researched, though in some cases partisan studies on these issues within a growing French historiography on Islam.

22. Of course, many German princes and volunteers had participated in the Crusades and the religious establishments remained critical of Islam; yet a direct, bipartisan relationship never occurred. The earliest German encounters with Muslims were through Austro-Ottoman warfare, when the Turks failed to capture Vienna in 1683. The Austro-Hungarian and Ottoman empires were neighbours and it was in their mutual interest to resist further open warfare. It was in 1878 following the Congress of Berlin that Austria captured Bosnia, a long-time Turkish province, and a new era in the relationship began.

23. For more on the Ghadr Movement and the trials, see Iftikhar H. Malik, *US–South Asia Relations, 1784–1940: A Historical Perspective*, Islamabad, 1988, pp.123–258.

24. Under the secret Sykes–Picot Agreement, France, Britain and Russia had already determined to parcel out between them the few remaining Muslim regions. While Wilson's idea of self-determination was put aside, his scheme of mandatory systems for certain regions was quickly adopted by these countries. After the October 1917 Revolution, Russia not only withdrew from the secret pact but also made it public. Under the Balfour Declaration of 1916, the British had already committed themselves to Jewish immigration into Palestine and the formation of Israel. This agreement with the World Zionist Organisation, meant to help European Jewry, was ironically to lead to decades of instability, misery, bloodshed and warfare in the Middle East.

25. Eventually the Indian National Army (INA) came into being, though many of its proponents were either arrested by the British or perished in the forests. Even Bose, generally known as Neta Ji, died mysteriously and the second phase in this trans-communal struggle came to a tragic end. For more on this, see Lawrence Gordon, *Brothers Against the Raj*, New York, 1992.

26. Though it is difficult to obtain exact figures on various Muslim communities in Germany, it is possible to offer rough estimates. There may be nearly 2 million Muslim immigrants of Turkish and Kurdish origin, followed by 600,000 Yugoslav Muslims, and 50,000 Moroccans. About 24,000 Tunisians, 75,000 Iranians and 35,000 Arabs (including Lebanese, Jordanians and Palestinians) make up this increasing diaspora. For details on demographic trends and figures, see Nielsen, *Muslims in Western Europe*, pp.25–7.

27. They claim to make up a quarter of the entire Turkish community, but this is not true. Unlike other Sunni Muslims, Alwis are less attuned to mosque-based practices, focusing instead on *dhikr*, or the recital of hymns. They are a sect distinct from the Alwis of Syria.

28. It may still be difficult to ascertain the total number of Afghan asylum seekers, but, largely based in cities like Hamburg, Hanover, Frankfurt, Bonn, Munich and Berlin, they have established their own ethnic contacts across the EU. Many of them are university graduates and former members of the Mujahideen groups, who left their native country following the civil war in the 1990s. Several of them have relatives across Western Europe, North America, Pakistan and Australia and have been immensely despondent about the future of their own country. (This information is based on extensive personal contacts with Afghan exiles in the West.)

29. This a group which emerged in British India in the early twentieth century and considers Mirza Ghulam Ahmad to be the promised messiah. The mainstream Muslims criticise Ahmadis for not openly and unequivocally subscribing to the finality of the prophethood of the Prophet Muhammad. In 1974, Pakistan's legislature declared them 'non-Muslims' and since then they have been migrating to the West. The Ahmadis make the earliest and the biggest Pakistani community in Germany with concentration in Frankfurt and Hamburg. Collectively, they make a middle class, prosperous community of professionals and have established their own diasporic links with similar Ahmadi communities across Europe and elsewhere. The spiritual leader of the community is permanently based in Britain. This information is based on personal surveys and informal interviews conducted in 1996, 1999 and 2000. They have their own satellite television channel called Muslim Ahmadiyya TV in London, with programmes in several languages.

30. Quoted in Nielsen, *Muslims in Western Europe*, p.187. Five Turkish women died in this arson attack.

31. In the summer of 2000, the author attended an interesting conference at Loccum, Germany on immigration policies and experiences in both Germany and the United States. Several German academics appeared to be receptive to a redefinition of German identity.

32. For further details, see Ingvar Svanberg, '[Islam in] The Nordic Countries', in Westerlund and Svanberg, *Islam Outside the Arab World*, pp.379–401. A number of Islamic manuscripts and miniatures were acquired during the early period and are preserved in various Scandinavian museums.

33. Based on personal inquiries in the region.

34. There are some known Muslim scholars based in Sweden, the leading amongst them being Professor Ishtiaq Ahmed at the University of Stockholm and Pervaiz Manzoor, a writer on Islamic issues.
35. This was observed through a personal visit and interviews held with a wide variety of communities in Sweden during the late September of 2001.
36. *The Encyclopedia of Islam* and the Leiden-based ISIM (The International Institute for the Study of Islam in the Modern World) are some of the notable Dutch efforts on Islam.
37. The southern regions still exude a 'Moorish' flavour. Allama Iqbal, in his visit to Italy in 1931, composed a moving poem, 'Sicily', combining personal pathos with nostalgia:

> Now weep blood, oh eyes, for the womb of the arts of Arabia stands there in sight
> Where the men of the desert whose ships made a playground of ocean once rushed to the fight ...
> As the nightingale-voice of Shiraz of Baghdad, and for Delhi Dagh shed bitter tears,
> As ibn Badrun's soul lamented when heaven ended Granada's opulent years,
> So to sorrow with you fate has chosen Iqbal, oh this heart that knows your heart so well!
> Whose annals lie lost in your ruins? – those shores and their echoless music might tell.
> Tell your grief then to me, who am grief, who am dust of that caravan whose magnet you were:
> Stir my veins – let the picture glow bright with fresh colour, the ancient days declare!
> I go with your gift to the Indies, and I who weep here will make others weep there.
>
> (From *Poems from Iqbal*, translated by Victor Kiernan, pp.30–3)

38. Several former Muslim kings, including Farouk of Egypt, Amanullah Khan and Zahir Shah of Afghanistan and, for a time, Muhammad Reza Shah of Iran sought asylum in Italy. In the 1990s, Italy's former prime minister, Craxi, lived in Libya to escape prosecutors in his native Rome. Following the terrorist attacks in the United States, the Italian prime minister, Berlusconi, described Western civilisation as superior to all, and many Muslim residents were screened by the security agencies.

7 IRELAND AND ISLAM: GREEN TWINS OR WORLDS APART?

1. Like their Chinese counterparts to the west, Irish labourers built the eastern portion of the railway lines and when in 1869 the tracks built by the Central and Union Pacific companies finally reached Promontory, Utah, the former partied on tea, whereas the Irish workers profusely consumed Guinness and whisky. In the process, the two sides missed each other and continued building parallel tracks in opposite directions

for quite some distance. Alistair Cooke, *America*, London, 1977, p.228; also, Maldwyn A. Jones, *The Limits of Liberty. American History: 1607–1992*, Oxford, 1996, p.287.

2. For more details, see Department of Foreign Affairs, *Facts About Ireland*, Dublin, 1995, pp.9–10.

3. Many such stereotypes are linked with an imperialist past. Asians, like the Irish, have also been the victims of similar racial stereotypes, though 'Paki-bashing' has been considerably more severe than anti-Irish discrimination. Unlike the Irish, Asians and Africans are further underprivileged because of a mix of colour-, culture- and class-based trajectories.

4. Three years earlier, the English ship, the *Matthew*, had successfully completed its voyage from Bristol to North America.

5. Nabil Matar, *Islam in Britain, 1558–1685*, Cambridge, 1998, pp.4, 36–8 and 189–90.

6. Ibn Khaldun remains one of the most widely quoted scholars. His cyclic theory of the rise and fall of civilisations on the pattern of human life and owing to intra-tribal solidarity (*asabiyya*) or dissension (*fitna*) respectively has generated a significant debate among international sociologists. For a detailed commentary, see Ernest Gellner, *Muslim Society*, Cambridge, 1993.

7. Quoted in Mamoun Mobayed, 'Muslims in Northern Ireland', *ISIM Nesletter*, October 2000, p.36.

8. For an early work on the interaction of tea and opium in China, see M. Greenberg, *British Trade and the Opening of China 1800–1842*, London, 1951.

9. Such contacts were apparent on the American East Coast, especially in New York, and involved activists like Lajpat Rai. For further details see Iftikhar H. Malik, *US–South Asia Relations, 1773–1940: A Historical Perspective*, Islamabad, 1988, pp.193–204.

10. Dennis Judd, *Empire*, London, 1998, p.3.

11. Other than John and Henry Lawrence, Michael O'Dwyer and Brigadier-General Dyer are some of the best-known names in recent British Indian history. For a recent study of the Lawrences, see Harold Lee, *Brothers in the Raj: The Lives of John and Henry Lawrence*, Karachi, 2002.

    Michael O'Dwyer began as an ICS in a Punjab district, eventually to retire as the governor of the province. For his life story, see *The Punjab As I Knew It*, London, 1925. General Dyer was responsible for the infamous Jallianwala killing in April 1919, when he ordered his men to open fire on a crowd gathered for some peaceful social activity. In the process, 379 people were killed, including women and children, and hundreds of others were grievously wounded. This massacre turned out to be a turning point in the Indian nationalist movement.

12. Joel Mokyr and Cormac O'Grada, *The Heights of the British and the Irish, c. 1800–1815*, quoted in C.L. Innes, 'Black writers in eighteenth-century Ireland', *Bullan: An Irish Studies Journal*, V, 2, 2000, p.81.

13. Of course, the pioneering study on the subject is by Edward Said, who not only coined the term, its theoretical postulation and multifarious dimensions but also underlined its epistemological bottlenecks encompassing a complex yet crucial philological domain. Power-centric as it

is, Orientalism remains the most crucial factor and the main trajectory of this uneven relationship between various ethno-cultural constellations. Said's empirical data comes from places like India and Egypt, as seen by the colonial administrator–scholars, reformers and missionary–intellectuals (such as Sir William Jones, William Wilkins, Horace Hayman Wilson, Abbe Raynal, James Forbes, Adam Smith, Jeremy Bentham, James Mill, Charles Metcalfe, Hector Munro, J. Malcolm, Mounstuart Elphinstone, Charles Masson, William Macaulay, Richard Burton, Monier-Williams, W.W. Hunter, Ramsay Muir, Charles Trevelyan, Alfred Lyall, Rudyard Kipling, E. M. Forster and many others), though it equally highlights the need for further research. Said's hypotheses, since 1978–79, have led to one of the few intensely debated intellectual themes of our era. In the early twenty-first century, postcolonial studies and comparative sociology are concentrating on the issues of gender, arts and political economy by focusing on terms such as neo-Orientalism, anti-Orientalism and post-Orientalism. See Edward Said, *Orientalism*, London, 1979; Bobby Sayyid, *A Fundamental Fear: Eurocentrism and the Emergence of Islamism*, London, 1997; and Alain Grosrichard, *The Sultan's Court*, translated by Liz Heron, London, 1998.

14. In England, such views were further elaborated by the Benthamite Utilitarians and moralists like William Wilberforce, who, while advocating the abolition of the slave trade and slavery, believed in Christianising the Afro-Asian communities.

15. Three such authors from the UP (Itisam al-Din, Mir Muhammad Husain and Abu Talib Khan), writing in Persian, left accounts of Britain in particular and of Europe in general. Other members of the Muslim elite, such as Murtaza Husain Bilgrami, Abdal Latif and Ghulam Husain Khan, wrote about the British residents in India. For a commentary, see Gulfishan Khan, 'Indian Muslim Perceptions of the West during the Eighteenth Century', D.Phil. dissertation, 1993, Oxford. The research was published in 1998 under the same title by the Oxford University Press, Karachi.

16. For more on him, see Percival Spear, *The Oxford History of Modern India, 1740–1947*, Oxford, 1965, pp.85–94.

17. Cited in C.L. Innes, 'Black writers in eighteenth-century Ireland', p.82.

18. *Ibid.*

19. Nini Rodgers, 'Equiano in Belfast: a study of the anti-slavery ethos in a northern town', *Slavery and Abolition*, XVIII, 2, 1997, p.80.

20. Quoted in Innes, p.86.

21. See M. Athar Ali, *Mughal Nobility under Aurengzeb*, Bombay, 1968; also Muzaffar Alam, *The Crisis of Empire in Mughal North India, Awadh and the Punjab, 1707–1748*, Delhi, 1986.

22. Fought in Bengal, this battle not only exposed the inherent weakness in the Indian administration but also showed the interpersonal rivalries amongst the Indians. The combined forces of the Mughal Emperor, Nawab Qasim of Bengal and the Nawab of Oudh failed to defeat the Company, which emerged as the ultimate arbiter, administrator and ruler of the Subcontinent.

23. Michael H. Fisher, *The First Indian Author in English*, Delhi, 1996, pp.211–12.
24. Quoted in Innes, p.86.
25. *Cork Gazette*, IV, 16 March 1793, quoted in Innes, pp.86–7.
26. Michael H. Fisher (ed.) *The Travels of Dean Mahomet: An Eighteenth-Century Journey through India*, Berkeley, 1997, pp.34–5.
27. Innes, p.90.
28. Fisher, 1997, p.68.
29. *Travels of Mirza Abu Talib Khan in Asia, Africa, and Europe, During the Years 1799, 1800, 1802, and 1803, and written by Himself in the Persian Language*, Vol. 1 translated by Charles Stewart, (London, 1814), referred to by Innes.
30. It was at the time of the auction of his portrait in April 2002 that an exceptionally laudatory comment was published in an influential English daily. His case study was used to remind people 'that the past was more cosmopolitan than is often painted by traditionalists'. 'And Mr Mohamed too: a good day to remember a great tradition', *Guardian* leader, 9 April 2002.
31. Gulfishan Khan, *Indian Muslim Perceptions of the West During the Eighteenth Century*, Karachi, 1998, p.100.
32. *Ma'asr-i-Talibi*, pp.36–7, as quoted in *ibid.*, p.217.
33. *Ibid.*, p.219.
34. For further details, see *ibid.*, pp.220–2.
35. His papers and archives at Trinity College, Dublin, may afford a researcher vital and diverse information on Ireland–India and Muslim–Irish relationship.
36. Sir Syed Ahmed Khan, *Musafiraan-i-London* (travellers to London), as quoted by Hasan Abidi, 'The Muslim woman voyager', *Dawn*, 30 December 2001.
37. Amidst the indiscriminate shootings of Palestinian protesters by Israeli troops in October–November 2000, many Irish civic groups supported the former. For instance, a letter appearing in a leading newspaper demanded a NATO-led military campaign against Israel. The writer censored Israel for brutalising the Palestinians and for flouting 50 UN resolutions, and demanded a review of Western policies towards Tel Aviv. See *Irish Times*, Dublin, 11 October 2000.
38. Located in the city centre, it is also known as Christ Church and is used for exhibits and special conferences.
39. It houses a mosque, offices of the Islamic Foundation of Ireland (IFI), a halal restaurant and a shop selling groceries and meat.
40. The complex is a magnificent structure with lecture halls, conference rooms, gym, shops and a restaurant and was opened by President Mary Robinson. Shaikh Hamadan Khalifa took over direct control of the building a few years ago after some bickering with the IFI, and the property is registered under his personal name.
41. This issue has been amply discussed in the media as well as by academia in Western Europe (and Turkey), whereas in the Republic it is a non-issue.
42. Apparently there is no rivalry between the IFI, the Islamic Centre and the Imamia Centre, yet sectarian and national tensions have not allowed a close coordination among the three. On the other hand, there is close

collaboration between the IFI, Belfast's Islamic Centre and other regional smaller centres in Galway and Cork.

43. He initially came to live in London and bought the Baroda House in Kensington but then moved to Dublin and was honoured as its free citizen. His priceless collection is a major attraction for academics, diplomats and tourists and some specimens are available on the internet as well (see under <www.cbl.ie>).

44. The author is indebted to the curator for this information. Another significant personal collection of Islamic art in the West is owned by David Khalili, an Iranian Jew living in London. In more recent years, Gulbenkian, an Armenian oil magnate, gathered a similar collection of Islamic art which he bequeathed to Lisbon and which is now accessible to the public.

45. There are various estimates of the Muslim population in Ireland, varying from 20,000 to 25,000. More than half live in Dublin, followed by Belfast, Cork and Galway.

46. Like Islam, which has many nationalist heroes and religious saints, Irish history too has its share of such prominent individuals.

47. The Irish people may drink coffee in the diaspora, but at home it is tea (Bewley's in most cases!) or Guinness – like Pakistanis, Afghans, Chinese Muslims, Arabs and Iranians, whose tea consumption is both timeless and limitless.

48. Pakistanis, Indians and Bangladeshis love cricket, whereas the Irish, like the Lebanese, are rugby fanatics, and, as with Arabs and Africans, football remains an Irish obsession. At another level, to all of them, the BBC remains the hallmark of authenticity.

49. This is not to say that the Irish were always well treated in the United States. Their poor origins and Catholic beliefs were resented by many racist groups in America, including the Ku Klux Klan. Books by Daniel P. Moynihan, Andrew Greeley and several other Irish-American authors have copiously documented such mistreatment. But in recent times, in the wake of the civil rights movement, such legacies have largely disappeared. Their white colour, middle-class stature and political clout have collectively helped the Irish to become integrated into US society, in contrast to several other communities, especially the African Americans.

50. In 1998, Afghanistan was targeted by the Clinton Administration for sheltering Osama bin Laden, the Saudi dissident, who was held responsible for attacks on the American embassies in Kenya and Tanzania. In late 2000, there were rumours of possible joint Russo-American military action against Afghanistan to punish its Taleban regime for sheltering Osama bin Laden. See *The Times*, 25 November 2000. The story covered two full pages of the broadsheet. In addition, there have been similar reports of joint Indian–Israeli schemes against the Muslim Kashmiri activists. Finally, sustained attacks on Afghanistan began in October 2001, leading to the dissolution of the Taleban regime. Simultaneously, Israel flexed its muscles against the Palestinians.

51. Ireland needs to establish its own worldview, otherwise it may also end up pursuing cliched attitudes and policies vis-à-vis Muslims, as is evident in other Western countries. Proper and cooptive initiatives can protect

Ireland from falling prey to xenophobia, racism and intolerance. Only time will tell how Irish people and institutions might change when it comes to perceiving and practising multiculturalism.

8 ISLAM AND THE UNITED STATES: NEW FRIENDS OR OLD ENEMIES?

1. Seumas Milne, 'The innocent dead in a coward's war', *Guardian*, 20 December 2001.
2. Luke Harding, 'A slide into chaos', *ibid.*, 10 December 2001.
3. Jonathan Steele, 'Fighting the wrong war', *ibid.*, 11 December 2001.
4. Nancy Dunne, 'US police on alert to stamp out hate crimes', *Financial Times*, 20 September 2001.
5. While commentators such as V.S. Naipaul and Polly Toynbee agreed with US policies and saw Islam being hijacked by the fundamentalists and terrorists, a host of other writers and pacifists, including Arundhati Roy, George Galloway, Isabel Hilton, George Monbiot, Jonathan Freedland, Robert Fisk, Tariq Ali and Noam Chomsky, considered the US campaign totally unjust and revengeful.
6. Chris McGreal, 'Africans angry at refusal to debate slavery reparations', *Guardian*, 1 September 2001.
7. The United States, Israel and a number of former colonial powers including the United Kingdom and France were resistant to the idea of tendering an apology on the issues of slavery. The British Labour government felt that such confession could result in legal intricacies and endless demands for reparation. On the other hand, Belgium was prepared to offer an apology to Africans. But the United States was resistant to the proposed condemnation of Zionism, the continued uprooting of the Palestinians and their targeted murders by the Israeli security forces. The United States sent in a low-key delegation led by the Revd Jesse Jackson, whereas such a pioneering international event expected the participation of Colin Powell, the first African-American secretary of state. The Bush Administration had already been threatening to boycott the conference and did so even at a preliminary stage. Eventually, a watered-down resolution, sponsored by the European Union, was tabled, much to the offence of the Muslim and African participants. The convenors – South Africa and the UN – accepted it only to prevent the first major international conference from failing on such a significant subject.
8. For the US interventions elsewhere, see Bianca Jagger, 'Selective justice', *Guardian*, 8 December 2001.
9. The term was used in reference to Islamophobia and some incomplete British legislative efforts to ban incitement to religious hatred. Madeleine Bunting, 'The new anti-Semitism', *Guardian*, 3 December 2001. Needless to say, several letters on the subject were critical of using the term for Muslims. Anyway, the House of Lords did not ratify the legislation.
10. One needs to remember the role of the local African chieftains and of some Arabs who operated as commissioning agents for the Europeans

in the slave traffic. But that still does not exonerate the Europeans, who were running chattel slavery and pursuing an immensely intricate and well-organised system of enslavement, shipments and auctions. Without a high demand and sophisticated networks, the manifold increase in the demand for slaves would not have been possible.

11. In the case of South Asia, the present author, like a few other historians from the region, has made an effort to study its relationship with the United States. See Iftikhar H. Malik, *US–South Asia Relations, 1773–1940: A Historical Perspective*, Islamabad, 1988; and *US–South Asian Relations: American Attitudes towards the Pakistan Movement*, Oxford, 1991. There are several region-based or bilateral studies with reference to the Middle East, Africa and the Far East. Many universities in the Muslim world have fully fledged postgraduate degree courses in American studies, and courses on US history and foreign relations remain well subscribed.

12. The names of such 'pioneers', and those of towns and regions across the Western hemisphere, resemble Arabic and Mudejar names and reveal an ongoing acculturative process, both in Iberia and in Spanish America.

13. It is important to remember the debate among historians on the relationship between racism and slavery. One school subscribes to specific misperceptions of Africa and racism leading to slavery, whereas the second school sees racism in the post-Emancipation period itself rooted in slavery. See Winthrop D. Jordan, *White over Black: American Attitudes Towards the Negro*, Chapel Hill, 1968. Jordan himself subscribes to the first position.

14. For a comprehensive study of African-American experience, see John Hope Franklin and Alfred A. Moss Jr, *From Slavery to Freedom: A History of African Americans*, Boston, 1996; for a critical and precise commentary on the current debate, see Peter J. Parish, *Slavery*, Keele, 1992.

15. This broad subject has given rise to thousands of books and articles, along with specific courses, fiction, documentaries and dissertations. For a historiographical overview, see Mark M. Smith, *Debating Slavery: Economy and Society in Antebellum American South*, Cambridge, 1998.

16. As well as the works on slavery mentioned above, important studies focusing on moral issues, immigration, economics, the North–South relationship, gender and constitutional issues continue to appear both within the United States and elsewhere. Some of the leading studies include: Ulrich B. Phillips, *American Negro Slavery*, New York, 1918; Herbert Aptheker, *Negro Slave Revolts*, New York, 1943; Robert W. Fogel and Stanley L. Engerman, *Time on the Cross: The Economics of American Negro Slavery*, Boston, 1974; Eric Foner, *Free Soil, Free Labor, Free Men: The Ideology of the Republican Party before the Civil War*, New York, 1970; Lawrence W. Levine, *Black Culture and Black Consciousness*, New York, 1977; Peter Kolchin, *American Slavery 1619–1877*, New York, 1993; James McPherson, *Freedom's Cry*, Oxford, 1997; J. H. Franklin and A. Moss, *From Slavery to Freedom: A History of African Americans*, Boston, 2000; Eric Williams, *Capitalism and Slavery*, London, 1964.

17. For more on the African-American abolitionists, see Benjamin Quarles, *The Black Abolitionists*, New York, 1974. For a primary source, see Frederick Douglass, *Narratives of a Former Slave*, New York, 1995. Douglass's

speeches, his high-profile role in abolitionism and his advocacy of political activism make him the most influential leader of his age. His autobiography, written with the encouragement of white abolitionists such as William Lloyd Garrison, and under various titles, catapulted him into the status of an activist–intellectual.

18. Washington was influential in ameliorating the conditions of freed slaves through his emphasis on industrial education. However, his acceptance of second-class citizenship for them did not go well with radicals like Du Bois. Washington remained the most important African-American leader from the 1890s until his death in 1915. See his *Up From Slavery*, New York, 1968 (reprint).

19. Playing multiple roles, Du Bois emerged as the most influential activist and propagandist of his age. His editorship of *The Crisis* – the monthly magazine of the National Association for the Advancement of the Colored People (NAACP) – and several books earned him a great following among middle-class African Americans. During his final years, he was deeply disappointed with the United States; he died in self-imposed exile in 1963 in Ghana. See his *The Souls of Black Folk*, New York, 1968; see also Stuart Hall, 'Tearing down the veil', *Guardian*, 22 February 2003.

20. Through marches, music and uniforms he cultivated a sense of pride among African Americans. His end came quickly in the 1920s, owing to his indictment for fraud and resultant incarceration, yet he remained a cult figure for subsequent generations.

21. For a comparative perspective on these leaders, see John White, *Black Leadership in America: From Booker T. Washington to Jesse Jackson*, London, 1994.

22. James Haskins, *The Life and Death of Martin Luther King, Jr*, New York, 1977; and Clayborne Carson (ed.) *The Autobiography of Martin Luther King Jr*, London, 1999.

23. Malcolm X remains a cult figure and Spike Lee's film has further internationalised his radical mystique. For more on his life, see Alex Hailey (compiler) *The Autobiography of Malcolm X*, London, 1998.

24. Whereas the films *Roots* and *Amistad* include Muslim characters, *Glory* portrays a monolithic image of African Americans without revealing some of the prominent Muslim characters in the 54th Massachusetts Regiment that fought against the Confederates during the Civil War. Led by a white commander, this totally African-American regiment stood up against the odds and established its own valorous records, though it took America more than a century to promote black soldiers. It took even longer – almost until the end of the twentieth century – for the US government to offer medals and special merits to black soldiers and officers for performing heroic deeds in defence of their country.

25. This film, even in its technical sense, was a landmark as it involved thousands of extras without employing a single black actor or actress. President Wilson was deeply impressed by D. W. Griffith's extravaganza, at a time when several African Americans, including women, had been lynched. It is only in recent years that Hollywood has done away with the prestigious Griffith Award, annually offered to a high-profile celebrity.

26. See Philip Curtin, *The Atlantic Slave Trade: A Census*, Madison, 1969; and David Eltis, *Economic Growth and the Ending of the Transatlantic Slave Trade*, New York, 1969.

27. For a more recent and comprehensive analysis, see Herbert S. Klein, *The Atlantic Slave Trade*, Cambridge, 1999. The author, through figures and graphs, assesses the African contribution to American society, culture and the economy.

28. Allan D. Austin, *African Muslims in Antebellum America*, London, 1997, p.5.

29. Some of his papers were discovered in 1994 though there are still vast gaps regarding his life and pursuits at various times.

30. During the early 1970s, one often heard of a small group of Native Americans who identified themselves as 'Red Muslims', without of course claiming to be Muslims as such.

31. The Black Panthers included individuals like Huey Newton, E. Cleaver and S. Carmichael and their activism remained confined to the West Coast, though this has been a subject of major historiographical debate. Even several years later, they make occasional headlines. See *Guardian*, 10 January 2002.

32. The two support each other, and during Jesse Jackson's campaign for the presidential nomination, Farrakhan made many supportive statements, which, in some cases, backfired.

33. For his views, see Warith D. Muhammad, *Focus on Al-Islam*, Chicago, 1988; and *Challenges that Face Man Today*, Chicago, 1985.

34. Leroi Jones, 'City of Harlem', in William Makely (ed.) *City Life*, New York, 1974, p.24. Harlem was 'the home of Negro's Zionism'. A. Locke, 'The New Negro', in Houston A. Baker Jr (ed.) *Black Literature in America*, New York, 1971, p.152.

35. The Reverend Dr Adam Clayton Power Sr of Abyssinian Baptist Church lived in a cold water flat 'with prostitutes living over me and all around me'. He preached what he called 'gospel bombardment' to the pimps, prostitutes, and keepers of dice and gambling dens who sometimes attended his prayer meetings. 'They seemed to shout the loudest for the Lord's forgiveness. Others never went to church.' Gilbert Osofsky, *Harlem, The Making of a Ghetto, 1890–1950*, New York, 1968, pp.7–8.

36. Quoted in Arna Bontemps and Jack Conroy, *They Seek a City*, New York, 1945, p.178.

37.

> He came to our house selling raincoats, and then afterwards silks. In this way, he could get into the people's houses, for every woman was eager to see the nice things the peddlers had for sale. He told us that the silks he carried were the same kind that our people used in their home country and that he had come from there. So we all asked him to tell us about our own country ... (Erdmann D. Benyon, 'The voodoo cult among Negro migrants in Detroit', *American Journal of Sociology*, XLIII, 6, May 1938. The quote is based on an interview with a respondent.)

38. He was reportedly the subject of certain secret files and disappeared before his real identity could be made public. Gilles Kepel, *Allah in the West*, London, 1997, pp.15–18. It is not known whether he moved to somewhere else or was killed in some encounter.
39. E.U. Essien-Udom, *Black Nationalism: A Search for an Identity in America*, Chicago, 1971, p.6.
40. John White, *Black Leadership in America*, p.153.
41. Mrs Coretta King saw in both of them the same desire for reforms, as they both believed in black empowerment and the incapability of Christianity to eradicate injustice. C.S. King, *My Life with Martin Luther King Jr*, New York, 1970, pp.256–7; also C.E. Lincoln (ed.) *Martin Luther King Jr: A Profile*, London, 1972, pp.66–7.
42. The march eventually took place and was widely discussed in the media. See *The Times*, 11 October 1995; and, Charles Laurence, 'Zoot-suited monk brings order to chaos: underclass hero revels in climate of hatred', *Daily Telegraph*, 17 October 1995.
43. Jesse Jackson also faced Jewish hostility for using anti-Jewish terminology and for supporting the Palestinians against Israel. For details, see Mattias Gardell, 'The Sun of Islam Will Rise in the West: Minister Farrakhan and the Nation of Islam in the Latter Days', in Yvonne Y. Haddad and Jane I. Smith (eds) *Muslim Communities in North America*, Albany, 1994.
44. Muhammad Ali is equally venerated by the Nation and by general Muslims in America and outside, and is seen as a role model by millions.
45. Francis Trix, 'Bektashi and the Sunni Mosque of Albanian Muslims in America', in Haddad and Smith, *Muslim Communities in North America*.
46. For more on South Asian diaspora, see Iftikhar H. Malik, *US–South Asia Relations, 1773–1940: A Historical Perspective*, Islamabad, 1988; *Pakistanis in Michigan: A Study in Third Culture and Acculturation*, New York, 1989; and *US–South Asian Relations: American Attitudes towards the Pakistan Movement*, Oxford, 1991.
47. This kind of literature is still not widely explored and our information remains confined to a few biographies. The host of letters, articles and diaries remain unconsulted. For celebratory accounts from three different regions, see Salom Rizk, *A Syrian Yankee*, Garden City, 1943; Azizi Ali, *Ali: A Persian Yankee*, Caldwell, 1965; and, Dalip Singh Saund, *Congressman from India*, New York, 1960. In more recent times, fictional pieces have emerged that offer a revisionist perspective on such multicultural themes. For instance, see Bapsi Sidhwa, *An American Brat*, London, 1994. The author is a Pakistani Parsi who has been teaching at prestigious American universities. A younger generation of authors such as Sara Suleri and Mohsin Hamid has been attempting interesting trans-cultural themes. As well as well-known Muslim scholars at various American universities, including the late Professor Ismail Faruqi, Hossein Nasr, Hafeez Malik and Anwar Syed, there is a growing number of Muslim journalists and businessmen, though institutional networking is still a long way off. Some Muslim intellectuals in the United States, such as Eqbal Ahmad, remain unequivocally critical of US foreign policies. See *Eqbal Ahmad: Confronting Empire*, interviews with David Barsamian, London, 2000.

The number of institutes on the Middle East and Islamic studies has been on a steady increase over the last four decades though one has to be guarded when it comes to any possible major shift in the US foreign policies or American public opinions towards the Muslim issues.

48. Madonna's eulogy of this classic Sufi treatise and translations of Omar Khayyam have made Sufi Islam a more appealing religion to those who seek succour in escaping from grinding materialism and intolerant individualism. The negative spotlight on Islam, especially in recent years, has also drawn attention to it at various levels.

49. Though they have mainly concentrated on the Arab diaspora, their recent works are more comparative in style. See A. Elkholy, *The Arab Moslems in the United States*, New Haven, 1983; Barbara Aswad (ed.) *Arabic Speaking Community in American Cities*, Staten Island, 1974; *Property Control and Social Strategies: Settlers on a Middle Eastern Plain*, Ann Arbor, 1971; N. Shahadi and A. Hourani (eds) *A Century of Lebanese Emigration*, London, 1992; Yvonne Haddad (ed.) *The Muslims of America*, New York, 1991; also, with Adair T. Lummis, *Islamic Values in the United States: A Comparative Study*, Indianapolis, 1992; and S. Barboza (ed.) *The American Jihad*, New York, 1992.

50. In his visit to South Asia, Clinton spent just a few hours in both Pakistan and Bangladesh compared to five days in India. The visit to Pakistan took place only after serious persuasion by the Pentagon. His message telecast to the Pakistani parliament had been recorded in India.

George W. Bush, notorious for his gaffes and lack of awareness of nuances, annoyed Pakistanis by calling them 'Pakis' in a telecast interview during the anti-terror campaign. His spokesperson did not even try to apologise. See *Guardian*, 9 January 2002 and editorial in *ibid.*, 10 January 2002. (Ironically, this was at a time when Pakistan operated as the frontline state against terror, though itself being threatened by India, but Washington was unwilling to offer assistance and succour.)

51. Media reports widely commented on the denial of civil liberties to more than 6,000 detainees of Middle Eastern origins. Arab–American and Muslim associations highlighted these violations of human rights, but John Ashcroft, the attorney-general, declared the national interest far superior to the rights of the detainees. News report on CNN, 10 January 2002, monitored in Oxford.

52. This is based on Paul Moss's report from Dearborn for BBC Radio 4, *The World Tonight*, 11 March 2002.

53. For instance, see Afif A. Safeeh, 'Dear Mr Cheney ...' (letter), *Guardian*, 12 March 2002.

54. It is important to remember that there are several Muslim bodies with a secular outlook and nomenclature which do not agree with a religion-centred approach by Muslim organisations.

55. One could mention the Virginia-based Institute of Islamic Thought, which publishes a quarterly, *The Islamic Journal of Social Sciences*.

Bibliography

REPORTS AND ARTICLES

Ansari, Humayun, *Muslims in Britain* (a report by the Minority Rights Group), London, 2002.

Benyon, Erdmann D., 'The Voodoo Culture among Negro Migrants in Detroit', *American Journal of Sociology*, XLIII, 6, 1938.

Carew, John, 'The End of Moorish Enlightenment and the Beginning of the Columbian era', *Race and Class*, 33, 3, 1992.

Carr, Matthew, 'Spain: The Day of the Race', *ibid.*

Davidson, Basil, 'Columbus: The Bones and Blood of Racism', *ibid.*

Frank, Andre G., 'Third World War: A Political Economy of the Gulf War and the New World Order', *Third World Quarterly*, XIII, 2, 1992.

Gellner, Ernest, 'Islam and Marxism', *International Affairs*, 67, 1, 1991.

Huntington, Samuel P., 'The Clash of Civilizations', *Foreign Affairs*, 72, 2, 1993.

Imam, Irna, *Home from Home: British Pakistanis in Mirpur*, Bradford, 1997.

Innes, C.L., 'Black Writers in Eighteenth-Century Ireland', *Bullan: An Irish Studies Journal*, V, 2, 2000.

Lewis, Bernard, 'The Roots of Muslim Rage', *Atlantic Monthly*, 266, September 1990.

Malik, Iftikhar H., 'Islamic Discourse on Jihad', *Journal of South Asian and Middle Eastern Studies*, XXI, Summer 1998.

Miller, Chris, 'The Price of Freedom', *Oxford Today: The University Magazine*, 11, 3, 1999.

Miller, Judith, 'The Challenge of Radical Islam', *Foreign Affairs*, 72, 2, 1993.

Rodgers, Nini, 'Equiano in Belfast: A Study of the Anti-Slavery Ethos in a Northern Town', *Slavery and Abolition*, XVIII, 2, 1997.

Runnymede Trust, *Islamophobia: A Challenge for Us All*, London, 1997.

Salame, Ghassan, 'Islam and the West', *Foreign Policy*, 90, Spring 1993.

Searle, Chris, 'Understanding Columbus: A Review Article', *Race and Class*, 33, 3, 1992.

UNDP, *The Arab Human Development Report 2002*, New York, 2002.

Wright, Robin, 'Islam, Democracy and the West', *Foreign Affairs*, 7, 3, 1992.

BOOKS

Abrahamian, Ervand, *Khomeinism*, Albany, 1994.

Ahmed, Akbar S., *Postmodernism and Islam*, London, 1992.

Akhtar, Shabbir, *Be Careful with Muhammad*, London, 1990.

Al-Azmeh, Aziz, *Islams and Modernities*, London, 1994.

Al-Radi, Nuha, *Baghdad Diaries, 1991–2002*, London, 2003.

Ali, Azizi, *Ali: A Persian Yankee*, Caldwell, 1965.

Ali, M. Athar, *Mughal Nobility Under Aurengzeb*, Bombay, 1968.

Alibhai-Brown, Yasmin, *Who Do You Think We Are? Imagining the New Britain*, London, 2000.

——, *No Place Like Home*, London, 1995.

Anderson, Benedict, *Imagined Communities*, Oxford, 1993.

Anderson, Sonia P., *An English Consul in Turkey: Paul Rycaut at Smyrna, 1667–1678*, Oxford, 1989.

Anwar, Muhammad, *Pakistanis in Britain: A Sociological Study*, London, 1985.

Aswad, Barbara (ed.), *Arabic Speaking Community in American Cities*, Staten Island, 1974.

——, *Property Control and Social Strategies: Settlers on a Middle Eastern Plain*, Ann Arbor, 1971

Austin, Allan D., *African Muslims in Antebellum America*, London, 1997.

Banton, Michael, *Ethnic and Racial Consciousness*, London, 1997.

Barboza, Steven (ed.), *The American Jihad*, New York, 1992.

Bell, Martin, *In Harm's Way: Reflections of a War-Zone Thug*, London, 1996.

Berger, Peter, *Holy War Inc.*, London, 2001.

Bhutto, Benazir, *Daughter of the East*, London, 1989.

Bodansky, Yossef, *Bin Laden: The Man who Declared War on America*, New York, 1999.

Bulliet, Richard, *Islam: The View From the Edge*, New York, 1994.

Chejne, Anwar G., *Muslim Spain: Its History and Culture*, Minneapolis, 1974.

Clayborne, Carson (ed.), *The Autobiography of Martin Luther King Jr*, London, 1999.

Cockburn, Andrew and Cockburn, Patrick, *Saddam Hussein: An American Obsession*, London, 2002.

Colls, Robert and Lancaster, Bill (eds), *Geordies: Roots of Regionalism*, Edinburgh, 1992.

Cook, Alistair, *America*, London, 1977.

Cooper, John, et al., (eds), *Islam and Modernity: Muslim Intellectuals Respond*, London, 1998.

Coughlin, Con, *Saddam: The Secret Life*, London, 2002.

Daniel, Norman, *Islam and the West*, Oxford, 2000.

De Las Casas, Bartolome, *A Short History of the Destruction of the Indies*, translated by Nigel Griffin, London, 1992.

Douglass, Frederick, *Narratives of a Former Slave*, New York, 1995.

Du Bois, W.E.B, *The Souls of Black Folk*, New York, 1968.

Eliot, Charles, *Turkey in Europe*, London, 1900.

Esposito, John L., *The Islamic Threat: Myth or Reality?* New York, 1993.

Essien-Udom, E.U., *Black Nationalism: A Search for an Identity in America*, Chicago, 1971.

Fallaci, Oriana, *The Rage and the Pride*, London, 2002.

Ferguson, Niall, *Empire*, London, 2002.

Fieldhouse, David K., *The Colonial Empires*, Basingstoke, 1992.

Fisher, Michael H., (ed.), *The Travels of Dean Mahomed: An Eighteenth-Century Journey through India*, Berkeley, 1997.

—— *The First Indian Author in English: Dean Mahomed (1759–1851) in India, Ireland, and England*, Delhi, 1996.

Fogel, Robert W., and Engerman, Stanley L., *Time on the Cross: The Economics of American Negro Slavery*, Boston, 1974.

Franklin, John Hope, and Moss, Alfred A., Jr, *From Slavery to Freedom: A History of African Americans*, New York, 1994.

Gellner, Ernest, *Muslim Society*, Cambridge, 1993.

Gordon, Leonard, *Brothers Against the Raj*, New York, 1992.

Griffin, Michael, *Reaping the Whirlwind*, London, 2001.

Grosrichard, Alain, *The Sultan's Court*, translated by Liz Heron, London, 1998.

Haddad, Yvonne Y. (ed.), *Muslims in the West: From Sojourners to Citizens*, New York, 2002.

Haddad, Yvonne Y., and Smith, Jane I. (eds), *Muslim Communities in North America*, Albany, 1994.

—— (eds), *The Muslims of America*, New York, 1991.

Hailey, Alex (comp.), *The Autobiography of Malcolm X*, London, 1998.

Halliday, Fred, *Two Hours that Shook the World*, London, 2002.

——, *Islam and the Myth of Confrontation*, London, 1996.

Haskins, James, *The Life and Death of Martin Luther King Jr*, New York, 1977.

Hiskett, Mervyn, *The Course of Islam in Africa*, Edinburgh, 1994.

Hourani, Albert, *Islam in European Thought*, Cambridge, 1993.

Inalcik, Halil, *The Ottoman Empire*, London, 1973.

Iqbal, Muzaffar, (ed.), *Colours of Loneliness: Short Stories from Urdu and the Regional Languages of Pakistan*, Karachi, 1999.

Jones, Maldwyn A., *The Limits of Liberty: American History, 1607–1992*, Oxford, 1996.

Jones, Terry and Eriera, Alan, *Crusades*, London, 1994.

Jordan, Winthrop D., *The White Man's Burden: Historical Origins of Racism in the United States*, New York, 1974.

——, *White over Black: American Attitudes towards the Negro*, Chapel Hill, 1968.

Kabbani, Rana, *Imperial Fictions: Empire's Myth of Orient*, London, 1994.

——, *Women in Muslim Society*, Cork, 1992.

——, *Letter to Christendom*, London, 1989.

Kepel, Gilles, *Allah in the West: Islamic Movements in America and Europe*, London, 1997.

Khan, Gulfishan, *Indian Muslim Perceptions of the West during the Eighteenth Century*, Karachi, 1998.

Kiernan, V. G., (translator), *Poems from Iqbal*, Karachi, 1999.

Klein, Herbert S., *The Atlantic Slave Trade*, Cambridge, 1999.

Kolchin, Peter, *American Slavery 1619–1877*, New York, 1993.

LeBor, Adam, *A Heart Turned East: Among the Muslims of Europe and America*, London, 1997.

Lee, Harold, *Brothers in the Raj: The Lives of John and Henry Lawrence*, Karachi, 2002.

Lewis, Bernard, *The Crisis of Islam: Holy War and Unholy Terror*, London, 2003.

——, *What Went Wrong? Western Impact and Middle Eastern Response*, New York, 2001.

—— (ed.), *The World of Islam*, London, 1997.

——, *Islam and the West*, Oxford, 1994.

——, *The Muslim Discovery of Europe*, London, 1982.

Lewis, Philip, *Islamic Britain: Religion, Politics and Identity among British Muslims*, London, 1994.

Maan, Bashir, *The New Scots: The Story of Asians in Scotland*, Edinburgh, 1992.

MacKenzie, John M., *Orientalism: History, Theory and the Arts*, Manchester, 1996.

—— (ed.), *Popular Imperialism and the Military, 1850–1950*, Manchester, 1992.

——, *Propaganda and Empire: The Manipulation of British Public Opinion, 1880–1960*, Manchester, 1984.

MacMaster, Neil, *Racism in Europe, 1870–2000*, Basingstoke, 2001.

Malik, Iftikhar H., *Islam, Nationalism and the West: Issues of Identity in Pakistan*, Oxford, 1999.

——, *US–South Asian Relations: American Attitudes towards the Pakistan Movement*, Oxford, 1991.

——, *Pakistanis in Michigan: A Study in Third Culture and Acculturation*, New York, 1989.

——, *US–South Asia Relations, 1773–1940: A Historical Perspective*, Islamabad, 1988.

Malik, Kenan, *The Meaning of Race: Race, History and Culture in Western Society*, Basingstoke, 1996.

Mansel, Philip, *Constantinople: City of the World's Desire*, London, 1997.

Matar, Nabil, *Islam in Britain, 1558–1685*, Cambridge, 1998.

Mernissi, Fatima, *Islam and Democracy*, London, 1993.

——, *Women and Islam: An Historical and Theological Enquiry*, translated by Mary Jo Lakeland, Oxford, 1992.

Miles, Robert, *Racism*, London, 1989.

Moore, Michael, *Stupid White Men*, New York, 2002.

Nielsen, Jorgen, *Muslims in Western Europe*, Edinburgh, 1992.

Omissi, David, *The Sepoy and the Raj: The Politics of the Indian Army, 1860–1940*, London, 1995.

Osofsky, Gilbert, *Harlem: The Making of a Ghetto, 1890–1950*, New York, 1968.

Parish, Peter, *Slavery*, Keele, 1992.

Rashid, Salim (ed.), *'The Clash of Civilizations?': Asian Responses*, Karachi, 1997.

Raychaudhuri, Tapan, *Europe Reconsidered: Perceptions of the West in Nineteenth Century Bengal*, Delhi, 1988.

Read, John, *The Moors in Spain and Portugal*, Totowa, 1975.

Richard, Jean, *The Crusades, c.1071–c.1291*, translated by Jean Birrell, Cambridge, 1999.

Rizk, Salom, *A Syrian Yankee*, Garden City, 1943.

Rodinson, Maxime, *Europe and the Mystique of Islam*, London, 1988.

Rushdie, Salman, *Imaginary Homelands: Essays and Criticism, 1981–91*, London, 1992.

Ruthven, Malise, *A Satanic Affair*, London, 1990.

Said, Edward, *Orientalism*, London, 2003.

——, *Culture and Imperialism*, London, 1994.

Saiyid, Dushka, *Muslim Women of the British Punjab: From Seclusion to Politics*, Basingstoke, 1998.

Sardar, Ziauddin, *Orientalism*, London, 2000.

——, *Postmodernism and the Other*, London, 1998.

——, *Barbaric Others: A Manifesto on Western Racism*, London, 1993.

Sardar, Ziauddin and Davies, Merryl Wyn, *Why Do People Hate America?* London, 2002.

——, *Distorted Imagination: Lessons from the Rushdie Affair*, London, 1990.

Sayeed, Khalid B., *Western Dominance and Political Islam: Challenge and Response*, Albany, 1995.

Sayyid, Bobby, *A Fundamental Fear: Eurocentrism and the Emergence of Islamism*, London, 1997.

Shahadi, N., and Hourani, Albert (eds), *A Century of Lebanese Emigration*, London, 1992.
Sherif, M.A., *Searching for Solace: A Biography of Allama Yusuf Ali*, Kuala Lumpur, 1994.
Smith, Mark M., *Debating Slavery: Economy and Society in the Antebellum American South*, Cambridge, 1998.
Solomos, John, *Race and Racism in Britain*, London, 1994.
Southern, R. W., *The Making of the Middle Ages*, London, 1953.
Spear, Percival, *The Oxford History of Modern India, 1740–1947*, Oxford, 1965.
Tinker, Hugh, *A New Kind of Slavery*, London, 1974.
Visram, Rozina, *Asians in Britain: 400 Years of History*, London, 2002.
——, *Ayahs, Lascars and Princes: Indians in Britain, 1700–1947*, London, 1986.
Washington, Booker T., *Up From Slavery*, New York, 1968.
Watt, Montgomery, *A History of Muslim Spain*, Edinburgh, 1996.
——, *The Influence of Islam on Medieval Europe*, Edinburgh, 1994.
White, John, *Black Leadership in America: From Booker T. Washington to Jesse Jackson*, London, 1994.
Zebiri, Kate, *Muslims and Christians Face to Face*, Oxford, 1997.

NEWSPAPERS AND MAGAZINES

Daily Telegraph (London)
Dawn (Karachi)
Economist (London)
Financial Times (London)
Guardian (London and Manchester)
Independent (London)
Irish Times (Dublin)
ISIM Newsletter (Leiden)
New York Times (New York)
News (London and Lahore)
Observer (London)
Reader's Digest (London)
Sunday Telegraph (London)
Sunday Times (London)
The Times (London)
Times Higher Education Supplement (London)
Washington Post (Washington, DC)

VIDEOS

Amistad
Birth of a Nation
Glory
Malcolm X
Roots

Index